D0214500

# Collaboration in Education

# Routledge Research in Education

For a full list of title in this series, please visit www.routledge.com

**3. Education and Psychology in Interaction**
Working with Uncertainty in Inter-Connected Fields
Brahm Norwich

**4. Education, Social Justice and Inter-Agency Working**
Joined up or Fractured Policy?
Sheila Riddell and Lyn Tett

**5. Markets for Schooling**
An Economic Analysis
Nick Adnett and Peter Davies

**6. The Future of Physical Education**
Building a New Pedagogy
Edited by Anthony Laker

**7. Migration, Education and Change**
Edited by Sigrid Luchtenberg

**8. Manufacturing Citizenship**
Education and Nationalism in Europe, South Asia and China
Edited by Véronique Bénéï

**9. Spatial Theories of Education**
Policy and Geography Matters
Edited by Kalervo N. Gulson and Colin Symes

**10. Balancing Dilemmas in Assessment and Learning in Contemporary Education**
Edited by Anton Havnes and Liz McDowell

**11. Policy Discourses, Gender, and Education**
Constructing Women's Status
Elizabeth J. Allan

**12. Improving Teacher Education through Action Research**
Edited by Ming-Fai Hui and David L. Grossman

**13. The Politics of Structural Education Reform**
Keith A. Nitta

**14. Political Approaches to Educational Administration and Leadership**
Edited by Eugenie A. Samier with Adam G. Stanley

**15. Structure and Agency in the Neoliberal University**
Edited by Joyce E. Canaan and Wesley Shumar

**16. Postmodern Picturebooks**
Play, Parody, and Self-Referentiality
Edited by Lawrence R. Sipe and Sylvia Pantaleo

**17. Play, Creativity and Digital Cultures**
Edited By Rebekah Willet, Muriel Robinson and Jackie Marsh

**18. Education and Neoliberal Globalization**
Carlos Alberto Torres

**19. Tracking Adult Literacy and Numeracy Skills**
Findings in Longitudinal Research
Edited by Stephen Reder and
John Bynner

**20. Emergent Computer Literacy**
A Developmental Perspective
Helen Mele Robinson

**21. Participatory Learning in the Early Years**
Research and Pedagogy
Edited by Donna Berthelsen, Jo
Brownlee, and Eva Johansson

**22. International Perspectives on the Goals of Universal Basic and Secondary Education**
Edited by Joel E. Cohen and
Martin B. Malin

**23 .The Journey for Inclusive Education in the Indian Sub-Continent**
Mithu Alur & Michael Bach

**24. Traveller, Nomadic and Migrant Education**
Edited by Patrick Alan Danaher, Máirín
Kenny and Judith Remy Leder

**25. Perspectives on Supported Collaborative Teacher Inquiry**
Edited by David Slavit, Tamara
Holmlund Nelson and Anne Kennedy

**26. Mathematical Relationships in Education**
Identities and Participation
Edited by Laura Black, Heather Mendick
and Yvette Solomon

**27. Science, Society and Sustainability**
Education and Empowerment for an
Uncertain World

Edited by Donald Gray, Laura Colucci-
Gray and Elena Camino

**28. The Social Psychology of the Classroom**
Elisha Babad

**29. Cross-Cultural Perspectives on Policy and Practice**
Decolonizing Community Contexts
Edited by Jennifer Lavia and Michele
Moore

**30. Education and Climate Change**
Living and Learning in Interesting
Times
Edited by Fumiyo Kagawa
and David Selby

**31. Education and Poverty in Affluent Countries**
Edited by Carlo Raffo, Alan Dyson,
Helen Gunter, Dave Hall, Lisa Jones
and Afroditi Kalambouka

**32. What's So Important About Music Education?**
J. Scott Goble

**33. Educational Transitions**
Moving Stories from Around the World
Edited by Divya Jindal-Snape

**34. Globalization, the Nation-State and the Citizen**
Dilemmas and Directions for Civics
and Citizenship Education
Edited by Alan Reid, Judith Gill and
Alan Sears

**35. Collaboration in Education**
Edited by Judith J. Slater and Ruth
Ravid

# Collaboration in Education

Edited by Judith J. Slater
and Ruth Ravid

Routledge
Taylor & Francis Group
New York   London

First published 2010
by Routledge
270 Madison Avenue, New York, NY 10016

Simultaneously published in the UK
by Routledge
2 Park Square, Milton Park, Abingdon, Oxon OX14 4RN

*Routledge is an imprint of the Taylor & Francis Group, an informa business*

© 2010 Taylor & Francis

Typeset in Sabon by IBT Global.
Printed and bound in the United States of America on acid-free paper by IBT Global.

All rights reserved. No part of this book may be reprinted or reproduced or utilised in any form or by any electronic, mechanical, or other means, now known or hereafter invented, including photocopying and recording, or in any information storage or retrieval system, without permission in writing from the publishers.

**Trademark Notice:** Product or corporate names may be trademarks or registered trademarks, and are used only for identification and explanation without intent to infringe.

*Library of Congress Cataloging in Publication Data*

Collaboration in education / edited by Judith J. Slater and Ruth Ravid.
p. cm.
Includes bibliographical references and index.
1. Interaction analysis in education.   2. Community and school   3. Educational planning—Social aspects   4. Instructional systems.   I. Slater, Judith J.   II. Ravid, Ruth.
LB1034.C64 2010
371.19—dc22
2009040021

ISBN10: 0-415-80621-6 (hbk)
ISBN10: 0-203-85470-5 (ebk)

ISBN13: 978-0-415-80621-3 (hbk)
ISBN13: 978-0-203-85470-9 (ebk)

*To my loving family collaboration: Jennifer, Denise, and Dina.*
*J. J. S*
*To my family with love.*
*R. R.*

# Contents

*List of Figures*      xiii
*List of Tables*      xv
*Acknowledgments*      xvii

Introduction: The *Meme* of Collaboration      1
JUDITH J. SLATER

**PART I**
**Professional Development Schools**      15

1    When a Look Back Can Be a Step Forward: An Analysis of Two
PDS Partnerships for Education Change and Improvement      19
LINDA A. CATELLI

2    Growing a Multi-Site Professional Development School      26
JOHN E. HENNING, BECKY WILSON HAWBAKER, DEBRA S. LEE, AND
CYNTHIA F. MCDONALD

**PART II**
**Consultation**      35

3    Schools of Ambition: Bridging Professional and Institutional
Boundaries      39
MOIRA HULME, IAN MENTER, DEIRDRE KELLY, AND SHEELAGH RUSBY

4    Ten School Districts and One University: A Collaborative
Consultation      47
MARY PHILLIPS MANKE AND RACHAEL MARRIER

5    Elementary Public School and University Partnership:
Promoting and Analyzing Professional Development Processes
of School Teachers      54
MARIA DA GRAÇA NICOLETTI MIZUKAMI, ALINE MARIA DE MEDEIROS
RODRIGUES REALI, AND REGINA MARIA SIMÕES PUCCINELLI TANCREDI

## PART III
## One-to-One Collaboration                                    61

6   Policy Development and Sustainability: How a Rural
    County Maximized Resources through Collaboration and
    Managed Change                                             65
    DAVID M. CALLEJO PÉREZ, SEBASTIÁN R. DÍAZ, AND ANONYMOUS

7   School–University Collaboration as Mutual Professional
    Development                                                73
    EFRAT SARA EFRON, MAJA MISKOVIC, AND RUTH RAVID

8   A Public/Private Partnership in a Diverse Community         80
    MARIA PACINO

## PART IV
## Multiple Configurations                                      89

9   Reflections on a Cross University-Urban School Partnership:
    The Critical Role of Humanizing the Process                95
    BABETTE BENKEN AND NANCY BROWN

10  A System's Perspective for Professional Development in
    Science and Mathematics Education: The Texas Regional
    Collaboratives                                             102
    JAMES P. BARUFALDI AND LINDA L.G. BROWN

11  Conducting Research that Practitioners Think is Relevant:
    Metropolitan Educational Research Consortium (MERC)        110
    R. MARTIN REARDON AND JAMES MCMILLAN

12  A Miracle in Process: What it Takes to Make an Educational
    Partnership a True Collaboration                           118
    KATHLEEN SHINNERS

13  Collaboration and Equitable Reform in Australian Schools:
    Beyond the Rhetoric                                        126
    JOANNE DEPPELER AND DAVID HUGGINS

14  Benefits, Challenges, and Lessons of Longitudinal Research
    Collaborations                                             134
    ELIZABETH A. SLOAT, JOAN F. BESWICK, AND J. DOUGLAS WILLMS

## PART V
## Postsecondary 143

15 Reciprocity in Collaboration: Academy for Teacher
   Excellence's Partnerships 147
   BELINDA BUSTOS FLORES AND LORENA CLAEYS

16 Reconceptualizing Leadership and Power: The Collaborative
   Experiences of Women Educational Leaders 154
   DEBRA NAKAMA AND JOANNE COOPER

17 A CLASSIC © Approach to Collaboration: Documenting a
   Multi-State University and Multi-School District Partnership 161
   JANET PENNER-WILLIAMS, DELLA PEREZ, DIANA GONZALES WORTHEN,
   SOCORRO HERRERA, AND KEVIN MURRY

## PART VI
## Technology Projects 169

18 School-University Collaboration for Technology Integration:
   Resistance, Risk-Taking, and Resilience 171
   CATHY RISBERG AND ARLENE BORTHWICK

## PART VII
## Interagency Collaboration 179

19 Project FIRST: Families, Intercollegiate Collaboration, and
   Routes to Studying Teaching 183
   MARY D. BURBANK AND ROSEMARIE HUNTER

20 Urban Teacher Residencies: Collaborating to Reconceptualize
   Urban Teacher Preparation 191
   WENDY GARDINER AND CARRIE KAMM

21 Sharing Power in an Interagency Collaboration 199
   JACK LEONARD AND LISA GONSALVES

22 Collaborating for Labor Consciousness: The Education &
   Labor Collaborative 207
   ADRIENNE ANDI SOSIN, LEIGH DAVID BENIN, ROB LINNÉ, AND JOEL I.
   SOSINSKY

**Conclusion**                                                           215

JUDITH J. SLATER


*Contributors*                                                          217
*Index*                                                                 227

# Figures

I.1     Flow of influence for school/university collaboration.     12

10.1    Components of a dynamic professional development
        system.                                                   105

# Tables

I.1     Slater's School/University Collaborative Matrix          10

17.1    Summary of Demographics for Six Collaborating
        Universities                                            164

# Acknowledgments

The editors would like to thank the SIG School/University Collaborative Research of the American Educational Research Association for their support and encouragement for this volume. We conceptualized this work through presentations and feedback from the membership over the last few years. Many of the contributors are SIG members who have dedicated themselves to the research and practice of school/university collaborative endeavors. We hope that this volume encourages others to undertake collaborative projects and that our shared experience guides them in their work.

Judith J. Slater and Ruth Ravid

# Introduction

## The *Meme* of Collaboration

*Judith J. Slater*

In education there have been attempts to alter the way we institute change in schools. Collaboration, whereas it is not a new idea, has provided the mechanisms that purport to change the way school problems are approached. The atmosphere of collaboration, or the uniting of two or more organizational points of view, has created a synergy of sorts in approaching the overwhelming circumstances of schooling today. Yet, have collaborative efforts provided permanent solutions and new ways of operating? Have they changed the life of schools and universities? Are they sufficient structures to serve schools in the future?

Much work has been done over the years on collaboration between universities and school systems. Nonetheless, the avenue for dissemination has not been great except for certain configurations such as professional development schools (PDS) or large grant funded projects. This situation may be an indicator of the temper of the times which is infused with accountability, testing, efficiency, and the need for quick results on the part of the school system, and with little reward for such work internally from the university.

There are problems also with the dissemination of university–school collaborative efforts, both psychological and practical, and involve at least some of the following aspects:

1. The nature of the professorship and its reward structure produces a time constraint for such work. Traditionally, the professorate is judged according to criteria of the triumvirate of research, teaching, and service. Research is judged based on a hierarchy of refereed journal publications and grants which are often valued more than that of action research or book production that takes a considerable time to bring to fruition and publication. Collaborations take time away from these more rewarded endeavors, particularly for beginning professors who may be advised to curtail such activities.

2. There is an element of site specificity involved in collaborations that results in a lack of or perceived lack of transferability. Each new instance or project has its own culture and organizational climate

that permeates all interactions that make it difficult to inform other projects, sites, and outsiders.
3. Collaborations often involve grant based funding for much of the work. There are questions as to the sustainability of the good work of the collaboration when funding ends.

The future of collaborative efforts once the initial funding discontinues is a threat to many partnerships. The issue of sustainability includes:

1. The evolution of projects into secondary and tertiary interactions among participants; whether or not the human connections and new methods of working together will extend beyond the project into the way each organization perceives and works with each other in the future.
2. There is a lack of models/theories in collaboration research that are true calls for praxis rather than the reporting of practice (Slater, 1996). Because there is a problem with duplication and sustainability beyond individual projects, calls for continued action and change efforts can subside over time, and traditionally, the institutional pull toward maintaining the status quo becomes the dominant impediment for change.
3. There is an inherent disinterest of local school systems to produce disseminated research. Instead they have a vested interest in lauding their own merits and duplicating programs from one site to another without regard for the differences in culture and population characteristics that may not allow such duplication to be successful.
4. As with most collaboration, there are always issues of control of innovations among participants. These can be salient or overt and can cause problems that detract from the creation of sustainable changes in the way two or more organizations work together on a particular project or influence future possibilities.

## WHAT CAN BE DONE?

Whereas the problems outlined above are not insurmountable, it may be helpful to understand the limitations to innovation that exist as salient characteristics of the environment in which collaborations occur. Understanding the source of the limitations to change can aid in creating a process to loosen the hold of the past on the possibilities of the future. The vehicle to understand this phenomenon is psychological, and it is termed *meme*. Dawkins (1989) coined the term *meme* to represent those elements of culture that are passed on by imitation. These *memes* are selected from other *memes* in a pool, some of which are favored in a particular environment, and they cooperate in mutually supported *memes*, termed *memeplexes*, that are hostile to competing ones.

According to Blakemore (1999) *memes* are instructions for carrying out behavior that exist in the brain, in books, in artifacts, in organization operations, etc. They are ideas and culture that evolve, because the *meme* does not duplicate exactly but is a product of imitation of a previous interaction with an idea. Therefore, ideas (such as collaboration) spread, and as they become more prolific, they may become false reconceptualizations of the original successful project that are adopted and adapted as practices or beliefs at each new site.

Whereas the spread of *memes* appears to be advantageous, in reality they do not operate in that way. *Memes* compete (there is variety in collaboration practices, in ways in which organizations work together), because *memes* change the selective environment to the detriment of the competition. That is, they shore up the environment that allows them to survive by increasing in complexity and design without a goal or an end point except to become more complex and keep others at bay. Competition among ideas is not encouraged in the world of *meme* replication, because the stronger and more complex *meme* always wins. It exhibits the best argument for sustainability and survival of itself (Blakemore, 1999). Thus, it is possible to have a *meme* for collaboration that is used to fit into a new situation that, in reality, is a mismatch for the environment. To know beforehand what the limitations of a particular collaborative design/configuration portends can help practitioners to select alternatives that better meet their needs.

The *memes* we have for our institutions (the university and the school system) are bureaucratic operations that guide and power the school system and define their own world, a world that is vastly different from that of the university. The *memes* that perpetuate such environments each try to maintain their own dominance and push out the other. What is needed is another *meme*, one that has instructions for imitation for a collective that better advances both of the organization's work. Why is this so?

a. *Memes* acculturate participants into a mode of operation of university and school interactions. They pass on information by universal Darwinist principles of variation, selection, and retention. Those *memes* that are imitated are the survivors, in a sense, of this process. But, the *memes* for collaboration are merely replicators that have an advantage; thus, they have the potential to spread and change the selected environment to the detriment of competing *memes* only if they are lucky. For example, a *meme* for collaboration is the PDS model, a contractual relationship whose parameters are defined by the participants beforehand, one whose boundaries are set. Yet, by definition, PDSs don't alter the beliefs of each institution, portent new ways to work together on other projects, or cause institutional retrospection about each organization's respective mission and goals. They offer shorthand, efficient ways for collaboration to be defined and enacted. Inventions, therefore, benefit

themselves, not the ever-changing landscape of the work environment of collaborations. As each site tries to duplicate the collaboration of another site, the *memes* of practice do not allow adaptation
but merely replicate what was successful elsewhere. We can know
the gene map for collaboration; we can share successful practices
with each other, but we cannot predict why some collaboration
will last and change the way the two organizations work together
and why others fizzle and end with no discernable effect on the
organizations. The question, if we embrace this idea of *meme*, is
how to imitate and adapt and change at the same time. Evidence
that this transformation may work is found in the opportunities
and interactions that participants have with each other beyond a
particular project. It is the keystone for a new way to work with
each other that is different than the past.

b. If we recognize that chaos is the rule (not the exception) and replication (like genes) cannot be planned to occur in exactly the same
way as it did before, the result is that there need to be new ways
of thinking and new ways of doing collaborative work that can
be tweaked as needed in particular circumstances that fulfill the
situational need. For example, one-to-one university faculty/insti-
tutional projects are grounded in situational needs; research for
faculty, problem solution and grant implementation for the school.
Yet, human interaction is a key to the success of this design, and
replication is difficult because each project has different participants. In addition, workers within the collaboration have to scout
out the "*memes* of practice" which limit opportunities for modifying the "*memes* in use" that permeate the beliefs of the participants and color their expectations, thus limiting their behavior to
act in ways that are not expected by their institutional memories.

c. We have to be clear about the need to work together to create a mutually supported *memeplex*. This enables organizations to replicate better as part of a group than any single entity can on its own in order
to solve problems related to schools and education. This provides a
rationale for extending the effort to continue and refine collaborations and to continue to research and support participation in them
for both the public school and the university. The goal of a complex
design, particularly interagency types, for collaboration is the mutuality of purpose and sustainability in other interactions to come.

## HOW TO DISSEMINATE NEW MEMES

According to Dennett (cited in Blakemore, 1999), *memes* produce second
replicators (words and cultural and organizational artifacts) which, in turn,
produce and enhance intelligence about some object or belief. These second

replicators are important to the analysis of collaborations, because they have the opportunity to transform both parent organizations. Where do they fit into the worldview the individual has of the organization?

Popper (cited in Blakemore, 1999) conceived of three worlds: (a) the physical objective world and the conceptions about that world that influence objects in it; (b) the subjective world of experience, feelings, emotions, and consciousness, where problems, hypotheses, theories and intellectual struggles go on; and (c) the world of ideas, language, myths and stories, art, technology, and mathematics and science, that exist autonomously even though they are products of man and they affect other worlds. It is the last, a world of ideas, which can change the physical world, affect experience, and lead to new structures. The selective imitation of *memes* is the idea that they take on a life of their own and serve as a mechanism for change.

For collaboration, that means there is much work to do to elevate our practice to the level of ideas, of *memes*, that can be replicated and have an impact on the subjective experience of participants and, thus, transform the physical world in which we try to create innovations. The question is how to make the move from the old *memes* to the new so that everyone accepts them as core beliefs about the way in which they behave within a collaborative structure?

## CULTURAL EVOLUTION

For collaborations to be successful there has to be the creation of a good second replicator. Each side must balance structural impediments of their own set of *memes* and their human altruistic behavior with a reciprocative cooperative stance. There need to be an evolution of new *memes* with behavioral instructions that change the culture among the institutions and the people in them. The need for *meme* production is hampered by a need for consistency and the avoidance of dissonance, so this is no easy task. Much of the work in schools is maintenance of the status quo of the strongest *memes*, and they pass on the behaviors that are "correct" and discourage those that are not. Therefore, to evolve new and more effective *memes* among institutions and the people in them, the following should be considered:

a. It must be clear what there is to gain by cooperating. Each side of a collaboration must be aware of and articulate a *meme* that is advantageous to each and that could not effectively and efficiently be accomplished if each side proceeded on its own.

b. There must be recognition that there is a danger in exploitation, much like religious zeal, when imitation goes too far and squeezes out any other new *meme* that is more serviceable. Collaborations must be flexible because they are less structural than they are day-to-day interactions among people. The power of the old *meme* is that it resists change; therefore, the new *meme*, the new enacted idea, must be made strong by being embraced by all participants.

c. There must be clarity in what to imitate. As we impart stories of the results of collaborations between schools and universities, the *memes* get stronger on those elements of a collaborative that could and should be passed on and disseminated. University faculties write and publish their success and schools laud their innovations. Of course those elements that are most transferable, sustainable, and adaptable are the *memes* that should be shared.

d. There has to be cognizance that imitation requires complex transformations of a point of view. *Meme* artifacts are easily transferred, but the underlying beliefs about the way two organizations must transform themselves for cooperative work is a much more complex process made more difficult when two different cultures collide.

e. Imitation requires actions of participants that show the *meme* is, in fact, being enacted, hopefully for the betterment of the collaboration. As Freire (1970) notes, without praxis, there is only the idea; without action, there is no change. Organizations and participant change is critical for collaborative work.

*Memes* look at the world with a particular point of view in terms of opportunity for replication. The *meme*, in effect, tries to make more copies of itself and eliminates any idea that would prevent it from doing so. There are many *memes* that preclude collaboration from being a dominant *meme*; a good second replicator is hard to come by. The power of the status quo, of imitation of an old idea or way of doing the work of schools in the real physical world, does not give way easily for new ones to replace it, sometimes not even when the old becomes inappropriate or ineffective. It is easy for the legislators and politicos, then, to take over the business of education and become the dominant *meme* it has been for a long time in both universities and in school systems. The work of schools has been driven by practices and over-verbalizations that freeze behavior into patterns of response in fear of reprisals (i.e., lack of funding, punitive standard setting, and efficiency of operation). These are smoke screens for action and ideas of *memes* that better serve education.

What then can we (those who do work on collaboration) create as a second replicator, a *meme* that is a good idea, a better idea for the mind and for the practice of education? We have to sell that altruism and cooperation are vital aspects of being human and that the structures described above have gotten in the way of the humanistic practice of educating children. There must be support for reciprocal altruism among institutions, helping others who will help you, in an open and trustworthy environment within and without those institutions that support change (Slater, 2006).

The environment must be psychologically open to working together in new ways and duplicating those *memes* that are better adaptations at solving problems than are now in place. We also must be careful what *memes* we aid and abet and which ones we have the opportunity to create in a complex environment that necessitates and calls out for cooperation and collaboration.

## THE TASK AT HAND

The rationale for this book on collaboration is twofold. First, the editors have presented a plethora of research on the state of the art for the practice of school/university collaboration by providing 22 examples of real projects from various parts of the world to show what structures are in place that facilitate collaborative endeavors. The only theory related volumes that try to synthesize such work are the two volumes written and edited by the authors: Slater's *Anatomy of Collaboration* (1996) and Ravid and Handler's *The Many Faces of School–University Collaboration: Characteristics of Successful Partnerships* (2001). These two books are seminal in that the first sought to explore the elements necessary for sustainable collaboration and the second to categorize the types that exist in the literature in order to provide a frame of reference for others doing this work.

As Hord tells us, research on university–school collaborations produces individual works that taken together, form a synthesis of research on organizational collaboration. One common strand among the various voices contributing to the body of research is the clarifying one, posing the question: "What counts as a collaboration?" (Hord, 1986). In 2001, Ravid and Handler sought to clarify collaboration for those involved in existing projects, and also provide them with an understanding of what contributes to operating conditions that help them to thrive.

From the extant literature at the time, the text posited four models of school–university collaboration: (a) collaboration between a university and a professional development school (PDS); (b) a consultation model; (c) one-to-one collaborations; and (d) multiple collaboration project teams under one umbrella organization acting as the facilitator.

Whereas each of these models encompassed most of the configurations existent at that time, these models do not embrace all of the emergent forms that collaboration has taken in light of the changing needs of both universities and school systems. To understand the need to revisit these models and adapt them, it was necessary to take a look at the emergent and alternative configurations that now are in use to make the models more inclusive.

Slater and Ravid, along with others, doing work in the field of university/school research, have come to realize that there is a need to establish a framework for the emerging narratives of collaborative efforts to be understood by others wishing to participate in these partnerships. Slater has designed a categorization schema, *Slater's School/University Collaboration Matrix*, (hereafter referred to in this volume as the "Slater Matrix"; Slater, Ravid, Shinners, & Catelli, *American Educational Research Association*, 2007) for the interorganizational theory and practice of collaborative institutional practices that serves as a framework for the way to talk about the practices in the field.

The Slater Matrix is an organizing feature and focal point of the text. Each of the contributing authors were given a copy of the Slater Matrix and instructed to select the most appropriate categorization for their collaboration by type. Each type is a unique category and is distinguished from other types by implementation criteria. Next, each author was asked to write their narrative according to each of the eight elements in the matrix.

To explain further, collaborations by *type* from the simplest to most complex include:

a. *Professional Development Schools*: contractual agreements between a university and school for teacher training and staff development.

b. *Consultation*: university faculty hired as consultant by a school system or a school site, either public or private, for a specific purpose or for a project.

c. *One-to-One*: usually university faculty conduct research, are asked for advice, or collaborate, often on a grant with a school system member, teacher, parents, or other school official.

d. *Multiple Configurations*: partnerships, networks, and research initiatives; large scale university or research center funded projects whose goal is dissemination of innovation and knowledge.

e. *Postsecondary*: usually community college and community/school driven projects whose focus is on increasing minority entrance into higher education.

f. *Technology Projects*: externally funded by grants and foundations to infuse technology and innovation into schools.

g. *Interagency:* a semi-autonomous systems approach to collaboration that is focused directly on creating institutional change, experimentation, development of organizations, and innovation and change.

Slater and Ravid were most gratified to find that the matrix worked to allow each author to categorize their project. Therefore, the basic tenets of the types of organizational collaboration in the matrix are utilitarian by definition.

The elements for each type of collaboration are listed. Examples are provided for each type of collaboration according to the following *criteria*:

a. *Organizational Involvement*: Who are the participants in the collaboration?

b. *Formal/Informal*: Is the collaboration contractual and legally binding by state or local policies, or is it an informal relationship among participants?

c. *Purpose*: What is the goal for each type of collaboration; who benefits and who participates; is the purpose teacher training, research, professional development, discipline innovation trials, etc.?

d. *Resources*: What funding sources are involved, such as grants, faculty formal assignments, outside sources such as business and industry; what material and non material resources are needed such as personnel, space, supplies, access, or faulty incentives to participate?

e. *Mutuality Level*: What is the power hierarchy in the collaboration? This varies and can be a one sided benefit to one of the collaboration partners, a community service benefit, or a mutually beneficial level that equally supports the work of the collaborating institutions.

f. *Resistance Sources*: Most collaborations encounter resistance of one sort or another, therefore knowing potential sources of resistance for each type of collaboration is important in order to anticipate problems that may occur with implementation; this resistance can come from participants, administration, bureaucratic rules and regulations, etc.

g. *Positives*: Benefits of each type of collaboration must be real and product oriented creating changes from the status quo for each organization and its participants.

h. *Limitations:* What are the possible limitations of the type of collaboration described by participants and would a different type of organizing scheme been more beneficial to achieve desired outcomes?

After categorizing themselves as a particular type of collaboration, authors were asked to address each of the eight elements in the body of their contribution.

The other task asked to be addressed by contributors concerns the *Flow of Influence for School/University Collaboration* diagram which depicts the power relationships among the collaboration participants. This is the second organizing theme for the examples in this book and is an important aspect of understanding the corporate culture and influence on collaborations and where those power structures wield their influence away from the academic environment of knowledge and innovation of theory and practice.

The primary participants in school/university collaboration are teachers, parents, administration, and school board for schools, and faculty and administration for universities. Yet, there are other sources of influence that impact this work. Increasingly, these sources of power and money have come from government through national, state, and local

*Table I.1*   Slater's School/University Collaborative Matrix

| Type | Organizational Involvement | Formal /Informal | Purpose | Resources: *personnel; space; access; supplies; incentives* **Support Funding:** *grant; faculty assignment; school/university funds; business, industry* |
|---|---|---|---|---|
| PDS | university school site | formal contract | preservice teacher training fellowship training training site inservice university course development peer relationships: training/teaching | institutional: time incentives personnel access, etc. |
| Consultation | university school system private organiza- tion | formal or informal | planned change university with school: administration faculty district staff teacher professional development university credit: advanced degrees alternative settings research facilitation | school funds |
| One-to-One | university school system teacher parents faculty | informal university advisory | faculty research project university driven agenda faculty advisor to school system: projects— long-term grant evaluation or participant: publications proposals projects | faculty time (research) |
| Multiple Configurations: partnerships networks research initiatives | university school system (K–12) research centers: private public K–6, 7–12 | formal informal | research and dissemination: sustainability, nnovation, policy target discipline innovation | grant |
| Postsecondary | university larger community community colleges | formal or informal | entrance to university for: special programs minority and less served | grant tuition staff |
| Technology Projects | many partners: school university business research centers government | formal | infuse skills prepare workforce future | grant foundation |
| Interagency Collaboration | varies beyond university/school | semi- autonomous systems approach | future oriented change efforts renewal redesign of: parent institution | multi-level from participants and externally |

| Mutuality Level: power hierarchy visible invisible | Resistance Sources: agenda served | Positives university school/system | Limitations university school/system |
|---|---|---|---|
| high (contracted) | school system university | contractual commitment | school system rules and regulations |
| high | school internal forces university faculty interest perceptions of expertise trust | information flow knowledge/expertise | one dimension limited sustainability |
| faculty driven or school driven low | school staff participation faculty research agenda | living laboratory | isolated benefit isolated results school permission givers |
| university driven entrepreneurial | depends on: type of project no. participants motivation control momentum | producers of knowledge | dissemination |
| low service to community | community college | minority/ disadvantaged support | outreach problems grant boundaries |
| one-way to school | creating teacher change | innovation | funding training support over time |
| institution building experimentation institution change data producer of knowledge focus on development | varied: requires sea change | upset status quo used to create policy innovation generate knowledge common good | difficult to put together requires change in: organizations participants |

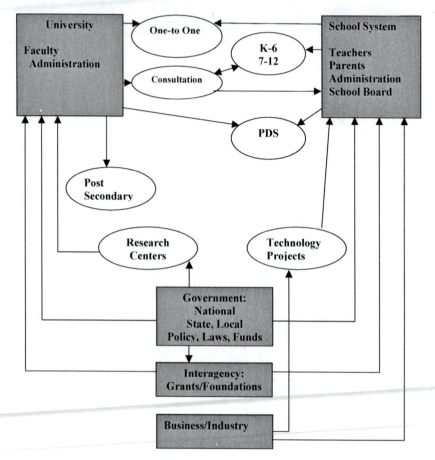

*Figure I.1*   Flow of influence for school/university collaboration.

policy or laws, and through funding criteria and accountability on the part of practitioners. These sources influence are for both the school system and the university through grants and/or foundational monies and research centers that disseminate and certify the success and failure of funded projects.

In less hardy economic times, interagency grants and foundations may be less likely sources of support, and influence for projects may come directly by business and industry going directly to school systems through funding, technological innovation support networks or resource allocation. Increasingly, schools and universities are not the only partners involved in educational partnerships. Both public and private monies from foundations and grants are now important influences and the sources of the funds become quasi-partners in the collaboration. The issue of how to sustain the collaboration once the initial grant money is over is emphasized in many of the examples provided in this volume.

This, on the surface, seems like a viable alternative in today's educational milieu, "he who holds the purse strings" often has tremendous influence on the collaboration, and brings another organizational structure into the mix. Contributors were asked to describe the power and influence sources and effect on their projects and we discuss this issue in the last chapter of this volume. At the beginning of each category/type the editors have provided a summary highlighting strengths and potential drawbacks.

The task of the contributors was to use the matrix as an organizer to describe their projects. Some examples referred to the parts of the matrix using the criteria as organizing headings, whereas others provided extensive analysis in their narrative, and all were asked to include lessons learned from their projects that could inform those wishing to begin collaboration. It is interesting to note that most of the chapters have as first author university faculty who were the first contact point for the call to participate. Yet, many engaged school project personnel in their written commentaries. As part of the culture of university faculty, and the pressure to publish, this is not unusual, but does highlight the fact that dissemination of collaboration resides almost exclusively with the university partners. Another observation is that most of the change occurring in the projects occurred in the schools, whereas the university structure and culture remained constant. Perhaps the reason for this is that the bureaucratic structure of the university is less hierarchical, tending to provide more opportunity for faculty to engage in innovation.

We hope the benefit of using the matrix and charting the flow of influence of power relationships to describe the 22 projects is that they give a focal point for the description of each of the examples and this ultimately can help others wishing to do collaborative work. Most important, it is an aide to decide which type of collaboration will most likely achieve the goals and purposes of new projects while being aware of the influences that impact on them when engaging in this type of work.

## REFERENCES

Blakemore, S. (1999). *The meme machine.* Oxford, UK: Oxford University.

Dawkins, R. (1989). *The selfish gene.* Oxford, UK: Oxford University.

Freire, P. (1970). *Pedagogy of the oppressed.* New York: Seabury.

Hord, S. M. (1986). A synthesis of research on organizational collaboration. *Educational Leadership, 43*(5), 22–26.

Ravid, R., & Handler, M. G. (2001). *The many faces of school–university collaboration: Characteristics of successful partnerships.* Englewood, CO: Teachers Ideas Press.

Slater, J. J. (1996). *Anatomy of a collaboration: Study of a college of education/public school partnership.* New York: Garland.

Slater, J. J. (2006). Creating collaborations: From isolationism to community. *International Journal of Educational Management, 20*(3), 215–223.

Slater, J. J., Ravid, R., Shinners, K. D., & Catelli, L. (2007, April). *Reviewing the structural and environmental elements of "The Many Faces of School–University Collaboration."* Paper presented at the annual meeting of the American Educational Research Association, Chicago.

# Part I

# Professional Development Schools

The first category listed in Slater's School/University Collaboration Matrix is Professional Development Schools (PDS). The rationale for placing this first is because it is the simplest type of collaboration and the least complex to understand. The reason for this is that PDS partnerships are formally arranged and/or contractually designed and understood by participants before undertaking such an endeavor. As such, roles, responsibilities, and rewards are clear. Often, the state designates the parameters of a PDS and both the university and school system administration agree up front to the guidelines that they must follow in the contract signed by designees from each institution; therefore, high mutuality is a built in dimension.

Most PDS encompass some configuration of preservice teacher training, inservice, university course development and delivery, peer training and teaching, and opportunity for research and development on the part of the university faculty involved. Resources, personnel, and access to the public school and to the university are part of the project, and it is known up front what the limits of such involvement will be.

The first example in this volume of a PDS is a retrospective look at 18 years experience with two long-term PDSs provided by Catelli. In her words, the aim of the projects she was a part of was "holistic–organic partnerships." The aim is clear: to improve K–12 education and professional education (higher education degrees for teachers). Most importantly, her analysis of the projects provides invaluable lessons to those embarking on this type of collaboration, and is particularly candid about the perils of untenured faculty using their time to do something which may not be valued by the university community, a theme also echoed in Slater's 1996 work, *Anatomy of a Collaboration*. In addition, untenured faculty are often powerless to make decisions within their own institution, as well as in the school system, whereas more power resides with the teachers used as adjuncts by the university to deliver coursework.

Catelli likens the process of this type of partnership to a "dance of the PDS" to keep it going. She offers valuable suggestions for leadership, funding, and institutionalizing successes. Catelli's story also illuminates the importance of the support of those in power at both the school and the university.

The second example of a PDS is provided by Henning, Hawbaker, Lee, and McDonald. They describe a 2-year project involving two community schools and a university where the first year of the project was its pilot year. In order to have buy-in from the stakeholders, a governing committee serving as a power base was formed to steer the development and activities of the project. One of the lessons learned from that pilot year was that change had to be made in small incremental steps. As with all change strategies, cultural elements of each organization must be understood by all participants as to why things are done the way they are done within each of the organizations. Big changes are short lived, and must be gradually introduced in order to become institutionalized. The pilot also found that open and clear feedback was necessary for all participants to feel informed and participatory. Along with this was the need for transparency so that resistance to innovation from any source was reduced. Bringing into the decision- making phase those who might have objections to the partnership also reduced potential resistance.

The second year of the project was formalized contractually with a clear statement of mission and purpose, the contribution and responsibility of each organization, the roles and responsibility of participants, the governance, and commitment of each of the three partners. This is one of the defining factors in PDS; that these elements are clearly stated and agreed upon by administration. For this project, the result of having a pilot led to more involvement, such as site coordinators, teacher incentives, and courses for mentoring preservice teachers.

Time for teachers balanced with their institutional demands, and time for faculty involvement, along with resource allocation and funding are major elements that impact on PDS success. It is clear that PDS is a collaborative model that can help foster the goal of "culture building" for school/university activities so that they become the norm and impact in positive ways on student success.

Some of the PDSs start organically, such as Catelli's example, and some start as the result of the work of a task force. In both cases, small incremental change in the way the institutions and individuals work together to implement change, highlight the need to manage the innovations. Lessons learned are to deal with individual negative feeling, involve those who object to elements in the operation and make them active partners in process, and listen to all concerns so that everyone feels that their voice is heard and taken seriously. PDSs also follow a long-term sequence moving from planning to piloting to articulating a formal agreement as in the Henning et al. example, and time must be both available and managed so that there is continuous progress. As shown in the Catelli project, participants need perseverance, and some associations can last as long as the five teachers she has worked with over 18 years.

PDSs can strive and succeed because they benefit both sides—the university and the schools. Each partner has different goals, needs, and cultures, but they can nicely compliment each other. The positive tone of the Henning et al.'s chapter and the long-term record of collaboration described in the Catelli's chapter are testimonies to the difficulties, as well as the positive outcomes to all participants.

# 1 When a Look Back Can Be a Step Forward

## An Analysis of Two PDS Partnerships for Education Change and Improvement

*Linda A. Catelli*

This essay focuses on two longitudinal school–college/university partnerships I have initiated and directed. The first one was at Queens College of the City University of New York (CUNY), and operated for 18 years under the title of Project SCOPE I (1980–1998). The project targeted the school's curriculum and the college's preservice and inservice teacher education programs, and then integrated them to effect change and improvement in K–18 education. The belief that fundamental change in education occurs through a holistic–organic approach to partnerships was an integral part of Project SCOPE's conceptual framework and theory. Aspects of that partnership were institutionalized and still exist today at Queens College.

In the latter part of 1998, Project SCOPE's holistic approach to education change was expanded and relocated at Dowling College and three school districts on Long Island. The project went under the title of Project SCOPE II—School–College Operation in Partnership Education. It included the core subject areas of an elementary-school curriculum, such as science and language arts. Project SCOPE II has been in existence since 1998 and continues to have a vibrant relationship with one of the original three school districts—the North Babylon School District (NBSD). In 2006, the Belmont Elementary School of the NBSD became a Professional Development School (PDS). It adheres to the essentials and standards for PDSs, as well as the basic tenets of a holistic–organic partnership. Both Project SCOPE I and II are categorized as PDS-type partnerships in that their goals are to improve pre-K–12 education, professional education (16–20), and student learning in a coordinative fashion. Grade levels 16 through 20 refer to master's and doctoral degree programs in education.

In this essay, I analyze and compare the two partnerships with reference to the major elements of the Slater's School/University Collaborative Matrix. Also, I comment on the type of relationship (symbiotic or organic) among the participants, the sources of power and influence, and how such factors impacted the partnerships. Finally, writing this essay has given me the opportunity to look back and reflect on my many years of partnership work. It has helped me to identify the important lessons that I have learned in directing these partnerships. The essay is written in my voice and from my perspective as the professor-director of two small PDS partnerships that envisioned a new integrative K–20 education system.

## PROJECT SCOPE I AND II: DESCRIPTIONS AND ANALYSES

### Organizational Involvement and Type of Agreement

In 1980, Project SCOPE I began at Queens College/CUNY. The partnership involved 15 teachers with me as its director. A handshake and a two-page description of the teacher's role in the partnership was our basic contract. At that time, I was an untenured assistant professor. I initiated the partnership with cooperating teachers who had agreed to work with one another in a partnership arrangement. Our purpose was to improve K–12 education and teacher education. Although I had subsequently received tenure years later, the 15 teachers and I were not able to influence important decisions that were made at the higher levels within the system. Nor were we in positions of power to deter some of the blows that came from CUNY's financial problems and restructuring efforts. At the time, much of my work with the 15 teachers took me off campus for a good part of the week. Subsequently, this prevented me from developing the type of social capital one often needs to survive well during adverse situations at a university. First lesson: Be aware of how important it is to network, and how important developing social capital is to your survival. Second lesson: Make sure you and your dean are on influential committees to provide the benefits of partnerships so that the partnership can ride the political waves during a crisis.

The teachers represented schools from New York City, Westchester County, and Long Island. The schools included two high schools, two middle schools, and three elementary schools. Two of the schools were private institutions and the others were part of the public education system. The mixture of grade levels, systems, and settings (urban and suburban) was important for providing Project SCOPE I with what it needed to conduct its experimental work and research. Also, the mixture provided diversity in terms of philosophical and curriculum viewpoints. Such diversity was the partnership's strength along with the fact that the 15 teachers knew what it meant to work together as a team and resolve conflicts in order to reach a common goal. There was no power play among the teachers. Their respect for one another's position and mine as director prevailed in many of our debates and monthly discussions. As adjunct employees of the college the teachers were by contract in positions to influence course content, and to make decisions about student grades. They were part of the CUNY system. This was by design. I, on the other hand, did not have a contractual position with the schools. This limited my influence and involvement in the schools' curriculum. Regardless, for most of the 18 years there was an *esprit de corps* among members. Eight of the 15 teachers remained in the partnership for all of its 18 years. A more organic type of relationship among all involved had developed.

Project SCOPE I consisted of 15 teachers representing their schools with their principal's approval. I represented my department and one teacher education program at Queens College. The program was in a subject that was considered by some as having low status in the world of academe—health and physical education. Influence and power sometimes reside in an academic discipline. We often wondered if we would have suffered as many blows when the budget cuts came if the partnership were in mathematics or science. However, we were able to sustain the partnership for three reasons: One, we were cost effective. Two, we had by that time established trusting, organic-type relationships. And three, SCOPE I was part of a larger formal partnership agreement that the college had with two schools. One of the two schools was a high school located on the campus of Queens College—the Townsend Harris High School. The other was a middle school based in the Borough of Queens, the Louis Armstrong Middle School (LAMS–IS 227). Each of the now nationally-recognized schools had formal written agreements with Queens College that were signed by the College's president and the chancellor of New York City Board of Education.

The then-president of Queens College, Saul Cohen, was an avid proponent of school–college partnerships. He had artfully designed contracts with the NYC Board of Education to begin LAMS, and to resurrect the Townsend Harris School on the Queens College Campus. SCOPE I operated within these two larger contracted projects. As director, this afforded me some influence and power in the early years to make important decisions. Also, I was asked by the president to serve on committees responsible for designing the new Townsend Harris School. Thus, in addition to a handshake with the teachers, there were two formal agreements between the college and the NYC Board of Education signed by the top CEOs. My work at both schools, coupled with the president's interest in partnerships, had contributed to my receiving tenure, and to securing resources. It is no secret that an active and visible college president and dean in partnership work are key factors for success. However, the bottom line is the teachers' involvement. The tangible benefits to them in their classroom, as well as the financial benefits they receive, are important to sustaining their involvement. In 1985, Saul Cohen left Queens College. Partnerships in education at Queens College lost their position as a top priority item. Lesson learned: Power and influence are fluid. They change when leadership changes. Timing is, indeed, everything. Therefore, one should capitalize on the good times; make significant strides and innovations as an investment in sustainability; and push for strategic planning in the partnering institutions to favorably position the PDS partnership.

Which institution's strategic plan do you operative from? Open conversations among partners and a detailed annual contract that includes such information are critical to answering that question. Ideally, the partnership should appear in both the college and the district's strategic plans. If not, then this sets the stage for an invisible imbalance of power that sets the partnership and its members up for eventual failure.

Whereas SCOPE I involved Queens College, a public institution and 15 teachers from public and private schools, SCOPE II involved Dowling College, a private institution with public school districts. Having experienced a small partnership project among 15 teachers, I decided to branch out and design partnerships with formal letters of agreement that would involve whole institutions—schools, school districts, and a college. I designed contracts, this time as a full professor. Rank makes a difference and affords you more authority. In 1998, Project SCOPE II at Dowling College involved 3 school districts and 30 elementary-school teachers who had volunteered to participate in the first phase of the partnership. This time the dean and superintendents signed the agreements.

Private higher education institutions that are tuition driven and reliant on changing markets often find it difficult to relinquish their autonomy in partnerships. Also, they are more comfortable with symbiotic-type relationships rather than organic ones that require functional interdependence. This is understandable in that private colleges need to shift gears and make decisions quickly in order to survive financially. What private institutions may have yet to fully realize is that they are in a better position than public ones to innovate and benefit from well-conceived partnerships. On the other hand, partnerships with public higher education institutions and K–12 school systems are sometimes easier to form because they are really in the same system. However, they are more difficult to sustain because of the large number of rules and regulations in the system. To make change occur at the program level there were fewer bureaucratic obstacles in the private institution than in the public one. This was a definite plus. Two lessons I drew from the experiences: One, the institutional context within which the PDS partnership resides—private and/or public systems—is a significant factor that must be considered early on in designing and operating the partnership. If it is not accounted for it will become a serious *limitation*. Two, in private institutions time must be devoted to understanding how the business mind and academic mind come together in order to meet the challenges. It is important for the director to recognize that higher education today in America is an industry and a big business. Private institutions, especially, need to be convinced that quality will turn into quantity in terms of enrollment.

In the second year of SCOPE II (1999), the college's financial situation along with problems occurring in the districts impacted our ability to grow. Thus, the number of school districts and schools dwindled to one school district and one elementary school. The partnership survived because of one teacher, Joan Carlino, who had emerged as a leader. The teacher worked closely with me. She was respected enough by her principal and her peers to have influenced them to stay onboard during this difficult period. Respect, in this case, translated into positive power and influence. Subsequently, we survived the 2 years of financial hardships. We continued the partnership with detailed written contracts that were now signed annually by the president, the dean, chairs, director of field placement, the superintendent, principals, teachers, and representatives from the union. Let me reinforce the idea that detailed, annual contracts between partnering institutions are crucial. However, informal agreements with handshakes with partnering teachers are invaluable! Both are needed for sustainability. The lesson I learned was that it is important, especially for organic partnerships, to empower and compensate teachers financially. This should be emphasized in their contractual partnership roles and responsibilities. Teachers and the professors sustain longitudinal partnerships. Administrators should have a supporting role. They come and go more frequently in longitudinal partnerships. That is why it is important to move quickly to institutionalize a partnership.

## Purpose

As mentioned previously, both partnerships are categorized as PDSs. Their mission is four-fold: (a) prepare preservice teachers; (b) enhance the professional development of inservice teachers; (c) improve student learning at both the school and university level; and (d) conduct innovative, collaborative research on learning and education practice. Their mission and vision necessitate a comprehensive approach to improving education and teacher education in a coordinative fashion. Lesson learned: For PDSs to become a reality and be successful on a large scale, a coalition of associations, agencies, state education departments, school and university boards, and unions is needed. PDSs have the potential to be laboratories of innovation or R&D centers for ushering in a new era in education. They are newer structures in education that require breaking the status quo. This is a daunting vision but a timely one for education in America.

## Resources

In both partnerships, I received three credits of released time to direct the operation. Currently, I receive an additional three credits a semester to conduct research that is often related to the partnership. Also, the college has hired and paid a liaison to coordinate activities between the school and college, and to provide professional development for teachers in their new role as supervisors of student teachers. In addition to receiving tuition waivers for serving as cooperating teachers, the PDS supervisors also receive payment for performing supervisory functions before or after school time. Also, the PDS teachers are hired and paid by the college to teach seminars and to co-teach an education course with me. The content of the course was approved by the college. The roles that the teachers serve in this PDS partnership include: host teacher, cooperating teacher, supervisor/mentor of student teachers, action researcher, course instructor, seminar leader, lead teacher, and member of the PDS Advisory Council.

## Limitations and Sources of Resistance

The limitations I confronted in both partnerships revolved around what I call the "three Cs"—commitment, capacity, and competency. It refers to the partnering institutions' level of commitment to the partnership's vision-mission; their capacity to enact the vision-mission; and their ability to sustain the PDS partnership. If one or two are assessed as low, they severely limit the development and vitality of a PDS. If all three are low and remain low, then it may be time to end the partnership. Lesson learned: Assess the PDS partnership periodically for the "three Cs."

In both partnerships, the financial stability of each institution and the frequent change of leadership were factors that prevented growth. Lessons learned: Involve members of the school boards and boards of trustees in PDS partnerships. Have board members along with the president and superintendent involved in fund-raising for the partnership. Their role is to raise funds and to remove pathological conditions that prevent the partnership from succeeding Also, have them interact annually with the students from partnering institutions so that may see the tangible results of partnership work.

In terms of *sources of resistance*, a college president who had previously served in the U.S. diplomatic corps once commented to me that it was easier to negotiate with the North Koreans at times than the faculty. It is enormously difficult to bring a whole school and college faculty in line with a PDS partnership. The cultures are so different. And the competing agendas within institutions are a daily reality. That coupled with tensions between administration and faculty present formidable sources of resistance. I have learned, though, that such sources of resistance can be confronted successfully with: (a) the creative design of the roles people serve; (b) the incentives they are offered; (c) the rewards they receive from the work; and (d) how much they are empowered.

## Mutuality and Positives

I can say with confidence that when a PDS partnership works well, both the school and the university benefit. Unquestionably, schools and universities are in a high state of being mutually beneficial to one another. This, in turn, benefits a state's efforts to improve and renew education. With time and persistence, everyone can be working on the same page. And if it is a true holistic–organic relationship, it is for the common good. This is an enormously complex agenda, especially in today's self-oriented climate. It is also complex because of hierarchical organizational structures that are entrenched in old-world management styles and norms. These are also *sources of resistance and limitations*. But, what I have learned is that they can be confronted, accounted for, and then changed. I know this to be so because I have seen it happen on a small scale. And that is a *positive*. Also, let me say that symbiotic-type relationships and projects in a PDS do exist. However, they must be placed within a larger organic framework in a partnership to secure its longevity. Lesson learned: Identify such projects and have individuals reveal their intentions, reasons, or motives for joining and remaining in a PDS. This helps to determine who is in it for the long run. Who benefits more? Who has more power? In a longitudinal PDS the benefits and power shift from time to time from the school to the university and vice versa. If both tip more to one side for too long then the situation may need to be confronted honestly. It is a delicate balance.

Finally, as a national movement, PDSs are gaining momentum and they are accruing evidence and research to demonstrate their value and impact in different arenas such as student learning, the achievement gap, teacher retention, teacher quality and efficacy, teacher-to-student ration, student engagement, and professional development. PDS partnerships are not fads. As I look back and then ahead, I can say that PDSs are waves of the future that represent the very best example of partnerships for education change, improvement, and renewal. Also, they present a refreshing pre-K to 20 vision of American education in the 21st century.

# 2 Growing a Multi-Site Professional Development School

*John E. Henning, Becky Wilson Hawbaker,*
*Debra S. Lee, and Cynthia F. McDonald*

The purpose of this chapter is to describe the evolution of a multi-site professional development school during its first 2 years. This initiative began as a pilot project intended to improve the quality of the field experiences offered at the University of Northern Iowa (UNI). At the inception of this project, it was not clear how we would move away from a traditional conception of school–university relationships. Our lack of a clear vision for specific outcomes in a multi-site professional development school caused us to place particular emphasis on growing the PDS through a collaborative process. This chapter provides a narrative of the journey, describes the resulting organization, and discusses the lessons we learned.

## ORGANIZATIONAL INVOLVEMENT

The three partner organizations represented in UNI's professional development school are the University of Northern Iowa, the Cedar Falls Community Schools, and the Waterloo Community Schools. The University of Northern Iowa has a large teacher education program (approximately 600 graduates per year) whose students move through three levels of early field experiences, many of which are located in both the Cedar Falls and Waterloo School Districts. In Cedar Falls, UNI students are placed in one high school, two middle schools, and six elementary schools. In Waterloo, UNI students are placed in three high schools, four middle schools, and 12 elementary schools.

## MUTUALITY LEVEL

Each of the three partners in the professional development school perceived a high level of benefit for participation. All three shared a common concern with the quality of teacher education. Many of UNI's graduates become teachers in the Waterloo and Cedar Falls Community Schools, and there is a long history of past partnership with these two school districts. Thus, representatives of the partner institutions entered the pilot project with positive expectations and a common agenda to improve field experiences.

## PURPOSES OF THE COLLABORATION

The impetus for beginning the Professional Development School Pilot Study began with the work of a task force appointed by the UNI provost. The task force consisted of various stakeholders representing the university, the College of Education, the university laboratory school, the teacher advisory board, and the alumni. The initial purpose of the task force was to make a recommendation concerning the future of the Malcolm Price Laboratory School. Although the committee could not agree on such a recommendation, the two local school superintendents crafted a proposal for starting a professional development school. This invitation was operationalized in the form of a pilot study proposal, which was unanimously recommended by the task force. The three purposes of the pilot study were: (a) to determine to what degree field experiences could be expanded beyond their current capacity; (b) to determine the value of providing additional structure and faculty supervision for the field experiences; and (c) to generate a PDS model based on NCATE's five standards for professional development schools.

## FLOW OF INFLUENCE

Upon approval of the project in early July 2007, the first step in implementing the pilot project was to call a meeting between university and school personnel. The two superintendents brought key school leaders, such as the elementary and secondary curriculum directors and the professional development director. The university was represented by the coordinator of field experiences, the director of teacher education, and the chair of the teacher education faculty. From this initial meeting emerged the Governance Committee that steered the activities of the PDS.

## Limited Emphasis on Advanced Planning

The second meeting of the Governance Committee was held on August 10, 2007. Although the tone of the meeting was very positive, there was a concern that because classes were to begin on August 25th, the pilot would benefit from a year of extended planning. However, engaging in a year of extended planning period was rejected for three reasons. First, a substantial budget for the project had been approved for the immediate fiscal year, and there was no guarantee that there would be interest in providing a comparable budget in the following year. Second, postponing immediate implementation of the pilot would sacrifice momentum and risk the inertia that ended previous attempts to initiate a PDS. Third, and most importantly, any planning would have been based on assumptions derived from pre-existing relationships. Therefore, even the most extensive plan would be outdated within a month of implementation. So, we took a deep breath and began.

## Planting a Seed and Letting It Grow

Starting the pilot project immediately offered several advantages over an extended planning approach. Instead of making decisions based on hypothetical information or data gathered in our old model, our decision making was stimulated by our engagement in the PDS pilot study. This enabled two powerful thinking processes: tacit thinking (Polanyi, 1958) and simultaneous thinking (Davis & Sumara, 1997). Thinking tacitly about a problem requires being immersed in its context; simultaneous thinking also requires a similar immersion as a way of processing all the possibilities.

## Managing Anxiety

To ensure the unimpeded evolution of the pilot study, we made a sustained effort to reduce the anxiety surrounding the change process. Three strategies were consistently and continually employed: (a) make small changes incrementally; (b) listen closely and respond quickly; and (c) make the process transparent.

### Make Small Changes Incrementally

Our primary approach to managing the anxiety associated with rapid and unscripted change was to make small changes incrementally. For example, we made only one initial change—the addition of supervision in the early field experiences in four pilot schools. This relatively small change was intended to break the current system from its inertia and trigger another small change, then another, and another; in other words, one small change set the conditions for the system to begin evolving. Because the initial change was small and relatively manageable, it limited the initial problems we had to address. This enabled us to respond to them in a timely way and thus reduce the anxiety of those involved.

### Listen Closely and Respond Quickly

Feedback is essential to the change process, and we solicited it often; for example, during casual conversations, supervisor meetings, presentations to teachers, and Governance Committee meetings. The willingness of stakeholders to speak freely was vital to eliciting accurate information on which to base our decisions. Therefore, it was critically important to make shareholders feel their comments were valued and appreciated, and under no circumstances to show any resentment or resistance to the feedback we received. We demonstrated we were listening by handling problems swiftly and decisively, thus establishing credibility with teachers, principals, and other participants.

### Make the Process Transparent

We also made the process as transparent as possible. A primary strategy was to include educators who may have been initially regarded as sources of resistance. In fact, this approach served as incentive for faculty to participate. Those involved were assured they could report events for their constituencies without fear of censorship or intimidation (i.e., serve as watchdogs). In this way, faculty who might have served as sources of resistance became insiders who identified problems and provided valuable feedback on them.

## RESISTANCE SOURCES

We treated problems encountered during the pilot study as indicators of the emergent organization of our professional development school. In the evolving context of our pilot study, three significant sources of resistance emerged: concerns about implications for the laboratory school, teacher concerns about university support, and principal concerns about being overburdened.

## Concerns about the Laboratory School

An initial concern came from some teachers and university faculty who worried that starting a PDS would cause the closure of the laboratory school. To manage anxiety from this quarter, we moved the conversation beyond debating whether a laboratory school or a professional development school was a better choice for our university. Instead, we emphasized the importance of engaging with local schools, deemphasized the idea of the PDS as an alternative to the laboratory school, and included numerous laboratory school faculty in the project.

## Teacher Concerns about University Support

The P–12 teachers also had a number of reservations about the project. After listening to an introductory presentation about professional development schools, a number of teachers had questions and comments. Their questions suggested a general concern that their administrators were committing them to more than they could handle. There was also a sentiment that the university had not been fully supportive in the past and some doubt expressed as to whether there would be follow up on this project.

An oft-asked question was: What will be different for us in a professional development school? When we answered this last question by referring to the addition of supervisors, concerns were raised about the nature of the supervision. We responded by continually repeating that teachers were in charge of their own classrooms, by sharing this feedback in our committee meetings, and by preparing our supervisors to manage these concerns.

Others wanted to know what they would receive in return for participating in the PDS pilot study. So to encourage participation, we initially offered teachers incentives such as library cards and tickets to musical performances. Later, when the Governance Committee identified inexpensive credits for licensure renewal as a powerful incentive, we offered graduate credits at a reduced cost for teachers who agreed to host field experience students. Three courses on mentoring preservice teachers were created to serve this purpose.

During the initial course, teachers were shown specific strategies for mentoring field experience students, such as how to get them involved in their classroom, how they could ask reflective questions, how to conduct inquires with them, and how to assess them. The teachers responded very positively to the course, demonstrating their eagerness to learn more, to participate more, and in general, to become more involved in the decision-making process. Their interest in learning more led to the development of a second and third course, both of which emphasized mentoring other teachers on mentoring.

## Principal Concerns

The PDS building principals played a critical role in the initial implementation of the project. They were highly supportive and invested considerable time and energy into persuading their teachers to take part in the project. However, feedback from principals indicated they strongly endorsed the position that teachers should be persuaded, not coerced, to participate. Principals also felt overburdened when asked to do additional tasks associated with the coordination of field experiences. To address these concerns, we appointed site coordinators and introduced the previously discussed incentives for hosting field placements. The site coordinators are teachers in the building who coordinate the field placements and generally serve as liaisons to the university. As new schools are added to the pilot project, principals typically express their appreciation for being relieved of these responsibilities.

## RESOURCES

The new resources introduced as part of the base budget for the pilot project came primarily from the central administration of the university. Funding from the central administration provided the supervisors, the site coordinators, and the supplies, such as evaluation forms, notebooks, mileage for supervision, and refreshments at mentoring classes. The central administration also provided teachers with access to some university services, including the university library and musical events. Finally, the central administration also provided meeting space, a $500 building gift as an incentive to participating schools, and reduced tuition for participating teachers.

Additional resources have come from three other sources. The College of Education has provided the funding to support the faculty resources needed for the project, including the PDS director, the coordinator of field experiences, and the lead supervisor. Grants have funded several special projects, for example, the development of a literacy PDS in an elementary school in Waterloo. And finally, the two partner school districts have continued to contribute resources they have always provided, such as meeting space, the teachers who served as mentors and site coordinators, the classrooms where preservice teachers engage in their field experience, and access to the classrooms for preservice teachers.

## POSITIVES

The resources invested in the pilot study by the university resulted in a number of positives for the three partners. First, the addition of supervisors and site coordinators provided new lines of communication between the schools and the university, producing an immediate improvement in the structure and organization of the field experiences. Second, the addition of the three courses on Mentoring Preservice Teachers provided a forum for teachers and university faculty to share ideas on improving the field experiences. This created richer and more interactive field experiences for preservice teachers and more leadership opportunities for mentoring teachers. Third, conversations begun among faculty members in PDS committees have led to the development of curriculum and instruction more supportive of field experiences.

At some future point, a significant number of teachers in the PDS may have either taken the mentoring courses or have received some form of professional development from teachers who have taken the courses. At this time, we can't be certain what impact this will have or what opportunities for further evolution it may offer us, but we are confident that the infrastructure of trusting relationships, a support system of new roles and responsibilities, an interwoven network of educators who value and engage in teacher education, and a foundation of successful joint initiatives will continue to spark and instigate ongoing innovations.

## INFORMAL TO FORMAL STRUCTURE

The response to the professional development school was so positive that in the second year of the project (2008–2009), the pilot was expanded to include 8 additional schools for a total of 12 schools: 2 high schools, 3 middle schools, and 7 elementary schools. In addition, the process of writing a formal statement of the partnership also began during the second year. Thus, representatives of the three partner institutions are currently crafting an articulation agreement that will delineate our mission statement, the contributions of each partner, the roles and responsibilities of participants, the governance procedures, and our commitment to diversity.

## LIMITATIONS

The most significant limitations for both school and university participants are time and resources. The primary commitment of the participants is to their own institution, and the demands made on them by that institution are substantial. Thus, teachers can be reluctant to engage in more professional development, even when provided without cost or obligation. Similarly, professors have limited time for field supervision or engaging with teachers, although they would readily acknowledge the value of doing so.

## LESSONS LEARNED

The professional development school pilot study began by making a single change in the previous approach to organizing field experiences. This initiated a collaborative process that led to a number of unanticipated innovations in our field experiences, including the addition of site coordinators, incentives for teachers, and courses for mentoring preservice teachers. We expect these changes to provide opportunities for further improvements in the next phase of our partnership. The following are some valuable lessons that we have gained from our experience.

### Grass Roots Support

From the beginning our PDS grew and developed from the needs of the stakeholders. By not imposing an arbitrary model at the outset, we allowed our understanding of the PDS to grow as we acquired more experience, thus providing stakeholders with a sense of ownership in the pilot project. Stakeholders agreed on a common purpose, shared the responsibility for meeting that purpose, and were willing to explore new ways of working together to achieve that purpose. The strong support the pilot project received from the leadership was a necessary catalyst in starting the project, but the direction of the project was fashioned on the ground, one field experience student, one teacher, one administrator, and one professor at a time.

## Professional Development

We discovered from survey and focus group data that mentoring teachers found significant benefit in hosting field experience students for self-reflection, for their teaching practices, and for their students. Similarly, we found that teachers responded positively to opportunities to work with university faculty, either as site coordinators, in connection with the Mentoring Preservice Teachers classes, or in collaboration with university liaisons. Our experience suggests that the opportunity to work with the university offered a powerful incentive for mentoring teachers.

## Culture Building

As the project unfolded, we began to realize that a significant part of implementing a professional development school is creating and sustaining a culture for school–university partnership activities. This occurred primarily through the development of structured activities that fostered dialogue and relationship building, for example, the Governance Committee meetings, the addition of site coordinators, and the Mentoring Preservice Teachers classes. Creating situations that bring educators from both the school and university together can significantly foster capacity building and distributed leadership.

## FUTURE DIRECTIONS

As we move forward, we are considering other ways to foster dialogue, relationships, and professional development opportunities. A primary approach is to provide additional opportunities for mutual professional development, such as co-teaching assignments that include both teachers and university faculty. Co-teaching assignments should offer teachers substantial opportunities to develop skills associated with teaching and leadership; similarly, they should offer professors exposure to current practice and access to field-based settings.

Our vision is to develop environments, instructional strategies, and dispositions that enable professors, teachers, and preservice teachers to work collaboratively to increase P–12 student achievement. Inevitably, continued funding will be a challenge as we move forward. But the direction we have chosen will continue to lead us to productive outcomes if we remain true to the most powerful lessons we have learned during our pilot project. School improvement and teacher education are inseparable: Fostering one inevitably benefits the other. Further, when schools and universities deliberately and systematically cultivate their partnerships, they can enhance the intended outcomes of both institutions to a greater degree than either could do separately.

## REFERENCES

Davis, B., & Sumara, D. (1997). Cognition, complexity and teacher education. *Harvard Educational Review, 67*(1), 105–125.

Polanyi, M. (1958). *Personal knowledge: Towards a post-critical philosophy.* Chicago: University of Chicago Press.

# Part II

# Consultation

The designation in Slater's Matrix termed *consultation* encompasses those projects that involve university faculty as consultant to schools or systems, and/or private organizations for either formal or informal use of their expertise. The purpose of this type of collaboration is varied and can range from a planned change, teacher professional development, research facilitation, grant development and implementation, or the implementation and delivery of university coursework for advanced degrees off-campus. In addition, it may be some configuration between the university and school administration, faculty, or administrative staff, requiring the special skills and expertise university faculty can deliver to the school system.

The resources for such collaboration are institutional in that they require time use for faculty and personnel and are usually compensated for in real and monetary form. In addition, access to the school system by university faculty is another positive of this scheme. Mutuality levels are high because this is often contractual and the parameters of the collaboration are designated and understood by all parties up front.

Whereas this formal interaction is clear, often the limitations are the university and/or school system that are resistant to these projects. Whereas the initiative to conduct research is valued by the university, and service and community involvement is important, the entrepreneurial nature of the work is often not positively viewed by chairpersons or others within the academic community. Likewise, the school system, by going outside of their own built-in process for training and expertise, has its own problems of acceptance of innovation and letting outsiders in on their perceived shortcomings and need for outside help. Therefore, faculty involved in this must garnish and sustain the trust of the school system personnel they interact with, and make sure that internal factors at the university itself do not result in punitive evaluation of how they spend their time.

The positive result of consultation is that it can prove to be a fruitful source of data for the university faculty who must publish as part of their research agenda, and for the school system to get state-of-the-art information and dissemination of best practice from the source of knowledge production.

Because of the nature of the contracted parameters of the partnership, collaboration is one-dimensional and may have limited sustainability. It is difficult, given all the other tasks required of university faculty, to maintain a high level of involvement over time with schools. Nor is it in their best interests to ignore the other things they are responsible for, such as teaching, service, and publication. On the other hand, the culture of systematic evidence-based decision making and research is not usually part of the operation of schools. They tend to respond more directly to immediate needs with short term solutions based on accountability factors evidencing success.

We offer three examples of the consultation organizational structure for collaboration in this section. The first, by Hulme, Menter, Kelly, and Rusby, describes an ambitious project involving three universities, the Scottish government, and over 50 high school sites in a school change effort for action research. The Manke and Marrier project has 10 school districts and a university informal grant funded consultation for new teacher induction. The last is the Mizukami, Reali, and Tancredi Brazilian consultation of a public university with a public elementary school inservice teacher education program. The inclusion of two consultation projects, one in Europe and the other South America, highlights the universality of the issues evident in conducting collaborative work.

Hulme, et al.'s 3-year project was initiated and funded by the Scottish government to enact school change through an action research model. The university support team was instrumental in streaming feedback to the school and community over three years of implementation. School communities were formed based on the idea that they would learn more together than they could alone, and each school formed a transformational plan that localized need for curriculum, teacher/student leadership, student learning, and community involvement.

The three universities each got contracts to conduct research on the project and serve as mentors and evaluators. Each site had university mentor and government representative for support along with a project manager, government research coordinator, and advisory group.

Resistance to the change effort, even though it was government initiated, was evident in school personnel who viewed this as something else imposed upon them, were skeptical about the research relevance, and were wary of being evaluated. Mentors spent more time than they were funded for on site in order to sustain dialogue and promote support for the program, and they had to negotiate with the school site leadership who acted as gatekeepers to innovation that came from without. The school coordinators who had responsibility to translate the plan into effective strategies of action research had to act as brokers between the teachers and the tasks, and sustain the innovations and build communities. The government support teams were advisers responsible for designing conferences and events, identify training providers and sites of excellence, and keeping the flow of communication open. These advisers were subsequently eliminated when funding was withdrawn under new government policies. Thus the flow of funds determined and sustained the high level of personnel needed for the work, but when that was eliminated, the government teams left and the project could not sustain itself.

Whereas mutuality was high among the stakeholders, in order to sustain this type of consultation government support is necessary for funding, school leaders need to be committed and provide resources and time for teacher evaluation, and the university departments of education need to support faculty and schools over time. Most importantly, there needs to be constant brokering to create communities of common enquiry such as those described in this consultation.

The Manke and Marrier consultation is between a university and 10 schools. It was an informal, but grant-funded project with compliance formality, whose purpose was to support new teacher induction through mentoring, seminars, professional development, and effective student teacher placement.

Mutuality for this project was potentially high as grants written by the Associate Dean at the university paid for faculty to deliver professional development for mentor teachers and substitutes so they could attend seminars offered by the university. Yet, resistance was exhibited with reluctance of some faculty to participate in subject areas needed for the training. They viewed this as beyond their responsibility as subject area specialists. One school district did not like the professional development activities and chose not to participate, and others wanted a calendar of planned activities which was not feasible for the university. These problems eroded trust among participants, a condition we see again and again in collaboration. University and school faculty have different agendas within and across their institutions. Yet, the consultation model has the potential to affect teacher training programs as described by Manke and Marrier, when the university faculty are willing to function as co-learners to build what they learned into their teaching at the university.

As seen in the previous project, when funding sources changed focus away from specific school district concerns, the configuration of the project was not sustainable. In addition, university problems of time, policies of space and resource utilization, and administrative support were apparent. Therefore, the power relationship of a top-down consultation model that was university initiated and funded by a grant had to be balanced with a conception of shared power and decision making among stakeholders. This, in turn, had to be balanced with personnel and leadership dynamics in order to sustain the partnership. Manke and Marrier rightly ponder the life cycle of collaboration. They question the influence of the university and the tensions of the implementation which are common whenever people come together and they do not share the same vision and have to break down barriers to implement change.

The last selection in this section is the Mizukami, Reali, and Tancredi consultation project in Brazil between a university and a public school to provide inservice teacher education. In addition to the problems discussed in the other projects in this section, they emphasize the problems of mutuality and resistance to change evident in the beliefs and suppositions underlying the process of collaboration. These problems, they state, are ones of contradictions, ambiguity, and truth in situations encountered. They conclude that trust in listening tolerance and being listened to seriously is something that participants need to do in order to maximize benefits of the collaboration.

Another area of contention is the dichotomy of methodology between what the educational literature considers collaborative research, action research, academic knowledge, and practical knowledge. Teachers feel, the authors state, dispossessed of knowledge learned from their experience, forced to adopt the academic stance. It is a difference in the academic paradigm and the practitioner paradigm, a real difference in world view of the enterprise of teaching and learning. Therefore, when in the midst of a change effort, it is imperative to know where each of the stakeholders is coming from and to work hard so that together an understanding is reached about the project at hand and how it fits into the reality of the everyday life in schools. This is particularly true of consultation where the initiation is most often from the university level.

# 3 Schools of Ambition
## Bridging Professional and Institutional Boundaries

*Moira Hulme, Ian Menter, Deirdre Kelly, and Sheelagh Rusby*

## INTRODUCTION

The Schools of Ambition programme (2006–2010) is a collaborative partnership between 52 high schools, 3 universities, and the Scottish Government Schools' Directorate. The role of the university-based Research Support Team is to stream formative feedback to the schools and wider education community through a 3-year period of school-initiated "transformational change." The programme is distinctive in Scotland in its promotion of an action research model within a national programme for school change. This chapter identifies the opportunities and challenges arising from participation in this innovative programme from the perspective of university, school, and government participants.

## BECOMING A SCHOOL OF AMBITION

The policy document *Ambitious, Excellent Schools* (SEED, 2004) set out a modernisation agenda for comprehensive schools[1] in Scotland. Teachers and schools were afforded greater freedom to tailor learning to the needs of their students. Within a framework of national guidance, schools were encouraged to explore flexible, creative, and innovative approaches to school improvement (Learning and Teaching Scotland, 2003).

In February 2005, local authorities[2] were invited to nominate high schools to participate in the programme with the stated aim that these schools "will stand out in their locality, and nationally, as innovators and leaders, providing ambition and opportunity for young people, setting an example to the whole community" (SEED, 2007, p. 1). The Schools of Ambition include "schools most in need of transformation—very often those contending with the most challenging local circumstances in Scotland—and schools that have strong ideas for transformation and can set new standards of excellence" (SEED, 2007, p. 1). The Schools of Ambition community is thus an eclectic mix of those schools judged to be most in need of transformation and a smaller number of high achieving, innovative schools with clear plans for the development of distinctive practice. The network is founded on the premise that schools can learn more together than alone (Lieberman, 1999).

Each school submitted a "Transformational Plan" outlining their priorities for change. Broadly defined common themes associated with national and regional priorities are discernible. These include enhancement and/or restructuring of the curriculum, initiatives to promote (teacher and student) leadership, student confidence and engagement with learning, and community involvement. Whilst there are common themes, the freedom to articulate flexible responses to specific local circumstances is a key feature of the programme. A commitment to self-evaluation is a condition of the award of School of Ambition status. In contrast to "outside-in" forms of evaluation, the Schools of Ambition hold responsibility for collecting and analysing evaluation information that will map distance travelled toward the achievement of locally defined goals.

Schools of Ambition receive additional funding of £100,000 (c. $148,800 USD) per annum for 3 years. This funding can be used to support changes to the school estate; promote new partnerships through community, college and business links; invest in curriculum and teacher development; or create new posts (such as specialist coaches or counsellors), including time-limited coordinator or project manager posts from within the school staff. Since its launch in 2005 the programme has expanded from 21 schools (tranche one) to 28 by March 2007 (seven additional tranche two schools), and finally 52 schools distributed across the 32 local authorities of Scotland by September 2007 (24 additional tranche three schools).

## RESEARCH TO SUPPORT SCHOOLS OF AMBITION

In June 2006, following a process of competitive tendering, a consortium of the Universities of Glasgow, Aberdeen, and Strathclyde was awarded the contract for *Research to Support Schools of Ambition*. There are two strands to this collaboration: (a) a *mentoring strategy*; and (b) an *evaluation strategy* to explore processes of change across the network and distil lessons learned. A mentor (or critical friend) from the university consortium and an advisor from the Government Support Team support each school[3]. The project is overseen by a programme manager and a part-time research coordinator within the Scottish Government Schools' Directorate, and is supported by a research advisory group with membership drawn from the policy, practice, and academic community.

The mentoring strategy includes:

- Support in refining teacher-initiated proposals
- Advice on issues of manageability/scope, stages, timeline, and resources

- Advice on ethical practice in practitioner research
- Advice on collaborative use of a bespoke Virtual Research Environment
- Advice on accessing electronic resources (research briefings for a practitioner audience)
- Support for data collection, analysis, and reporting
- Support in compiling a "Telling the Story" electronic portfolio for dissemination purposes
- An annual evaluation conference for teacher researchers

Each mentor offers 3 days on-site support to the school each annum, supplemented by telementoring through the Virtual Research Environment, email, and telephone contact. The evaluation of the programme has involved annual rounds of semi-structured interviews with members of the leadership team and teacher researchers in each school, plus an online questionnaire to all school-based participants and telephone survey of community partners involved in supporting each school during this period of significant change.

## HOW DID THE UNIVERSITY BENEFIT BY THIS PROJECT?

Involvement in the Schools of Ambition programme encouraged reflection on the value of supporting teacher research, the impact of partnership working within the wider context of university work, deliberation on what counts as research evidence in this context, and how it would be judged in terms of academic rigor. In common with other European countries, in Scotland there is a move toward career-long professional learning. The *Common European Principles for Teacher Competences and Qualifications* (European Commission, 2009) recommended teacher education programmes across the three cycles of higher education (bachelor, master's, and doctorate within the meaning of the Bologna Process) and the provision of formal and informal professional development opportunities across teachers' careers. The Schools of Ambition programme has strengthened relationships between experienced teachers and teacher educators, helping to bridge the school–university, research–practice divide and sustaining research engagement beyond award bearing courses (such the Chartered Teacher Programme or the Scottish Qualification for Headship). The Universities of Glasgow and Aberdeen have moved toward inquiry-oriented preservice teacher education programmes through the provision of master's level components (Glasgow) and the development of the Scottish Teachers for New Era programme (Aberdeen; based on the U.S. Teachers for New Era programme supported by the Carnegie Foundation). Working in a longer-term project (2006–2010) allowed for growth in understanding as schools came on-stream in three successive tranches for a period of 3 years.

University mentors accrued experience over time and were supported by the involvement of an external facilitator—an experienced researcher within the lead university, but outside the project team—who supported the development of a supplementary 'reflexive strand' to this work.

## BUILDING COMMUNITIES OF ENQUIRY

### University Mentors

Whilst much has been written of the progressive possibilities of teacher research and the benefits of extended opportunities for professional collaboration (Cochran-Smith & Lytle, 1999; Hargreaves, 1994; Lieberman & Pointer Mace, 2008), there are fewer accounts of the complexities of collaboration and partnership (Bullough, Draper, Smith, & Birrell, 2004; Carlone & Webb, 2006). Aspirations for "expansive organisational learning" are played out within existing work cultures (Hodkinson & Hodkinson, 2003; Wenger, 1998). School–university research partnerships are built on histories of previous partnership work and are influenced by preconceptions of research and its relevance to the pragmatic concerns of classteachers (Peters, 2002; Smedley, 2001; Stronach & McNamara, 2002).

The university team encountered a range of reactions at the inception meeting held in September 2006 with headteachers/principals from the first 21 schools. These reactions include: (a) *resentment* at having to engage with an additional, and unexpected, demand within the programme; (b) *skepticism* about the feasibility of developing an evaluation strand within existing school plans; (c) *questioning of the relevance* of "academic" research to the school-led ethos of School of Ambition; and (d) a recognition among some school leaders that evaluation could proceed in tandem with curriculum development and that the involvement of mentors might serve to *support capacity building* within a model of school-led change.

Consequently, in the first year of the programme mentors committed greater time than was funded to visit schools and build relationships that might sustain and deepen professional dialogue as the programme developed. An initial generic model of "outside-in" research workshops was abandoned in favour of more responsive modes of engagement. Mentors encouraged the formation of school enquiry groups, negotiated on a case-by-case basis to reflect each school's current situation, expectations, and aspirations. Guidance materials were provided to support the development of protocols and the configuration of enquiry teams.

By the end of the second year, 15 of the 28 schools in the programme (54%) had formed an enquiry/evaluation group with up to eight members. This process was sometimes interrupted by recurrent changes in school staff; varying degrees of preparedness to devolve responsibility and opportunities beyond school management teams; negative connotations attached to research and continuing suspicion about the role of evaluation within school, especially in relation to peer observation. School leaders commonly acted as gatekeepers, moderating the transfer of new practices from outside collaborators.

The limitations of externally imposed or "contrived collegiality" (Hargreaves, 1994) are well documented. Mentor engagement requires sensitivity to the many competing demands on busy teachers' time, and a preparedness to work flexibly within the shifting timescales that mark the peak and troughs of evaluation activity across the school calendar. Throughout this process, it was important to maintain critical friendship in providing feedback to scaffold further reflection, development, and improvement action. An understanding of the distinction between *doing* a time-bound work-based project and adopting an "inquiry stance" to professional practice (Cochran-Smith & Lytle, 2001) is of significance here. Extending evaluation approaches beyond routine data gathering (attendance, attainment, exclusion, and participation rates) to include consideration of "soft" (qualitative) indicators and the involvement of students (and other stakeholders) as co-investigators has proven particularly challenging.

## School Coordinators

The possibility of embedding an inquiry stance within school improvement planning is highly dependent on the role of the school coordinator, who is both strategist and advocate. The coordinator works with members of the senior management team to translate the transformational plan (or "vision") into an actionable strategy, supported by cycles of action research. Effective coordinators adopt an extended role, aligning development and research plans with the day-to-day concerns and priorities of class teachers.

Collaboration within schools has proven most effective where the appointed coordinator is a senior and respected colleague, who is afforded adequate time to respond to the operational challenges of leading evaluation, and who possesses the necessary interpersonal skills to grow a culture of enquiry within situational constraints. The tenacity and skill of the school-based coordinator are important in sustaining momentum across interrelated strands of activity and in promoting opportunities for collegial learning.

Coordination is inhibited by well-documented barriers such as the segmentation of time, space, and school curricula within subjects and stages (Hargreaves, 1994, 2003). Prospects for the sustainability of initiatives may be diminished by workload intensification and where insufficient attention is afforded to the importance of community building. School coordinators frequently play an important brokerage role in responding to these challenges by: (a) raising the profile and communicating the relevance of Schools of Ambition activities; (b) inviting participation from peers in promoted and non-promoted posts and across curriculum boundaries; (c) encouraging acceptance of professional enquiry as a valuable professional development practice; (d) creating spaces for the self-determination of teacher research priorities; and (e) extending the focus of enquiry beyond the school walls through the involvement wider community stakeholders.

## Government Support Team

The team of advisers are experienced teachers seconded from local authority Advisory Services to the national Schools of Ambition Support Team. They provide regular networking opportunities through day conferences and residential events for school leaders. In addition to identifying links between schools (with shared development priorities), the advisers identify relevant training providers and sites of good practice outside the Schools of Ambition network. They are able to provide linkage and improve the flow of communication between the schools and other strands of the policy community, such as Learning and Teaching Scotland (the main organisation for the development of the Scottish curriculum), the schools' inspectorate, and local authority officers.

The advisers may be seen to occupy a somewhat ambivalent position characterised by proximity to and distance from policy and practice communities. Their peripatetic role, "hot desking" within the schools' directorate and working from home to coordinate networking events and regional school visits, is likely to engender a sense of "uprootedness" (Wenger, 1998, p. 110). Their influence within policy circles is linked with the life cycle and standing of the programme, which was adversely affected by a change in government. In March 2008, it was announced that the new administration would not continue to support the programme when current commitments to the existing 52 schools are met in 2010. The programme manager and seconded advisers now face the additional challenge of sustaining levels of commitment and influence in a shifting policy landscape.

Whereas the mentors and advisers share a common commitment to building capacity, they have different roles and responsibilities within the programme. Mentors focus on the development of systematic professional enquiry and advisers monitor and support school compliance with programme objectives. Within this model of collaboration, enquiry and accountability are two sides of the same coin and levels of mutuality are high. The negotiation of shared understandings is important. In common with school communities, the advisory team has limited experience of engagement with educational research and is primarily immersed in a "discourse of delivery" (Fielding, 2003). The facilitation role played by the government research coordinator, appointed for her experience in working across sectoral and professional boundaries, is particularly important in weaving together the strands of support within the programme, drawing together the complementary roles and expertise afforded by the various partners.

## CONCLUSION

The Schools of Ambition programme is an innovative way of providing support for schools that are going through a period of significant change, often in challenging circumstances. *Research to Support Schools of Ambition* illustrates the complexities of working across professional and institutional boundaries. The issue of "fidelity" in school–university partnerships is well observed (Campbell & Keating, 2005). Within the Schools of Ambition programme, fidelity is pertinent to: (a) *national government* support for the programme (over a change in administration and lead personnel); (b) *school leaders* commitment to integrating development and research in school improvement planning (as stipulated within the award of School of Ambition status) and, following from this, the provision of adequate resource for teacher evaluators (including time for reflection and joint work); and (c) the fidelity of *university departments of education* to maintaining support for schools over an extended period of time.

Although the schools vary in many ways, new relationships between research, policy, and practice are becoming visible as they engage with a research orientation. These relationships are complex, highly contingent, and affected by power imbalances and status inequities. Our experience through the Schools of Ambition programme has highlighted the significance of time scale and information flow in networks characterised by contrasting allegiances. Constant brokering has proven of paramount importance in creating a community of enquiry from diverse communities of practice (Wenger, 1998). Sustained interaction between university mentors, school personnel, and government advisers ("boundary encounters") in the production of evaluation plans, reports, and portfolios ("boundary objects") has strengthened a sense of collective professional commitment. The experiences of the Schools of Ambition suggests that the pursuit of evidence-informed practice in education requires an understanding of collaboration as social practice and demands serious consideration of the micro-political and relational dimensions of partnership.

## NOTES

1. Non-selective, publicly funded secondary schools (students aged 12–16 years)
2. There are 32 local authorities (or local councils) in Scotland. Each local authority has responsibility for local delivery of education and children's services.
3. Advisers are seconded from positions within local authority Advisory Services for the duration of the Schools of Ambition programme.

## REFERENCES

Bullough, R.V., Draper, R. J., Smith, L., & Birrell, J. R. (2004). Moving beyond collusion: Clinical faculty and university/public school partnership. *Teaching and Teacher Education, 20,* 505–521.

Campbell, A., & Keating, I. (2005, September). *Shotgun weddings, arranged marriages or love matches? An investigation of Networked Learning Communities and higher education partnerships in England*. Paper presented at the British Educational Research Association annual conference, University of Glamorgan.

Carlone, H. B., & Webb, S. M. (2006). On (not) overcoming our history of hierarchy: Complexities of university/school collaboration. *Science Education, 90*(3), 544–568.

Cochran-Smith, M., & Lytle, S. (1999). *Inside/outside: Teacher research and knowledge*. New York: Teachers' College Press.

Cochran-Smith, M., & Lytle, S. L. (2001). Beyond certainty: Taking an inquiry stance on practice. In A. Lieberman & L. Miller (Eds.), *Teachers caught in the action: professional development that matters* (pp. 45–60). New York: Teachers College Press.

European Union. (2009). *Common European principles for teacher competences and qualifications*. Retrieved July 13, 2009, from http://ec.europa.eu/education/policies/2010/doc/principles_en.pdf

Fielding, M. (2003). The impact of impact. *Cambridge Journal of Education, 33*(2), 289–295.

Hargreaves, A. (1994). *Changing teachers, changing times: Teachers' work and culture in the postmodern age*. New York: Teachers' College Press.

Hargreaves, A. (2003). *Teaching in the knowledge society: Education in the age of insecurity*. Maidenhead: Open University Press.

Hodkinson, P., & Hodkinson, H. (2003). Individuals, communities of practice and the policy context: School-teachers' learning in their workplace. *Studies in Continuing Education, 25*(1), 3–21.

Learning and Teaching Scotland. (2003). Focusing on curriculum flexibility in secondary schools: A paper for professional reflection. Dundee, Scotland: Learning and Teaching Scotland.

Lieberman, A. (1999). Networks. *Journal of Staff Development, 20*(3), 43–44.

Lieberman, A., & Pointer Mace, D. H. (2008). Teacher learning: The key to educational reform. *Journal of Teacher Education, 59*(3), 226–234.

Peters, J. (2002). University–school collaboration: Identifying faulty assumptions. *Asia Pacific Journal of Teacher Education, 30*(2), 229–242.

SEED. (2004). *Ambitious, excellent schools: Our agenda for action*. Edinburgh: Scottish Executive.

SEED. (2007). *Schools of Ambition. Scottish executive news*. Retrieved July 2, 2007, from http://www.scotland.gov.uk/News/News-Extras/schoolsambition

Smedley, L. (2001). Impediments to partnership: A literature review of school–university links. *Teachers and Teaching: Theory and Practice, 7*(2), 189–209.

Stronach, I., & McNamara, O. (2002). Working together: The long spoons and short straws of collaboration. In O. McNamara (Ed.), *Becoming an evidence-based practitioner* (pp. 155–170). London: Routledge.

Wenger, E. (1998). *Communities of practice: Learning, meaning and identity*. Cambridge: Cambridge University Press.

# 4  Ten School Districts and One University

## A Collaborative Consultation

### Mary Phillips Manke and Rachael Marrier

Over the past 7 years, 7 to 10 school districts, with student populations from 250 to 5,000, and over 30 Education Unit faculty and staff at the University of Wisconsin–River Falls have worked together. The collaboration has been informal in that there were no contractual arrangements for its work, but the existence of the grant funding and its requirements led to some formal elements.

The purpose of the collaboration, determined in a planning meeting, was to support new teacher induction by implementing rigorous mentoring and support seminars for all new teachers, to provide professional development to teachers, and to improve the quality of student teacher placements.

Education Unit administration and school administrators met in a steering committee. Professional development and new teacher induction were offered for credit. Activities were offered without cost to the districts, except costs for substitute teachers for the mentor trainings. When possible, these occurred before the school year began.

Professional development opportunities offered for teachers were diverse. Model Academies in mathematics, science, and language arts provided co-learning for teachers and faculty. Each occurred twice a year on a Friday evening and Saturday. These events became extremely popular with teachers. An annual technology workshop day led to significant changes in technology provisions and use in the districts. Lesson study training and support for teams from three districts lasted only 1 year, as administrators found it too difficult to schedule time for the necessary planning, observing, and evaluating. Both teachers and administrators valued the outcomes, and would have liked to continue.

The mutuality level of the work was potentially high. Scholarship of Teaching and Learning (SOTL) grants for faculty teaching courses for preservice teachers were added. Content faculty worked with teachers to improve their own teaching and they were required to spend time in the teacher's classroom and invite the teacher to their own. A second grant provided summer seminars in content and curriculum development for teachers. Most of the content seminars were taught by faculty who participated in the Model Academies; some of these faculty have also received SOTL grants.

Districts could involve teachers in a high quality mentor training program to improve the quality and retention of new teachers. Smaller districts could meet the requirement for support seminars even when they hired only two or three new teachers in a year. Many student teaching supervisors went to the mentor trainings. The academies and summer seminars helped the university meet its obligation to provide professional development for teachers in the region.

There was some internal resistance to the goals of the collaboration on both sides. Some faculty did not see professional development for working teachers as their responsibility, and thus did not participate. The representative from one district disapproved of the nature of professional development activities in which teachers from the district were participating. Some district representatives wanted all events for a year to be fully planned and scheduled in advance, which was not feasible within the university structure. This resistance, often expressed in indirect ways, gradually eroded trust levels within the collaboration.

Decision making in the collaboration rested for over five years with the Steering Committee. The Associate Dean chaired the committee, coordinated the partnership, and wrote for the grants, building on the original planning meeting. The number of districts involved has varied from 7 to 10; the faculty members involved have varied widely, and the activities supported by the partnership have also been diverse. A core Steering Committee leadership group from four of the districts has been a constant, though new members have joined the Steering Committee as job changes took place or as districts were added.

A year ago, the districts initiated a grant-funded regional partnership to continue the new teacher induction portion of the work. The university served as fiscal agent and as a site for the mentor trainings and support seminars for new teachers in this grant. Because funding for the original grant was almost gone, steering committee meetings ended. These changes reduced communication among the school and university leaders, and contributed to a sense of distrust on both sides at the governance level.

Teachers and faculty, nevertheless, continued to value the experiences the partnership provided for both new teacher induction/support and professional development. Unlike many such partnerships, the work was multi-dimensional. However, basing the partnership on grant funding led to limited sustainability. Currently, no solution for a future without grant funding has been found. It seems more likely that grant funding will reappear for the professional development than that it will for the new teacher induction piece.

The UW–System grant funding, which ranged from $25,000 per year to $60,000 per year over a period of 7 years, was a major resource. It has provided essential clerical support for the grant at the university, and allowed credit to be offered to participants in most activities. Other funding from an ESEA grant administered through the state supported the summer seminars.

Most recently, the Wisconsin Department of Public Instruction provided funding that supports mentor training and new teacher support. Another important resource has been the New Teacher Center–Wisconsin, closely affiliated with the New Teacher Center–California at UC–Santa Cruz. At first, trainers from NTC–WI provided the mentor training; now district grant leadership, trained by NTC–WI leaders, provides half of it.

Some suggest that relying on grant funding precluded developing both sustainability and solid and trusting relationships among the leadership. The collaboration assumed that limited funding for both public schools and universities in our state made it impossible for schools to pay for the partnership activities. This may be true, but as long as everyone believes that it is true, there will be little movement toward sustainability. An optimist might say that now, as the grant funding is running out, everyone's attention will turn to finding resources for continuing what is most valued.

Whereas the associate dean convened and chaired the Steering Committee, decision making has usually been collaborative. Certainly mutual benefits have accrued. The collaboration is most visible in the districts; many teachers have participated in the partnership. University faculty involved in the grant (including student teaching supervisors participating in mentor training, faculty participating in the model academies, SOTL grants, summer seminars, student technology leaders offering workshops for the technology days, travelling to schools to support teachers' technology efforts, and the dean's office and support staff managing the offerings) are aware of the partnership, but those not participating have little knowledge of its activities.

Participation by district leadership has been somewhat uneven. Four district leaders have formed a core group of strong participants. Three of these now function as mentor trainers. The smallest and most distant districts have been least participatory in leadership, but their need is great, and they want their teachers to participate. (The smallest district, with just 250 students, has only a half-time superintendent/half-time high school principal and a half-time elementary principal/half-time first grade teacher.) Three other districts have participated when interested in specific initiatives.

Some university faculty, whose roles would make them ideal participants in the grant, do not see it as part of their responsibility. (Faculty has not been paid for participation, except for those leading the summer seminars.) Some staff members have resisted changes in university practices recommended by the Steering Committee.

The final source of resistance has been from grant funders at UW–System, who have shifted the focus of grant funding away from the concerns of districts in the grant. A positive result of this resistance, though, has been the movement of the new teacher support activities into the hands of a consortium of the 10 districts. It now handles and organizes this work and is attempting to develop a stronger support structure for it.

The university contributed people with a strong commitment to mentoring and supporting new teachers and providing teacher professional development. Our state is currently listed as 49th in support for public universities, and over time these funding limitations have brought our Education Unit to a point at which all available staff time is used to prepare new teachers, with few resources available to provide professional development or support once they are in the field. With grant funding, the college was delighted to be able to provide this missing link over 7 years. Training many teachers in our local districts as mentors was also a benefit as it improved their effectiveness as cooperating teachers with our student teachers and interns.

The university's mathematics department in particular, as well as individual faculty from other departments in the College of Arts and Sciences, has done exceptional work in building partnerships with teachers and making positive changes in both university and PK–12 teaching and curriculum. These people brought great willingness to function as co-learners with teachers, and to build what they learned into their work at the university.

The districts also had people who were strongly committed—far beyond the norm in our state—to mentoring and supporting new teachers. When our partnership began, two districts had jointly received a state grant to develop mentors, whereas another had a separate grant for the same purpose. Other districts were rapidly moving forward in technology development, and contributed the efforts of both administrators and teachers who led our work in sharing new technology through all our districts.

Nevertheless, we recognize weaknesses in the partnership, and realize that those weaknesses may lead to its dissolution. The financial resources that we had could fund many activities—especially the core activities of mentoring and support for new teachers and teacher professional development. Resources of time and person-power were far less abundant. The task of administering a program so wide-ranging and complex was sometimes overwhelming to those who had chosen to assume it. In addition, changes in university policy about the use of space in its buildings were a frequent problem.

The mathematics department is deeply committed to teacher professional development, as are a number of faculty in English/language arts. The science departments, located at two ends of the campus and in two colleges, and unused to working together, have not responded as strongly to this opportunity. A few faculty have participated fully, but none of the science departments has committed to the goal of co-learning and change for both teachers and faculty.

Uneven participation by the schools in the governance process has been a major limitation. Of the 10 districts, two were added recently and are the smallest and among the most distant. These did not participate to any extent in the planning and decision making of the Steering Committee. Two others, part of the collaboration from the beginning, have participated only occasionally. Two more have participated regularly, but never taken leadership roles. The remainder is the solid four who have provided most of the leadership. The convener of the Steering Committee has consistently tried to elicit more active participation from all members, but with limited success. Unfortunately, the agendas from the four leadership districts did not always have full buy-in from other districts, which has reduced the overall effectiveness of the partnership. On the other hand, the consistent participation of teachers from all the districts and their enthusiasm for the partnership's offerings are probably the strongest indicators of its success.

## POWER RELATIONS IN THE COLLABORATION

Throughout the partnership, decision making has been intended to be collaborative. Because the Associate Dean wrote the original grant proposal, the leadership and framework of activities came from her knowledge of the obligations of the University and the needs of participating districts. She understood the dynamics of each district's needs, and her work with preservice teachers let her understand the need to improve teacher quality and increase student achievement at the classroom level. Her vision of collaboration led the way for the partnership. Her influence was strong in paving the way and supporting the key ideas behind the group's work. Also, the university could serve as fiscal agent for grants.

An important challenge to sustaining the collaboration has been the issue of shared power and decision making. In 7 years, the group has moved from a highly structured original grant that outlined specific timelines, participation, budgets, and evaluations, to seeking sources of funding to sustain the work that has become part of each individual district's core structure of teacher induction. Other initiatives have been less supported by the districts, but still drew high teacher attendance at events. This division of support lends an interesting lens to the influence of each party on the group's work.

Hank Rubin, in his book, *Collaborative Leadership*, writes that collaboration is "a purposeful relationship in which all parties strategically choose to cooperate in order to accomplish a shared outcome" (2002, p. 17). The choice to cooperate demands that participants constantly balance their individual institutional needs with the needs of the partnership. For a collaboration to be completely successful and sustainable, the needs of the partnership must match each individual institution's needs for partnership activities. Add to the mix individual members' personal needs for active leadership and/or power within this structure, and the dynamics of the balance become delicate.

When the partnership began, the structure of the PK–16 grants was a good vehicle for the group's clearly articulated vision of its goal and activities. Members could see and support the group's shared purpose. The administrative influence of the University remained high, providing the framework and ideas for activities, and leading the organizational aspects of regular meetings, including agendas, e-mail reminders, and follow up notes. Individual school districts benefited from the activities without having to do much work beyond communication within their home districts to teacher participants.

In time, the original grant ended and the vision for PK–16 collaboration to improve teacher preparation and induction was solidly established. Because some of the initiatives were very powerful, they became institutionalized within home school districts. Work of the partnership began to move toward finding funds to sustain and further existing programs. At the same time, core members who had been satisfied with the strong influence and work of the University began to seek more influence in the partnership.

All collaborations have life cycles, but without a strongly articulated overall vision that the collaboration itself can reflect on and call attention to, the balance between individual needs and the needs of the partnership became harder to achieve. In the area of teacher induction, the group now struggles to decide whether to bring in outside facilitators/organizations or to grow its own leaders to support regional needs. As core participants have grown professionally, personal ties to teacher induction facilitation have been a source of challenge in choosing a future.

In teacher professional development, the university's influence and ideas have been met with less enthusiasm recently. Some feel they are not a true part of the decision making process. Some have felt they are "rubber stamps" for university plans. When a meeting to come together for input was offered, a less-than-full conference room filled with tension generated few new ideas. Because these issues have not been honestly worked through, and without a unifying document or articulated philosophy to ground the work of the group, achieving successful collaborative balance is now a challenge.

This discontent comes partly from personal desires for active leadership. As the partnership has matured, personality styles have conflicted and personal and professional gain have become contentious. Working styles have conflicted, and the desire to have more decision-making authority has been a subtext. This discontent has generated new regional partnership meetings at school district sites, with school district representatives taking the lead in teacher induction. The university sees this as a desirable outcome. The partnership wants the benefits that the university can offer the teachers, such as credit for professional development, leadership in new teacher support seminars, fiscal agency, and physical facilities for activities related to teacher induction, but also wants to go its own way.

The university also wants the partnership to continue to bring K–12 and university faculty together at the Model Academies, deepening content and pedagogical knowledge. The Scholarship of Teaching and Learning project and the annual technology day are also bridges between teachers and university faculty. They actively engage the partners in sharing lessons, team teaching, and the planning/teaching/reflecting cycle, bringing improved instruction to preservice teachers and PK–12 students. The active participation of its teachers in these events shows the support of the partnership for these initiatives.

The PK–16 collaboration members continue to work together on teacher induction and professional development of working teachers. Working relationship and dynamics have changed (and will continue to grow) but still hold the potential to expand and affect hundreds of teachers in the St. Croix Valley of Minnesota and Wisconsin.

## LESSONS LEARNED

It is challenging to balance a partnership with so many members. The likelihood that a partnership of 10 school districts and a university will develop conflict and dissent over time seems high. Over 7 years, members of the group have changed in their ambitions and intentions, developed new ideas about what the outcomes of the partnership should be, and disagreed about one another's working styles and practices. Careful attention to these issues from the beginning might have made a difference in the comfort levels of members of the partnership, but its activities might not have been much affected.

The termination of grant funding is the primary reason for the partnership's likely dissolution, but outside funding, needed to create the partnership, reduced everyone's responsibility for its continuation. In other parts of Wisconsin, districts are paying the costs of mentor training and new teacher supports. It is hard to know in retrospect whether such an approach would have been possible for these districts.

Seven years is a good run for a partnership, however, and possibly most of the activities will continue with new funding arrangements.

## REFERENCES

Rubin, H. (2002). *Collaborative leadership: Developing effective partnerships in communities and schools.* Thousand Oaks, CA: Corwin Press.

# 5 Elementary Public School and University Partnership

## Promoting and Analyzing Professional Development Processes of School Teachers

*Maria da Graça Nicoletti Mizukami,*
*Aline Maria de Medeiros Rodrigues Reali,*
*and Regina Maria Simões Puccinelli Tancredi*

### ORGANIZATIONAL INVOLVEMENT AND PURPOSE

This chapter reports the results of a 6-year research project conducted by a public university in partnership with an elementary public school (Grades 1–4), both from the city of São Carlos/SP, Brazil, concerning a thematic program of applied research called "Public Teaching." This program was sponsored by the FAPESP/São Paulo State Foundation for Research Support, as an educational public policy. The program addresses the improvement of the quality of teaching and schooling processes through an inservice teacher education program developed in the workplace.

As action collaborative research, it was characterized by the development of intervention strategies that allowed the construction and implementation of a pedagogical process shared by its members, as well as the consolidation of the professional autonomy of the teachers involved.

Reflecting the theoretical orientation, the methodological approaches include: descriptive and analytical studies; follow-up studies; ethnographic studies; case studies; and the use of several data sources (participant observation, diary entries, interviews, portfolios, and different kinds of documents), pertinent to each of the issues studied.

The basic concern related to the understanding and promoting of teachers' professional learning and development processes was investigated in relationship to the following question: To what extent a partnership process allows us to know, understand, and promote professional development of schoolteachers? The process sought to promote reflection on pedagogical practices through planned intervention.

This question was investigated in two phases. The first phase (1999–2000) considered how a constructive/collaborative intervention that draws on the reflection on the teachers' practices in their workplace be considered and used as a successful strategy for promoting and improving pedagogical actions.

In this phase, the research's main goals were to: (a) construct knowledge about professional development of teachers' and the best way to investigate such issue; (b) construct knowledge about the process of conceptual development (related to the teaching and learning processes and the educational phenomenon) and of practices made possible by the use of a constructive/collaborative approach; (c) promote the professional development of teachers through reflection on the pedagogical action; (d) promote the adequate utilization of different spaces of knowledge, especially the school library, with emphasis on the development of abilities, the skill to browse, and the ability to utilize the various sources of information; (e) assess a methodology of a school-based inservice teacher education; (f) assess the tools constructed and utilized; and (g) offer contributions and guidelines for the development of preservice and inservice teacher education programs.

The second phase (2001–2003) was aimed at implementing the knowledge base collectively constructed by the schoolteachers in the first phase. This phase considered how elementary schoolteachers "translate" the knowledge base for Grades 1–4. The goals of this second phase of the project were to analyze: (a) different individual "translations" of the elementary schoolteachers related to the constructed school collective project; (b) how the schoolteachers perceive the contributions of constructive/collaborative work at the individual and group levels, and apply them to their professional development; and (c) how all of the above contribute to the school as a learning community.

## PARTICIPANTS, RESOURCES, AND DEVELOPMENT OF THE PROJECT

The participants integrated a group formed by 23 professionals from a public state school (20 schoolteachers, the principal, the pedagogical coordinator, and the library assistant), 5 researchers from the Federal University of São Carlos–SP, and 3 specialists from different subject areas. Eighty percent of the elementary school professionals participated in the 6 years of the project. Schoolteachers and specialists received scholarships from the "Public Teaching Program" sponsored by FAPESP.

During the first year we dealt with situations that could be considered as reflection-on-action, with narratives that make beliefs, values, and personal theories of the participants evident. Relations between conception, practice, and dimension of the professional development were also investigated during this period. Finally, because this project was the first collective experience in research for all the participants, a common language was established to enable the participants to communicate.

From the second year of the project on, a strategy for the promotion and investigation of learning and professional development processes was progressively constructed. The teaching and learning experience, as described by the school teachers are:

> [S]tructured situations of teaching and learning planned by the researchers and schoolteachers, implemented by the schoolteachers, collectively discussed, and originating from issues chosen by them individually or by the group. These experiences are circumscribed processes—which may imply actions involving small groups of teachers or classrooms (teachers and their students)—usually deriving from practical difficulties related to the understanding of curricular components, school daily activities or challenges posed by public policies. (Mizukami et al., 2003, p. 34)

This strategy proved to be a powerful tool for the investigation and the intervention. The teaching and learning experiences developed during the research's first phase were: knowing the school students; teaching and learning Portuguese; teaching and learning mathematics; teaching and learning science; constructing the school knowledge base; school–family interactions; assessing students; assessing and attributing grades to our students; utilizing the school library as a resource; using children's literature for story telling; knowing and interpreting the Brazilian National Curriculum Guidelines; specifying pedagogical discourse versus contrasting personal and collective theories; sharing personal and professional stories with peers; and sharing professional lives.

During the research's second phase, teaching and learning experiences were developed that were translated into a collective project for classrooms. This included the water project, the cultural plurality project, the health education project, and the sex education project.

In order to offer an overview of the teaching and learning experiences developed during the project we present one of them: The school–family interactions: "Let's help our children."

This teaching and learning experience was designed to promote teacher professional development in order to overcome school failure and improve teacher quality, focusing on encouragement of parent participation. Several meetings were held between researchers and teachers to discuss parent participation in their children's school life and the need to recognize the parents' point of view about certain school-related themes.

The experience's goals were: to face a common preconception assumed by the schoolteachers that their students' families don't have interest in their children's schooling processes; to analyze how the families conceive of the school, the schooling processes, and the relations with the school; to understand the families expectations about the school and the teachers; and to discuss how to face learning difficulties from different points of view, including those of teachers, parents, principal, and pedagogical coordinator.

Several data sources were used: a survey directed to the families constructed collectively by the teachers; participant observation; a report, made by the teachers, regarding the aforementioned survey; and collective discussions involving teachers and families.

Many methodological questions were raised during the project's development. They predominantly refer to the process of investigation made by a team of researchers from different backgrounds that continually performed many diverse roles.

As described by Wasser and Bresler (1996), participants faced a continuous process of testing and clarifying interpretations. This demonstrates the importance and complexity of the issues related to beliefs and suppositions underlying the interpretative process. The group members had their roles and positions changed when they observed the concerns, themes, questions, and problems of the other members. This process allowed each member to see the data from new perspectives. The group also faced situations that involved ambiguity and truth. Contradictions arose in the face of different types of knowledge. Uncertainties were found in problematic situations; perplexities, difficulties, and obstructions were present in the interpretative process. To Wasser and Bresler, trust as moral and political instance is of extreme importance because the dialogical inquiry must, by definition, comport a certain amount of ambiguity which can be considered in different ways, depending upon the circumstances under which they are created.

From this perspective, trust is a necessity for collaborative projects such as this. It is, nonetheless, a complex and multifaceted notion. The kind of trust needed goes beyond mere listening and tolerance. It includes the certainty that the message of whoever speaks will be taken seriously and will, in a sense, affect the outcome of the project. There is also the trust nurtured by conversational inquiry—the one members must have for the group to tolerate ambiguity, misunderstandings, clash of points of view, and continuous discussion, even when it becomes uncomfortable to put oneself in another's shoes. As was stated by Slater (1996), "Action is dependent on the dialogue of trust, and decision making is directed by the relationship established by participants and the positive outlook they have about the life of the system in which they are participating" (p. 33).

Methodologically speaking, this project faced dilemmas relating to what educational research literature considers as collaborative research, action-research, academic knowledge, and practical knowledge (academic research and practitioner's research); that is, academic paradigms versus practitioner's research.

By assuming a constructive/collaborative approach, we are at the same time aiming to investigate the professional development process of elementary school teachers and to promote said process for all members of the group (university and school). This process takes into account the peculiarities of this kind of research and the still-recent dilemmas of investigations that involve researchers in the investigated situations as participants and co-authors of the actions.

The present research group was initially seen as having a fixed structure in the project. However, this structure went through changes when members started to create an identity for the group by assuming different commitments, creating rituals and routines in order to give it form (e.g., labeling activities, structuring meetings, and publishing reports), and creating explicit group-related values. During the 6 years of this project the participants have given interpretative meanings, raised ideas, contested opinions, redirected processes, and reaffirmed or reformulated convictions in ways that make it impossible, currently, to establish clear lines between individual contributions. Many of the individual contributions were possible only through the group. The construction of the group process and of the group itself as an interpretative tool went through various individual and collective understandings which generated many changes to the project. These changes, in turn, redirected it to the investigated problem, as well as to the formative and investigative processes under consideration. The professional development process, previously seen as unidirectional, became known as bidirectional, that is, part individual and part group work. The interpretations that, in the beginning, tended to be more topic-oriented started to assume a process orientation. The project also underwent different processes of decision making that affected the group construction in relation to the theoretical and methodological orientations to be adopted. During this process, the concept of "interpretative zone" was especially important to understanding the different group dynamics. The processes throughout the project were slow, arduous, and engrossing to all the participants. The progress and success achieved were nonlinear for every person involved.

## COLLABORATIVE PARTNERSHIP: CHARACTERISTICS, DIFFICULTIES, LESSONS AND CHALLENGES

We successfully constructed knowledge related to the professional development processes of the schoolteachers. Such construction was possible through the collaborative partnership and the results were discussed with the schoolteachers on a regular basis.

A project such as this provides challenges, difficulties, and lessons inherent to the peculiarities of the adopted model. In that sense, the project's development revealed that:

1. The confrontation of conceptions allowed the teachers to make clear to themselves what they thought and to note the differences among them, along with what is imposed by the actual public policies. But this dynamic demands time, the tightening of relationships, and the

guarantee of the possibility of the existence of diverse ways of thinking and acting in a school.

2. The inclusion of the research group in the school's environment and the construction of a shared program of professional development is a process that can be considered unstable and needs to be rebalanced at any given moment. This requires a high degree of participant involvement. At some points, processes of legitimization or non-legitimization of the discourse over pedagogical practice became noticeable, demanding constant review of the dynamics of the school group that had to be rethought and redirected continually. The construction of partnership implies the constant reanalysis by schoolteachers, the researchers, and the combined group as a whole through a process of continuous negotiation.

3. The "teaching and learning experiences" revealed themselves as powerful strategies of intervention and shared work, allowing the development of continuous reflexive processes. By using these experiences it was possible to: (a) analyze the teachers at different stages of their professional learning process; (b) understand specific learning by the teachers in specific contexts that challenged them to reflect, verbalize their beliefs, and describe their practices, taking experience into account; (c) construct situations of reflection-on-action with narratives that made beliefs, values, and knowledge evident; (d) visualize everyday school situations that require decision making, interpretation, evaluation, and the elaboration of new plans of action from the teachers in a non-intrusive way; and (e) access the classroom processes effectively developed by the teachers.

4. The analyses made by the researchers and their theoretical explanation often produced a response by the teachers of "not knowing something." The teachers disqualified the researchers' theories by invoking specific contexts of pedagogical practices utilized by the elementary school, that the researchers were not aware. The most evident difficulties faced by the teachers were related to processes of implementation of educational public policies. The majority of those influences did not reach the school and the classrooms. When they did, the language, format, and concepts were so difficult to understand that they were hard to transform into classroom daily activities (e.g., The Brazilian National Curriculum Guidelines).

There is no illusion that the teachers have changed or will change their way or their teaching practice simply due to hierarchical power. During the inservice teacher education program, there is a need to build a network of interactions that allow teachers to invest in the process of using new knowledge, reflecting on their practice, without the need to defend themselves from attempts to impose changes they do not comprehend. What we usually call "resistance to change" seems to be much more related to the teachers' resistance to being dispossessed of their knowledge learned from experience and training.

At some points, processes of legitimization or non-legitimization of the discourse over pedagogical practice became noticeable, demanding constant review of the dynamics of the school group that had to be rethought every step of the project, for redirectioning. The construction of partnership implies constant negotiation of participants. This is a slow, laborious, and arduous systematic investment of participants.

## CONTRIBUTIONS AND POWER ISSUES

The project's results allowed us to affirm that constructive/collaborative research models can improve the professional development of teachers because they promote opportunities for them to reflect on their practice, share criticism, and support change. A tremendous emotional involvement of the schoolteachers and other members of the school community in the development of the project were observed. The schoolteachers created diverse strategies in order to deal with different content and looked for varied and unusual sources of information.

From the first "teaching and learning" experience to the last, the data showed that the following elements were improved: the sharing of information, the utilization and the construction of diverse instructional material, varied teaching strategies, communication and collaboration between school teachers, and respect for differences. It was also observed that the teachers involved in the experiences became more risk taking, flexible, assertive, and autonomous.

There were several factors that contributed to the success of this experience. These include the individual contribution to the dialog of the broader group; the existence of common themes that directly involved all the schoolteachers; time allotted for discussion (among peers within and across classrooms/grades and with the participants from the university); and the creation of place and opportunity to venture into areas that they had not dared in the past, and to face the possibility of failure. This project also empowered participants to create a basis for a sustained learning community.

## REFERENCES

Mizukami, M. G. N. et al. (2003). *Escola e Aprendizagem da Docência. Processos de Investigação e Formação.* São Carlos, SP: EdUFSCar, INEP, COMPED.
Slater, J. J. (1996). *Anatomy of collaboration: Study of a college of education/public school partnership.* New York: Garland.
Wasser, J. D., & Bresler, L. (1996). Working in the interpretative zone: Conceptualizing collaboration in qualitative research teams. *Educational Researcher,* 25(5), 5–15.

# Part III

# One-to-One Collaboration

As described in Chapter 1, the type of collaboration termed *one-to-one* usually involves university faculty who are interested in conducting research in an area of interest to them, or a situation where there is some benefit to the university for a particular project with a local school system that involves university faculty, resources, or expertise. Often, school system personnel ask a faculty member for advice concerning an issue or problem and they seek state-of-the-art information concerning the situation. Another form of one-to-one is collaboration on a grant-based project that requires participation of university faculty members and this may be initiated by a school official, teachers, parents, or other school-based person.

The three representative selections in this section are: (a) Callejo and Diaz's description of a university/school district professional development project to provide workshops for teachers to more effectively utilize legislatively mandated assessment data in their practice; (b) Efron, Miscovic, and Ravid's description of three case studies where school teachers and their university partners engaged in collaborative action research; and (c) Pacino's chapter about a public school/faith-based university initiative to provide summer facilities and coursework for low-income Latina gifted students.

The Callejo and Diaz project clearly shows the power of legislative stakeholders as rule maker and driving force in the data collection and assessment of progress of a school district. The overwhelming influence of mandated change on the school district curriculum led administrators to reach out to the university to hire a university faculty member to provide professional development workshops that would empower the teachers to use the mandated data assessment results in a way that would inform them as practitioners using the information as a tool for student intervention. The chapter describes the goal of the workshops as one that would give teachers ways to meliorate the atmosphere of fear over the use of the information, hostility toward the administration that might target them to raise scores, and possible insubordination to protest the pressure they were under. It was evident that the information provided in the workshops had the potential to alter their work environment so that they could use the data in a way that gave them more autonomy. Yet, the perspective of the different world view that divides the legislation and mandates from actual teaching practice is creating a situation where the power is so overwhelming that rather than compromise with an unmovable source, strategies for use and practice become the only solution. Thus, the university people are important mediators between policy and practice and provide proactive solutions in a tense situation.

The Efron, Miskovic, Ravid chapter includes three case studies where teachers and their university partners engaged in collaborative action research. The three teachers were former students in the faculty's graduate research courses and agreed to participate because they were interested in teacher action research and engaging in collaboration with a university partner. Each dyad of school–university partners designed their own research project based on their interests, schedules, and availability. Data collected included observations, interviews, email communications, and a focus group discussion with the teachers.

The three partnerships were informal and were carried out as a result of mutual interest of the school and university partners. The level of trust was high and both partners felt free to express their needs and thoughts. The school and university partners had different roles and agendas in each of the cases, but in all the partners complemented each other in what they brought and contributed to the partnerships.

Pacino's chapter describes a school system's need for university involvement. In a time of low income and budget cuts, school districts have come to rely more on alternative methods to deliver programs. The initiation of a collaboration project by the school district is an important part of this project. They turned to the university because that was where the facilities and faculty were to deliver a summer program for the low-income Latina gifted students. The faculty benefitted because they were paid, and the university increased their summer enrollment, and recruited future students in return for providing space. Whereas the mutuality is high in this project, it is interesting to note the limitations evident in the definition of roles, undue influence, real and perceived, and misconceptions about the verbal agreement between the two institutions. These problems become evident anytime there are groups of people interacting and making decisions from their own organizational perspective. It is the same world view orientation that the Callejo and Diaz project referred to in this section. Whereas administrators are invested and supportive, and the project is deemed successful, internal every-day interactions often are stressful and very time consuming.

These three examples illustrate that when there is a need for human resources and training, the one-on-one configuration for collaboration is a good choice. These projects were successful in achieving their goals and the choice of one-to-one was appropriate. Monetarily, both parties benefit, and guidelines for implementation are clear. These are time constrained projects, definitive in parameter, goal oriented, and easily assessed. But they are not long lasting by design and involve a limited number of university faculty. Therefore, when using this configuration there are isolated benefits and results, they impact in a non-systemic way on the two organizations, and the school system defines the parameters of the collaboration.

# 6 Policy Development and Sustainability

## How a Rural County Maximized Resources through Collaboration and Managed Change

*David M. Callejo Pérez, Sebastián R. Díaz, and Anonymous[1]*

This chapter outlines a strategy for facilitating professional development in public schools by relating the narrative of the events that occurred during summer 2007 and 2008 in rural West Virginia. The professional development initiative provided implementation sessions for 60 administrators and 500 teachers of a rural school district in northern West Virginia. The chapter describes the formation of the collaborative relationship; explains the particular approaches used in the professional development; and discusses findings and conclusions.

## THE COLLABORATIVE FORMATION

Several themes guided the design of the collaboration related to data analysis of Adequate Yearly Progress (AYP), which is mandated under the No Child Left Behind (NCLB) legislation. The first was using data differently depending on the purpose: (a) reporting data (e.g., NCLB AYP); or (b) informing strategic planning and decision making. Data reporting is a reactive process that is guided primarily by the needs of the stakeholder, in this case the mechanisms of NCLB legislation. The latter purpose involves strategic planning and decision making, which comprise a proactive process guided primarily by the needs of the school district. The summer curriculum helped participants compare and contrast the two and understand their roles in carrying out both processes within the school district as they improved instruction to meet AYP, especially with special education and African American subgroups in mathematics and reading.

A second theme of the summer program was that as with many aspects of school curriculum, the use of school data was informed by both espoused theories and practice considerations. A problem arose because many of the stakeholders failed to acknowledge the "disconnect" between the two perspectives. Participants were asked to address candidly and explicitly how data collection *actually* occurred within the school district, and how this differed from expectations for how data collection *should* occur. This ensured that all stakeholders (at the policy, administrative, and classroom levels) found a place to articulate their responsibility for the strategic plan, mission of the schools and district, and external/internal assessments that guide curriculum and instruction. Power relationships that existed in the past—the control of state personnel over data management—were challenged. The transparency of the process opened the door for individual schools and district to articulate their mission to the school board and state. Last, the communal relationship between North County[2], and the two researchers challenged the traditional bureaucratic process of university–school consulting.

A third theme guiding our initiative was that adopting effective data utilization (perceived or real) was more so an *affective* challenge than *cognitive*. One indicator of success for the summer workshops was the extent to which participants understood and appreciated how their colleagues within the district saw and used data. For example, teachers used data primarily to guide their own classroom instruction. A principal or superintendent, however, used the same data to help ensure district-wide compliance with NCLB mandates; ultimately many began to discuss how the responsibilities associated with a particular role dictate how data are used.

## STAKEHOLDERS

Identification of stakeholders emerged from a set of conversations and surveys with teachers, school personnel, and the community. Teachers were the first step in data collection and the last step in curricular and policy enactment, thus it was important that teachers become involved in those decisions. The district had struggled with school administrators' management styles. West Virginia school districts are rural and, by their nature, independent. Although the state organizes districts by county, local control remains powerful, and constituents are highly involved in school decisions. School administrators were the most powerful agents of the school in the community, whereas the school board was elected by district, which led school board members to intercede on behalf of individuals and schools. This system relied on personal politics where transactional leadership created a political system of resources, curriculum, and access. NCLB changed many of these relationships by directing resources through the Office of Federal Programs, central district administration, and Department of Education. In 2007, the school district continued to operate through transactional policy, resources, curriculum; educational policy operated on institutional rules whereas curriculum was determined at national and regional levels.

It was important to provide empowering opportunities for teachers to create curriculum and assessment. The superintendent believed teachers needed to be involved in decision making and assessment. Classroom benchmarks were the first issues with which teachers needed to become empowered.

According to Paulo Freire (1970), empowerment emerges from individuals' awareness of their own consciousness. We hoped to provide platforms for teachers by re-interpreting the role of assessment within the classroom by engendering strengths to enliven change. Teachers, most from the area, had historically led movements such as educating miners, increasing college attendance of graduates, and leading the change for better healthcare for children. In the last 25 years, increased federal dollars and jobs in the county and changes in teacher education shifted the focus away from local activism and local assessment to accountability and standard-driven teaching assessment. Given this history, a powerful foundation for change existed; it was then our primary purpose to enliven it for change in assessment.

## CONTEXT FOR COLLABORATION

Our collaborative agreement emerged from a small conference workshop where we discussed how to change evaluation in school districts. Our study revealed teachers and school administrators wanted to be more involved in evaluation and assessment in their schools as NCLB and state regulations re-defined AYP. The shifts in personnel attitudes and assessment influenced administration to change their approach. After a conversation with the directors of federal programs, student services, and technology, we concluded that our connection would emerge from evaluation and assessment that met human needs. In our second meeting, using the theories of Eliot Eisner (1979/2000), we developed a coherent approach that all stakeholders needed to: (a) feel competent; (b) belong; (c) feel useful; and (d) feel optimistic. After a month-long exchange of ideas in October 2006, we met again with North County Schools to create a framework for district-wide strategies to develop and use assessment. Given the previous themes and needs of the district, we determined a strategy for our collaboration. The district should construct and deliver workshops that build on teachers' interest, knowledge, and disseminated data from the district-wide assessment. A second idea was discussion of student learning and assessment at school team meetings. Third, teachers were encouraged to reflect on and study classroom practice. This three-tiered approach sought to form coherence between classroom and school practices, and district policy. Next was organizing these ideas into goals and objectives. We hoped to explore what occurred when curricular choices enhanced ideas and habits put forth by schools and stakeholders involved in the assessment and evaluation culture.

With the director of federal programs, we established program goals in January 2007. Data were systematically collected and led to early returns on the investment in faculty-led data analysis that brought teachers and administrators together to establish a strategic plan culminating in a summer training to establish baseline data and begin long-term quality improvement.

## THE PROFESSIONAL DEVELOPMENT'S IMPLEMENTATION

This section describes the county's investment to meet the needs they perceived would emerge from data analysis. Apart from hiring consultants and using technology, the school district paid teachers their daily rate to participate in the process to create an incentive to work with data. The superintendent and school board believed that the work conducted during the two-day session would become part of schools' strategic plans presented each fall. Those assessments and work plans reflected school-wide strategies to develop and use assessment from teachers'/schools' points of view, including: (a) workshops that build on teachers' interests and knowledge; (b) team meetings where teachers/ administration discuss student learning and assessment; and (c) individual study, classroom practice, and reflection.

### Formative Assessment

Popham (2008) identified four levels of formative assessment: (a) teachers collect evidence to inform decisions; (b) students self-assess; (c) a systemic formative assessment culture exists in the school; and (d) the entire district adopts an assessment program. Stakeholders needed to value an open community in which freedom of expression would be protected, civility affirmed, and appreciation and understanding of individual differences honored. Some ideas emerged from the conversations on empathy and power of becoming invested stakeholders. One such idea was that power comes from data-driven decision making and addressing unmet standards, so we met with teachers at 24 schools to help disseminate state data and embed the practice within each school.

We had to address three issues before any implementation: (a) time management; (b) appropriate learning opportunities; and (c) alternative data sources. Time management was the most important as teachers felt their time limitations would make it impossible to address an evaluation program. Also, we believed that state-centered standards were not providing room for appropriate learning opportunities. The problem was that the standardized testing program was not in line with the West Virginia learning standards. What should they teach to, state or testing standards? Many felt that although the system provided "tons of data," it was never used to evaluate performance. Stories of collected data gathering dust in filing cabinets were common; with no systemic knowledge management system, why were teachers, administrators, and schools collecting data?

### Curriculum

The curriculum we developed reflected our own diversity of perspectives as hired faculty consultants: one a historian and qualitative researcher and the other a statistician. We wanted the curriculum to reflect the qualitative/

quantitative continuum. Furthermore, given NCLB's focus (to a fault) on quantitative measures of student achievement and school effectiveness, we wanted participants to experience a complex mix of subjective and objective factors that inform student achievement. We included a variety of teaching and learning styles, including commonly used technology. Our curriculum was delivered on two separate days. On the first day, administrators and other program facilitators participated in a day long *train-the-trainer* session that replicated the actual training day for teachers. On the second day, workshops were conducted throughout the school sites with smaller groups of teachers. Although as consultants we were not able to work directly with all participating teachers, the district utilized Adobe Connect™ to facilitate online discussions among the multiple sites on this second day of training.

## Microsoft Excel Templates

Microsoft Excel files were shared with all participants via the district's website. Microsoft Excel was chosen as the platform because of its availability and because it would force participants to combine professional development related to data and computer skills. On both days of training, participants were able to download the Excel files. We wanted to demonstrate that with simple tools accessible to any teacher, the analysis of achievement data is feasible. It was important to demystify the process of analyzing data.

## FINDINGS AND CONCLUSIONS

Our findings revealed that organizational, curricular, measurement, and political factors impact North County's ability to effectively evaluate student achievement and revise the curriculum in a data-driven fashion. Teachers' responses to the training yielded valuable insights regarding their perceptions of time available to engage in evaluation initiatives. Data implications arose as another primary issue. Consistent with feedback from other consulting contexts, teachers of North County feel they do not have enough time to adequately perform their jobs. Therefore, any new initiative such as ours needed to be perceived as valuable before teachers will buy in to the process. Data was a main focus of the intervention we designed and implemented for North County School District. Much as we tried to instill an appreciation for how data can inform teaching and learning, teachers' candid perspectives revealed North County's organizational beliefs and attitudes toward teaching and learning. Stakeholders' attitudes toward data varied along a continuum, from teachers' view of achievement data as a tool for designing interventions for individual students to the assessment movement's view of data for the purposes of assessing large groups of students.

One of the challenges for NCLB is that, although the legislation's acronym alludes to a focus on the individual student (No Child), it is focused on assessing aggregate trends in student achievement data. Teachers have a difficult time understanding this population-oriented view of testing. America's education system parallels its healthcare system in that both teachers and physicians are not naturally inclined to approach their work from a population-based perspective. Through both training and self-selection, teachers' approach their profession as one in which interventions are to be geared to the individualized needs of single students rather than the collective needs of the group. By contrast, legislators who authored NCLB, designers of large-scale achievement tests, and many school administrators are much more interested in schools' overall success rates as measured by AYP. This fundamental difference in worldview of "what it means to be an educator" serves as a divisive element between teachers and other stakeholders, in particular school administrators. Teachers want data to inform how they can intervene with the individual student, whereas administrators want data to inform broader programmatic efforts. This divisiveness results in a back-and-forth volley of criticisms. At one end, teachers popularize the kneejerk backlash toward the *irrelevance of objective tests*, whereas testing advocates criticize teachers' unwillingness to be held accountable. Subsequent responses to these criticisms further the divide.

This divisiveness is enforced by another cultural element common among teachers, namely their strong sense of professional independence. Compared to many professions, teachers work autonomously without direct supervision, often in professional isolation. For this reason, the spreadsheets in our intervention addressed individual-focus needs of teachers and aggregate-focus needs of administrators. This approach helped the two groups gain an appreciation for the others' perspective. Teachers' affective orientation toward data revealed positive feelings such as appreciation for being able to work together with other teachers, receiving data training in a student-centered fashion, and being able to participate actively in data analyses. Negative feelings included elements of fear, hostility, and insubordination. As consultants, we developed pre- and post-measures that would determine the impact of our training on teachers' and administrators' attitudes regarding achievement data. Our return was lower than expected. In the second year, we discovered that teachers feared their particular individual responses would be sought out by administrators. Regardless of whether such fears are justified, this finding demonstrates that in order to achieve success with any data initiative, affective concerns that have little to do with the objective quantification of achievement need to be first addressed.

Teachers also revealed feelings of hostility toward administration. In particular a perception that any data-related initiative as some form of punishment targeted at them individually. This sentiment highlights the lack of understanding among educators regarding the pressures at the national, state, and local community levels that result in efforts for accountability. Teachers fail to understand that the large-scale call for increased achievement testing is not the result of one administrator's motives, but is instead a social response to public education. These feelings of hostility and how they are personalized demonstrate a professional view contextualized in the context of individualized relationships versus organizational dynamics.

Teachers, however, were not the only stakeholders who exhibited fear regarding data initiatives. We believe our professional development initiatives, although beneficial, resulted in missed opportunities for effective change. In Year 1 of the initiative, we succeeded in helping teachers overcome their fear of software, technology, and quantitative achievement data. In Year 2, we encouraged teachers to consider further how the Excel data could inform curriculum at the classroom level. We had hoped, and this is where the opportunity was missed, that data would be used further to address the complex psychosocial dynamics that impact student achievement district wide. We believed that our proposal to pilot a faculty development program aimed at this need may have been somewhat threatening for administrators. School districts often analyze data in a reactive fashion for the purpose of complying with mandates such as NCLB. More ideally, educators can analyze data in a proactive fashion for the purposes of engaging in data-driven decision making and planning strategically for the future. Although this latter approach is fraught with complex feelings, politics, and organizational dynamics, this proactive approach is how data analysis needs to be conducted.

Warnings abound regarding education's need to become more data-driven. More than 15 years ago, Drucker (1993) warned that "no other institution faces challenges as radical as those that will transform the school. The greatest change, and the one we are least prepared for, is that the school will have to commit itself to results" (p. 209). He wrote that technology's impact would be limited in the transformation of education to improving how we gather the same data. One of the *new things* educators will be doing soon is large scale Knowledge Management. Kerr (2001) and Dalkir (2005) both emphasize that since knowledge is now central to society, the field of Knowledge Management has emerged as a framework for designing an organization's goals, structures, and processes so that the organization can use what it knows to learn and to create value for its customers and community. Although much has been written regarding *21st Century Skills,* to be successful in this century, public schools and teacher preparation programs need to change essential organizational behaviors in several important ways: (a) transition to evidence-based and data-driven approaches to decision making; (b) increase the transparency with which they serve the needs of the public; and (c) work more intimately with one another in planning strategically for and addressing the state's public education needs. This increased scrutiny on schools, however, will filter down to an increased scrutiny on universities and colleges of education that prepare future teachers.

Currently, there is no panacea for the complex challenges school districts face with respect to satisfying multiple stakeholders' demands for fostering student achievement. Even though our initiative enjoyed reasonable success in helping teachers and administrators develop better skills and attitudes regarding achievement data, the initiative also highlighted for us the complexity of this phenomenon.

## NOTES

1. We use *anonymous* because our third author could not reveal his/her name due to political and programmatic changes occurring within the school district in the last 6 months.
2. North County is a pseudonym for the school district where this collaboration took place.

## REFERENCES

Dalkir, K. (2005). *Knowledge management in theory and practice.* Amsterdam: Elsevier Butterworth Heinemann.

Drucker, P. F. (1993). *Post-capitalist society.* New York: HarperCollins.

Eisner, E. (2000). *The educational imagination.* New York: Prentice Hall. (Original work published 1979)

Freire, P. (1970). *Pedagogy of the oppressed.* Boston: Continuum.

Kerr, C. (2001). *The uses of the university* (5th ed.). Cambridge, MA: Harvard University.

Popham, J. (2008). *Transformative assessment.* Washington, DC: ASCD.

# 7 School–University Collaboration as Mutual Professional Development

*Efrat Sara Efron, Maja Miskovic, and Ruth Ravid*

This paper describes three examples of one-to-one school–university collaborations. In all cases, each one of us—the university partners—collaborated with a teacher who was enrolled in preservice or inservice graduate teacher education programs at our university. The teachers, who taught in different schools, were former students in our research classes. We invited interested students to participate in a collaborative action research with them and three teachers expressed their interest. Even though all three collaborations fell under the heading of "One-to-One" collaboration, each partnership was very different depending on the needs of the teachers, availability of both partners, and interest of the partners. The lengths of time the collaborations took place were also different, ranging from 6 weeks to 8 months. The collaborations were informal, in that no contracts were signed.

School–university partnerships have been around for many years and have been used to meet different needs and address different goals. Research on school–university partnerships has documented that there are different stages or levels of interdependence, as is reported by Borthwick, Stirling, Nauman, and Cook (2003). Borthwick et al. stated that the interdependence may include cooperation, coordination, and collaboration. Whereas there are many advantages to these collaborations, there are also barriers. Brewster and Railsback (2001), in their comprehensive report on supporting beginning teachers, emphasized the importance of time, funding, and a shared interest in ensuring the success of collaboration between universities and K–12 schools.

The literature that documents the work of teachers as researchers is extensive (e.g., Burnaford, Fischer, & Hobson, 2001; Cochran-Smith & Lytle, 2009; Hubbard & Power, 2003; Phillips & Carr, 2006; Stringer, 2004) and highlights the positive effects of practitioner research on novice and veteran educators as it furthers their personal and professional development and enhances their own understanding and competencies. Researching their own practice helps educators face challenging situations and contributes to their ability to understand and solve problems. However, whereas teacher action research is often touted and promoted as an important aspect of teacher empowerment, studies about teacher action research are often conducted by university professors who study teachers or their student-teachers that are engaged in action research (e.g., Moore, 2006). In our collaboration with the teachers on researching their own classes, we followed the perspective of doing research *with* teachers, rather than *on* teachers, and we sought to initiate, support, and nurture the partnerships that we formed where all partners—both school-based and university-based—would benefit and grow professionally.

We have been interested and involved in school–university collaboration for many years. We have experienced several models of collaborations, similar to those described by Ravid and Handler (2001). The three of us are faculty members at National-Louis University, a private university in the Chicago area, with a well-established and highly-regarded college of education. We have taught graduate-level research courses to preservice (MAT) and inservice (MEd) students for many years and have been trying to promote the idea that teachers, as well as other educational professionals, should engage in practitioner research and study their own settings.

Because the school teachers that chose to collaborate with us differed in their educational context, personal experience, and level of confidence with action research, different collaborative relationships emerged. In all three collaboration teams, the teachers actively participated with their university partners throughout the research process, from the initial design to the implementation and evaluations of the action research projects. Each team adapted a variety of data collection strategies to capture and reflect the particularity of each partnership circumstances. In addition to our visits to the classrooms of the three teachers and ongoing communication with them face-to-face, by phone, or via email, we also conducted a focus group where Maja met with the three teachers after the end of the school year. The focus group provided an opportunity for the three teachers to meet and interact with each other. Additional sources of data were teachers' journal postings describing their teaching and action research experience, and teachers' work that resulted from their action research projects.

The three school teachers in our study were Jacob, Ana, and Wendy. Their three university partners were Efrat, Maja, and Ruth. Following is a description of each partnership and its unique characteristics.

## JACOB AND EFRAT: COLLABORATION
## AS A MENTORING PROCESS

Jacob is a career-changer in his 50s. He taught a self contained classroom of seventh- and eighth-grade students with emotional and behavioral disorders. There were eight students in the class, six males, and two females. All but one was African American. Most of the students were below grade level in reading, writing, and math. Several of the students were medicated in order to control behavior or emotional disturbances. One of the male students was hospitalized in a psychiatric ward of a hospital, one of the two female students became pregnant during that year, and the other was incarcerated for a long period of time. The nature, goals, and methods of the collaboration between Efrat and Jacob were an outgrowth of the particular needs and problems Jacob faced in his first year of teaching.

As Jacob started his first year of teaching his self-contained class, he shared via emails his sense of dissonance and confusion. Jacob felt that his academic coursework did not adequately prepare him for the challenges he faced. He also felt lack of support from the school administrators as he struggled with insufficient materials and supplies, and nonexistent appropriate curriculum guides. Attempts to make the learning experience meaningful and creative were criticized and mocked by his school administrator.

For 3.5 months Efrat and Jacob met once a week at Jacob's school. Each visit entailed an observation followed by self-reflective interview on the teaching and on individual students' involvement. Ideas were raised on how to improve the teaching or how to assess the learning. Students' work and special projects, as well as informal surveys (students' academic work and behavior self evaluation), were analyzed. Additionally, Jacob, a prolific writer, sent Efrat via emails journal narratives describing particular events that took place on that day, and shared his feelings, successes, frustrations, and self-questioning.

The collaborative partnership established and examined ways to exercise action research that supports the beginning teacher in the challenging inaugural year as he grappled with issues such as focusing student attention, exploring approaches that suit him, and evaluating the effectiveness of his teaching strategies. Though, clearly, the collaborative relationship has not solved all, or even the majority of the challenges that Jacob faced, it did assist him to gain a sense of control over his work and the circumstances in which he practiced.

Both Efrat and Jacob agreed that this kind of collaborative/mentoring relationships should become part of the initiation to teaching practice so that the novice educators can acquire a sense of self-efficacy and expertise to be effective teachers.

## ANA AND MAJA: COLLABORATION AS A MEANS OF UNCOVERING A REFLECTIVE TEACHER

Ana was a fourth-year special education teacher in a Chicago suburban middle school. For 8 months, Maja visited Ana's classroom regularly, which resulted in observational, interview, and written reflection data. As a White teacher in her late 20s, Ana's main goal was to become a culturally responsive teacher to her mostly African American male students.

Ana understood the research process as educating herself further about the needs of her students, some of them labeled as early as kindergarten as emotionally and behaviorally disturbed, and helping them negotiate the complex interplay of race, gender, and academic achievement. Whereas at the beginning of this research Ana's knowledge was fragmented and mainly anecdotal, the end of school year marked a shift in her understanding.

Maja and Ana had multiple conversations after the observations of classroom dynamics. For Maja these occasions were a place to clarify field notes and for Ana to actively reflect on the teaching process and find ways to understand her own and her students' words and actions. A reflection of Ana's growing awareness is her enrollment in a doctoral level class that Maja taught on race, ethnicity, and education, where Ana became deeply immersed with literature, which "gave name" to the experiences of her students. She began to question her assumptions about the ways that her school system responds to minority students, and how the politics of exclusion trickle down to her own classroom.

Whereas it would be flattering to assume that this uncovering of a reflective teacher is a result of year-long collaboration, it is worth noting that Ana arrived at the point where, in the words of Schwandt (2000), "acting and thinking, practice and theory, are linked in a continuous process of critical reflection and transformation" (p. 191). We contend that this collaboration influenced this teacher to tap into her own professional and personal self to become aware of larger societal and political forces that inevitably affect both her and her students.

## WENDY AND RUTH: COLLABORATION IN A CLASSROOM ACTION RESEARCH

Wendy was a student in two of Ruth's research classes, with the second class taken during her first year of teaching. Wendy was a career-changer and was new to teaching but was confident in her abilities and had strong organizational skills, both in class preparation and her willingness to do action research.

Because Wendy and Ruth got together late in the year, Ruth visited Wendy's class only a few times during the last few months of the school year. Wendy taught three sections of math and two sections of language arts (both regular and accelerated levels). She estimated that her students were roughly 80+% white, several Asians, and one African American. Wendy said that her students were very compliant, fairly respectful, and that they got along well with their peers. A number of Wendy's students were routinely pulled out of her classes for additional support.

The communication between Wendy and Ruth was mostly through email, although phone calls were also made when necessary. While visiting Wendy's classroom, she and Ruth also discussed various issues, such as the challenge of teaching students of various levels in Wendy's classes, lesson planning, and being a first-year teacher. Wendy has enjoyed a strong well-organized induction program in her school and got along well with her colleagues and administrators. She did not need support or guidance from Ruth and was attracted to the partnership because of her interest in continuing doing action research.

Based on their mutual interest in the topic, Wendy and Ruth collaborated on the process of creating a survey to assess the attitudes of Wendy's students toward homework. Together, Wendy and Ruth administered the survey to Wendy's students. While Ruth volunteered to enter the survey data and run the statistical analyses, both Wendy and Ruth reflected and analyzed the data together, looking for insights into middle-school students' attitudes toward homework and implications and practical suggestions for Wendy as she was preparing to start her second year of teaching in the same middle school.

## SUMMARY

There are multiple ways and approaches to one-to-one collaboration, which can be designed and implemented by the partners to fit their needs, interests, and schedules. In our three cases, Jacob saw this project first and foremost as a mentoring relationship between him and Efrat. Ana saw the collaboration with Maja as personal growth and learning how to be culturally responsive to her African American students. Wendy was already interested in action research and Ruth served mostly as a facilitator and collaborator. This flexible implementation attests to the advantage of noncontractual one-to-one collaborations. It allows university faculty to serve in multiple roles by responding to the needs and interests of the teachers and their particular educational settings.

Robinson and Darling-Hammond (1994) identified 10 characteristics required for achieving successful school–university collaboration:

1. Mutual self-interest and common goals
2. Mutual trust and respect
3. Shared decision making
4. Clear focus
5. Manageable agenda
6. Commitment from top leadership
7. Fiscal support
8. Long-term commitment
9. Dynamic nature
10. Information sharing and communication (pp. 209–217)

Our small scale, open-ended, one-to-one collaboration efforts achieved 7 out of these 10 characteristics (we did not meet characteristics 6, 7, and 8). Maybe due to the fact the collaboration was informal and was self-chosen by the participants rather than imposed by outside power, the relationships between us and the teachers were based on mutual respect and trust. We communicated often via email messages, had long informal conversation each visit, and at times even met over a cup of coffee just to keep up with each other lives. The focus, length, and nature of the collaboration were based on shared decision making, reflecting the teachers' and faculty members' mutual common goals and self-interests. The collaborations were a direct response to school-based practice and teachers' needs, and allowed dynamic evolvement of the projects. On the other hand, because there was no commitment from top leadership at our university or the teachers' schools and no financial support or release time, our efforts were done voluntarily and were completely dependent on the strong interest of all partners in school–university collaboration.

Whereas the resulting changes were limited and local, we feel that the collaboration extended our knowledge about classroom research and teaching and learning. For all of us it was a professional development experience. The classroom teachers were introduced to innovative experimentation, and we, the university professors, were involved in bringing theory in action. For all, it was an example of how educators can become actors and change agents in the school reality.

We do have to acknowledge, though, that in spite of the shared decision making, the one-on-one school–university collaboration is not necessarily an equal partnership. In our collaborations, the role of the university partner as a mentor and advisor was often evident, perhaps due to the fact that all three school partners were former students of the university partners.

In many one-on-one school–university collaborations, the university partner is the one who initiates the collaboration and is usually expected to plan and report on the action research project. Many school-based practitioners do not have the time, expertise, or incentive to document the partnership, analyze the data collected, or write a final report. These usually are assumed to be the responsibility of the university partners, although these partners are likely to seek the input, support, reflection, and approval of the school partners. Presenting and sharing the study's outcomes at professional research conferences is another obstacle to active participation by the school-based partners who often do not have the means or the time to co-present with their university partners.

Our experiences demonstrate the advantages of one-to-one school–university collaborations. The teachers had an opportunity for professional growth, reflection on their practice, and working closely with their former professors on a topic of their choice. As faculty members, we benefitted mostly by gaining access to schools and classroom, and working closely with our former students on action research projects. The three of us also enjoyed the opportunity to work and collaborate with and support each other.

The main difficulty all of us encountered was the additional time invest-ment that was required. This was more of a problem for the teachers who did not have active support by their administrators and colleagues or time release for their work with us. After one year, all of us were heading in different directions and the partnerships ended. Another limitation is the small scale of the partnerships. Working with a single teacher in a school cannot possibly have a systemic effect on the school. Rather, the positive outcomes are for the teacher-collaborators and their students.

After reflecting on our experience and considering the positives and neg-atives of one-on-one collaboration, we find that we are highly supportive of this form of school–university collaboration, which we view as a win-win situation for all participants.

## REFERENCES

Borthwick, A., Stirling, T., Nauman, A. D., & Cook, D. (2003). Achieving success-ful school–university collaboration. *Urban Education, 38,* 330–371.

Brewster, C., & Railsback, J. (2001). *Supporting beginning teachers: How admin-istrators, teachers and policymakers can help new teachers succeed.* Northwest Regional Educational Laboratory. Retrieved July 16, 2007, from http://www. nwrel.org/request/may01/textonly.html

Burnaford, G., Fischer, J., & Hobson, D. (2001). *Teachers doing research: The power of action through inquiry* (2nd ed.). Mahwah, NJ: Lawrence Erlbaum Assoc.

Cochran-Smith, M., & Lytle, S. (2009). *Inquiry as stance: Practitioner research for the next generation.* New York: Teachers College Press.

Hubbard, R. S., & Power, B. M. (2003). *The art of classroom inquiry: A handbook for teacher researchers* (rev. ed.). Portsmouth, NH: Heinemann.

Moore, R. (2006). Taking action: Assessing the impact of preservice teaching on learning. *Action in Teacher Education, 28*(3), 53–60.

Phillips, D. K., & Carr, K. (2006). *Becoming a teacher through action research.* New York: Routledge.

Ravid, R., & Handler, M. G. (2001). *The many faces of school–university collab-oration: Characteristics of successful partnerships.* Englewood, CO: Teacher Ideas Press.

Robinson, S. P., & Darling-Hammond, L. (1994). Change for collaboration and collaboration for change: Transforming teaching through school–university partnerships. In L. Darling-Hammond (Ed.), *Professional development schools: Schools for a developing profession.* New York: Teachers College Press.

Schwandt, T. A. (2000). Three epistemological stances for qualitative inquiry: Interpretivism, hermeneutics, and social constructionism. In N. K. Denzin & Y. S. Lincoln (Eds.), *Handbook of qualitative research* (2nd ed., pp. 189–214). Thou-sand Oaks, CA: Sage.

Stringer, E. (2004). *Action research in education.* Upper Saddle River, NJ: Pren-tice-Hall.

# 8 A Public/Private Partnership in a Diverse Community

*Maria Pacino*

Partnerships and collaborations between local K–12 schools and universities are usually developed for the primary purpose of allowing teacher candidates to engage in fieldwork experiences under the mentorship of practicing teachers. Most of these relationships are within public institutions. However, collaborations beyond fieldwork and student teaching are becoming increasingly more prevalent because they provide an opportunity for university faculty and K–12 teachers to engage in meaningful research centered on theoretical and pedagogical issues which lead to best practices in teaching and learning and in providing opportunities for K–12 learners in diverse communities. This chapter presents an example of such a collaborative project between a school district and a university.

## ORGANIZATIONAL INVOLVEMENT

The school district and the university were already engaged in a number of highly effective partnerships involving the School of Education, including programs to bring children in elementary grades to the university for a variety of activities. In 2000, the district was seeking a place to house a summer program for third–fifth grade Gifted and Talented Education (GATE) students. The assistant superintendent approached the dean of the School of Education and Behavioral Studies to discuss the challenges the district had encountered. The dean, the assistant superintendent, and the coordinator for the district's GATE program met to discuss their proposal.

The dean then met with the university president to discuss the proposal and the university role and responsibility in the proposed partnership. Although the university has a program to provide scholarships for local high school graduates, few students were taking advantage of this opportunity. The dean and university president felt that a partnership would be beneficial to both institutions and it would provide an opportunity for the university to recruit high achieving students from the district's two high schools.

## PURPOSE

The purpose of this partnership is to provide Latino gifted students, from a low income community, with an opportunity to experience life in a university campus and to realize that they have the potential to attain a college education and become professional contributing members of a pluralistic democracy. This is also an opportunity to bring parents along and provide them with the tools to encourage and assist in their children's educational journey. Although not stipulated in the verbal agreement, another outcome would be that this project/partnership would provide an opportunity for collaborative research. This chapter is an example of such research endeavor. Data discussed in the chapter come from interviews, surveys, observations, parent, teacher, and student evaluations; general demographic data for both institutions; and school records open for examination.

## FRAMEWORK

The framework for this paper is based on Slater's School/University Collaboration Matrix, review of literature on successful partnership models, and, to a lesser extent, on research for K–12 gifted programs. Marshall (1999) argues that: "Each partnership takes on a different flavor and reflects the variety of needs, opportunities, and philosophical beliefs held by the partnering institutions and individuals" (p. 400). In writing about her own partnership experience, Marshall asks an important question: "Who were the learners in this partnership?" (p. 403). This question reinforces the fact that partnerships can only be successful when partners are involved in a reciprocal teaching and learning experience. The success of partnerships depends upon the communication, relationship, and commitment of all the people involved.

Horowitz (2005) notes three important steps in successful partnerships: the need to recognize the pattern of involvement within partnerships; the need to communicate effectively among partners and with the community; and the need to have a clear definition of the roles played by all stakeholders involved. This seems to be a very important piece of the relationship. The partnership must create a sense of empowerment within K–12 settings to ensure continued progress, even when the university partners may no longer be present at the school site. Instead of creating a state of dependence, it must foster a sense of interdependence and offer additional sources of support within the school and community. A network of support and relationships will ensure ongoing progress.

Stephens and Boldt (2004) propose questions within a complex process of rhetoric, reality, and intimacy. One of the central questions is the mutual reciprocity of contributions and benefits. The authors also mention personality differences, philosophy of teaching and learning, collegiality, communication, and coordination as possible barriers to effective partnerships. They argue that for successful relationships to occur, all of those involved in the partnership must be willing to face their own limitations and inadequacies, and admit their own vulnerability. It is important to identify the needs of the institutions involved and how those needs impact participants in terms of institutional beliefs, policies, and practices.

The school district believes that the GATE program is designed to provide "a comprehensive continuum of services and program options responsive to the needs, interests, and abilities of gifted students and based on philosophical, theoretical, and empirical support" (AUSD GATE Program District Plan, 2004–2005, p. 1). All students are eligible for the program and approximately 20% of the district's students are identified as gifted each year. The identification process includes traditional and nontraditional research-based methods: (a) standardized testing and authentic assessments, such as portfolios; (b) report cards, observations, checklists; and (c) nominations/referrals by teachers, parents, and students themselves (self and peers).

The philosophy, identification, and criteria process, including multiple assessments, used by the school district are consistent with similar programs and the research in the field, as recommended by the National Association for Gifted Children (Coleman, 2003). The district also takes into account the ethnic diversity and socioeconomic status of the student body by promoting and supporting the inclusion of African Americans, Latinos, and other minorities. Students in GATE programs tend to have a higher rate of high school academic achievement and graduation which leads to successful college attendance and graduation.

## FORMAL/INFORMAL

The partnership involves a public school district and a private, faith-based university. A verbal agreement was reached between the university and the school district, and the 4-week, 5-hour per day program, started in the summer of 2001. Although the contractual agreement between the institutions is not written, it is a rather formal verbal commitment which provides benefits to both partners.

The agreement between the school district and the university calls for the university to provide university facilities for the GATE program and free college credit classes for high school students. The district develops the elementary curriculum and provides the teaching staff for the elementary students. The roles and responsibilities of the partnership were discussed in depth between the representatives of the two institutions and shared with members of the school district and the School of Education. The GATE program takes place at the university for one month each summer.

Demographics from participating partners are as follows: the city of 47,150 people is 64% Latino with a per capita income is $13,412.00; 29% of the population makes less than $25,000 per year; 44% of the population is comprised of children are under 18 years of age. The school district has 11,100 students; 79% are Latino; 42% are English Learners (EL); 75% are on the reduced lunch program; and 10% are listed as homeless. The university is predominantly Caucasian with 20% Latino students, primarily in the School of Education.

## RESOURCES

There are numerous resources needed for this GATE program; facilities, salaries, and supplies are shared by the school district and the university. Teacher salaries and supplies for all third–middle school students come from the school district. This includes books and other classroom supplies, transportation, and daily lunches. The university provides: high school students' tuition for science and English courses, textbooks, faculty course salaries, and a stipend for the program's university coordinator. Expenses for facilities, including high tech rooms; computer lab use; and writing assistance for the high school students are paid for by the university. The district teachers and coordinator develop a differentiated, accelerated, enriched curriculum with tiered assignments to meet the needs of the third–middle school GATE students.

Each summer at the end of the program, the university provides a reception for all participants, including parents, school district representatives, university administration, and community members. Usually the university president, the assistant superintendent, and the mayor address the students and parents and strongly encourage the importance of a college degree. The program started with 50 students, 4 district teachers, 1 professor, and the district coordinator. Currently, we have approximately 250 students, 10 school teachers, and coordinators for the district and the university.

The university, in consultation with the school district, also organizes parent information meetings, guided by university faculty and staff, meant to engage the parents in supporting educational giftedness by: becoming advocates in their children's future college education; addressing child development issues, especially with gifted students; protecting the children from the influence of neighborhood gangs; and affirming cultural differences as assets in a pluralistic society.

## MUTUALITY

The mutuality level of the partnership and the flow of influence seem to be equally shared within the hierarchical power of both institutions for most aspects of the GATE program. There is a high level of reciprocity because the agenda benefits both the school district and the university. Within the K–12 administration, the superintendent, assistant superintendent, and the school board provide the financial support and resources needed in the GATE summer program. The K–12 district has autonomy over the selection of students for the program, curriculum, pedagogy, classroom rules and policies, and activities for the third–middle school students. The K–12 teachers have autonomous involvement in the development, implementation, and evaluation of the creative curriculum and pedagogy for the third–middle school students. Within the university administration, the president and the provost provide the facilities for program, including fees and textbooks for the students taking the college courses. Other university members involved in the program include the two faculty members teaching the college courses, English and science; other faculty whose students are fieldwork participants in the elementary and middle-school classrooms; and university staff, such as undergraduate registrar, facilities management, campus safety, lab supervisors, library personnel, marketing and public relations personnel, and many others. University faculty and staff have autonomy over the university policies and services which support the program. The coordinators, for the district and the university, keep in touch for effective communication and cross-cultural understanding among institutional members. It is also important to note the community involvement in this project, including the mayor and the local Rotary Club which funds the science boat fieldtrips for the high school students.

## RESISTANCE

Tensions always arise in defining the roles of the partners involved. When it is perceived that one partner is exerting more influence than another, there may be a level of mistrust, disengagement, resentment, lack of cooperation, and counterproductive attitudes. These dispositions will affect the outcome of the partnership. University professors must be careful not to project an attitude of superiority which can cause mistrust, anger, and lack of communication from K–12 teacher-colleagues. K–12 schools must see their university partners as colleagues with the common goal of improving student outcomes. Minor resistance incidents are to be expected in a program which involves several people from both institutions. Examples of these tensions, which could be perceived as resistance, include: waiting for campus safety to open classroom doors; lack of understanding from certain university faculty and staff for having children on campus; and facing traffic jams when parents pick the children each day. There are occasional minor misunderstandings between the K–12 teachers and some of the university's staff members; however, these incidents are fairly easily resolved, usually by the program coordinators. Another perceived resistance came from one of the professors who felt that some of the high school students did not seem well prepared for the rigor of a college course. Another potential concern refers to the separation of church and state when public school teachers and students are in a faith-based university.

## LIMITATIONS

One of the limitations of the project, as expressed by students, teachers, and parents, is that the program is only one month long with a very intensive schedule and curriculum. Another limitation is the fact that there is a waiting list and not enough funding to expend the program. Yet another limitation might be not allowing other districts (of higher income levels) and children of university employees to participate in this program. However, the program was purposefully designed to empower Latino, low-income students from a local, diverse community, and provide them with tools for a successful college education journey.

## POSITIVES

The success of the partnership evolved from the way the partnership was approached, the clarity in the agreement of responsibilities between partners, and the reciprocity of benefits to each partner. Students who attend the GATE program seem to have a positive attitude toward attending college. Both institutions believe that the university campus environment had an impact on getting students interested in attending college. The high school students and their parents were highly enthusiastic when they met with one of the university admissions officers and were eager to explore college opportunities. Students benefit from the available university scholarships. Three of the parents of GATE students enrolled in the degree completion program and later completed a teaching credential. In addition, the partnership provides an opportunity for collaborative research between the two institutions and for community involvement, including participation from the mayor and the local Rotary Club. In the last 3 years, the local school district has allowed university teacher credentialing students who teach at a private, faith-based, K–5 school to do part of their student teaching during the Gate program.

Partnerships will not succeed without building relationships and the understanding of reciprocal teaching and learning experiences for all partners. It is apparent that this reciprocal collaboration has touched the lives of many people in this diverse community. One of the high school students expresses her views on the GATE program:

I have been coming to [the university] since I was in third grade. It is a fun way of learning something new. The [university] summer school has been extremely beneficial for me and my future plans for attending college. Through these classes, I learned a wider perspective and understanding of things I can apply in my future and I get college credit.

The success of the partnership can be measured by the mutual respect and a collaborative spirit in which both partners benefit and by its successful outcomes:

- The partnership is reciprocal, as outlined in the agreement between the two institutions.
- The program has grown from 50 to approximately 250 students, 10 third–middle school teachers, and 2 university professors.
- Several students who attended the GATE program in earlier grades returned the following years.
- Students' interest and attendance in college has risen over the years, as evident by the number of college applications submitted to the private institution.
- University scholarships for the local school district rose from five to seven from previous years.
- The first student who attended the program at its various stages graduated from the university partner in 2008.
- Parents valued the collaboration between the district and the university and some of them are graduating from college.
- Undergraduate education students participate in the partnership, as part of their community service for the course Diversity in the Classroom.
- Teachers from a private K–5 school, credentialing candidates at the university, were able to do part of their student teaching experience with the teachers from the public school district during the GATE program.
- The partnership provides an opportunity for intentional collaborative research between the two institutions.
- Community involvement, including the mayor and the local Rotary Club which funds one of the fieldtrips, and participation of the city's mayor and other community members.

## LESSONS LEARNED

As with any partnership, lessons learned provide an opportunity for ongoing evaluation of the collaboration in terms of communication, expectations, and outcome. Although this has been a very successful endeavor for several years with very few challenges, the coordinators should reflect on the following:

1. Ponder the advantages and disadvantages of having a verbal agreement versus a written one.
2. Ensure continued open, effective communication skills.
3. Make changes according to feedback from end of program evaluations.
4. Collaborate more fully in preparing the district yearly report.
5. Consider more systematic classroom observations with feedback.
6. Evaluate syllabi and possibly suggest curricular and pedagogical issues to university faculty.
7. Engage in more intentional research opportunities, including, perhaps, the impact of separation of church and state in a collaboration project between a faith-based university and public school district.

## REFERENCES

*AUSD GATE Program District Plan.* (2004–2005).

Coleman, M. R. (2003). *The identification of students who are gifted.* Washington, DC: National Association for Gifted Children.

Horowitz, J. (2005). Partners in reform: The California Academic Partnership Program shows schools how to form lasting partnerships that help students to succeed in college. *Leadership, 34*(4), 16–19.

Marshall, C. S. (1999). Constructing knowledge about teaching and learning in early childhood teacher education because of a partnership. *Education, 119*(3), 400–408.

Stephens, D., & Boldt, G. (2004). School/university partnerships: Rhetoric, reality, and intimacy. *Phi Delta Kappan, 85*(9), 703–707.

# Part IV

# Multiple Configurations

Multiple configuration collaborations can involve partnerships, networks, and/or research initiatives with involvement of university, school system, and research centers of private, public, and K–12 involvement. They can be both formal and/or informal, aimed at doing research and dissemination of policy, innovation, and sustainability data. They can also target innovation or a discipline for research purposes. Multiple collaborations are usually grant driven; the university most often takes the lead in these complex projects which can be initiated by entrepreneurial faculty.

Because of the multiple levels of collaboration, resistance can come from any of a variety of sources depending on the participants and their parent organizations. Sources of resistance can be over type of project, number of participants, motivation, control, or maintaining motivation and involvement. The positive outcome of this complex project is that there is heightened production of knowledge and innovation that has the potential to be widely disseminated. The limitation is that the information never gets to those who are responsible for implementation, or that it is hard to translate for the practitioner.

There are six examples provided for multiple collaborations in this section. The first four are collaborations from the U.S, and the last two are examples from outside the U.S.

The first multiple configuration is the Benken and Brown 5-year teacher development and professional development in a collaboration project of a university and charter district K–12. The university, as authorizing agent for the charter district, formally was the responsible party to meet the goals of the project, but there were no formal contracts involved. However, most of the work described in this endeavor was outside the regulatory agreement. The project was undertaken in the context of an urban minority setting with mathematics as the focus. Students in the district were not able to pass the mandatory testing and there was a large teacher turnover; therefore, consultants from the university initially delivered courses and pedagogy for math teachers for certification. The project started in Grade 6–12 schools and by the third year, the learning community was expanded to include K–5 education sites.

The university provided funds, stipends for faculty, release time, internal grants and administrative support, all garnishing high mutuality of purpose. They also garnished urban fieldwork placement, content area instruction for teachers, and a research opportunity. Teachers got credit and stipends for certification, and school administration saw this as a positive to improve teacher performance and thus raise student achievement.

Resistance changed over time. Benken and Brown note that personality is a factor that needs to be taken into account. The university people must nurture trust and a sense that they are empathetic to the teachers and understand their perspective. In addition, there are questions of power and intention to contend with. The university had the resources and authorization, and they set the agenda, yet they must not be viewed as information givers but as collaborators in achieving common shared goals. Acceptance takes time, and this is one of the lessons of this example. The human aspect must be taken care of through honesty and the building of cooperation. In order for learning communities to be created, all participant organizations must share common goals and each must understand the way the other operates and what they have to contribute to achieving those goals. University faculty have to understand and empathize with the school personnel and there must be a balance among personal and community goals of all members.

Barufaldi and Brown describe a large statewide professional development collaboration aimed at improving the teaching of mathematics and science involving 36 science and 24 mathematics regional projects, each autonomous in operation. Although each collaborative is autonomous, they must subscribe to important common elements of professional development. In order to participate, there are competitive formal contracts annually that provide funding from grants, foundations, and large corporations.

The nature of the model, duplicated at each site across the network, sustains the collaborative through the integration of the network of facilitators, teachers, and stakeholders. Using a trainer-to-trainer model, a cadre of participants is trained and they bring back their skills and knowledge to the local collaborative. A support system of master teachers, mathematicians, scientists, instructional specialists, and science and mathematics teachers all share the professional development tenet of bringing the real world to the classroom.

Material resources are important for the project. They include: the flow of monies to the teachers who train; a formal budget for the grant process that is operational for the site; tuition for teachers from the university and community college; faculty participation as specialists with cutting edge information to share; and resources from community sources.

Barufaldi and Brown emphasize that trust and responsibility of the participants is an important element in making this project successful. The university is a large source of power and support because they have the responsibility to garnish soft money from various sources. Yet all participants share in their collaborative groups, respect others, cultivate norms of the group, and express common expectations in a flexible environment that makes it their own.

Reardon and McMillan describe a multiple collaboration that has been in operation for 18 years involving seven school districts and a university school of education. The goal of the formal collaboration is to enhance professional development, conduct and disseminate research to improve practice, and to ultimately influence student learning. Organizationally supported by a central coordinating office housed in the university, the oversight is by a consortium of superintendents, research director, school board members, and faculty. The position of consortium Chair rotates among the superintendents. This long-term collaboration has high visibility and it benefits from strong university and school leadership.

Funding for the office, staff, and incentives for research is on a per-pupil basis with the onus on the school districts. All other resources, including the graduate assistant and space, are provided by the university. When a large study is conducted the principal investigator, usually from the university, gets time release, an adjunct to cover classes, and a stipend at the conclusion of the study.

The mutuality level is high and collegial, there is open dialogue between the dean and the director, and the project is viewed positively by the community. However, there is also some resistance. The cost of membership, on a per-pupil basis, is high and is a disincentive for some districts to participate. Some research results are not accepted for fear that the particular sites may not be seen positively. In addition, time for research is seen by some teachers as a detractor to instructional purposes. In some instances, the activities of the collaborative and the research findings that are available are not well publicized among the schools.

Reardon and McMillan offer that the positive nature of the relevancy of the research conducted, and the efficient and helpful way it is disseminated is an important result of this collaboration. The goals of community, university, and school districts that they hold in common are achieved, and the power of competing for grants with a united front shows the power of collaboration.

The fourth U.S. collaboration in this section is the one described by Shinners. Fully funded through a multi-year federal grant, this multiple configuration involved six K–12 school districts, the university, and graduate Fellows in marine biology who received professional development training with teachers in summer institutes focused on science literacy.

Formally designed, this project was grant driven with clear reporting, evaluation, role definitions, and hierarchical structure within and among institutions. The goals were to bring research-based content into classrooms and to differentiate Fellow and teacher methods of science instruction to include inquiry and field-based activities. In addition, as Shinners notes, the goal of extending behavioral expectations across institutional boundaries and how to mobilize that effort is an important lesson to be learned from multiple configurations.

Whereas mutuality was high and benefits accrued to all participants, the grant was university centered, controlled, designed, and implemented. It was the university that awarded stipends, obtained the resources, provided training, determined the structure, and selected participants. Resistance of school partners resulted from the bureaucratic structure and hierarchy inherent in their mode of operation. Principals could subvert project schedules by controlling teacher time and as permission givers for field experiences, and schools could vie for advantages. Yet, there was a shared vision and common need for professional development and little monetary resources to provide for it internally by the schools.

Lessons learned from this project are that participants need to know and understand the feasibility of expectations and the organizational structure of each of the partners and that the collaboration works to create an autonomous structure for itself. Cross-project communication and planning aids in meliorating scheduling, cooperation, and coordinating large scale projects. Shinners concludes that time is needed to build partnership skills and develop a shared language and expectations.

The last two projects in this section are multiple configurations from countries other than the United States. The first is from Australia, and the second from Canada. Although the governments and culture of each vary, the issues identified in this type of collaboration are similar to the other four examples.

Deppeler and Huggins describe an 8-year university faculty and secondary school collaboration whose purpose is to bring social justice to disadvantaged children by connecting school improvement with teacher professional learning and assessment. High mutuality exists for this project. The university contracts for teacher professional development, obtains government grants, and evaluates the program. The school volunteers to participate and gets resources (tuition, release time, research expertise) leading to master's degrees. There is shared authority, responsibility, and accountability.

As with any collaboration project there was some resistance and tensions, internal problems, and wielding of power that the leaders dissipated. When possible, the university encouraged the local sites to handle problems as they arose that were specific to them. Building trust with others was seen to be an important component to sustain this project over time. Teachers tended to see the value of the project as short term normative understanding and action based behavior. University people had long-term goals typical of their commitment to research and knowledge production. To sustain the collaboration these had to be moderated and understood by each and creative solutions found so that the individuals on each side felt empowered and a part of a larger community that could solve the problems together. Deppler and Huggins found that making teacher successes visible was an effective way to manage teacher resistance.

The last project in this section, described by Sloat, Beswick, and Willms, is that of a 5-year early reading literacy monitoring system for at risk K–2 students. Five school boards and a university institute came together to design, implement and test strategies in 26 schools, including those of First Nations students.

The entire first year of this project was devoted to planning and buy-in of all participants as they worked out the details of the collaboration. This "partner-informed consultation process" had the design in place before funds were sought from the government and agencies. The mutuality was high as a result and was both top-down and bottom-up, with information flowing both ways through a liaison position who also monitored test data and developed intervention strategies based on information collected.

The researchers were responsible for leadership in the design, implementation of a timeline, materials, training and data analysis, as well as funding for the entire effort. A project on this scale required high administrative costs, and whereas monetary resources were high, not all avenues of research were brought to fruition. Meanwhile, resistance by teachers, already under time constraints and a high workload, took time to alleviate.

The spirit of collaboration in this project and others in this section in a multiple configuration relies on equity of partners, sharing, and having similar points of view and common goals in order to create meaningful change. That change is both in policy and practice, in ways to view and enact innovation, and to share power and use it effectively to benefit teachers and students.

Problems occurring include sustaining the project over multiple years while maintaining an authentic spirit of collaboration. This is difficult in that there often are personnel changes, conflicting views of top-down initiatives with corresponding power structures directing the research, and instances where the research findings benefit university purposes more than they do the site.

# 9 Reflections on a Cross University–Urban School Partnership

## The Critical Role of Humanizing the Process

*Babette Benken and Nancy Brown*

There exists much research regarding successful professional development (PD) programs that ultimately lead to improved student learning and achievement (e.g., Darling-Hammond, 1999). Yet, designing PD remains a complex and challenging endeavor; this body of work is usually reflective in nature, often jumping into what was learned in an existing, already successful collaborative. Rarely is a specific road map with the basics of how-to provided. What is missing is a careful description of how partnerships are formed, particularly what is needed before beginning to work collaboratively toward the established goals in the PD program. Additionally, there is little work that outlines impediments to progress, as well as how partners overcome challenges; these stories would help others in their decision-making, both during program development and implementation.

In this chapter we outline details from our cross university–school partnership, what we learned to be essential for any partnership, and how to begin the difficult endeavor of collaborating with multiple and diverse constituents toward meaningful teacher development.

## AUTHOR BACKGROUND

As teacher educators, friends, and former colleagues, we closely connect our research and teaching, allowing our instruction to function as a foundation for our research. We seek to contribute to what is known about teacher learning and knowledge, as well as how to best structure PD for both prospective and practicing teachers. What has made this work both interesting and possible was that during this collaboration, we were at the same university, yet in different units (a school of education and a department of mathematics in a college of arts and sciences); we were connected by our common perspectives related to teacher education and the important role a teacher can play in transforming schools (Borko & Putnam, 1996). In this partnership we served numerous roles, including consultants, project directors, instructors, researchers, and learners.

## THE COLLABORATION: A COMPLEX WEB OF ROLES

This long-term (5 years, 2003–2008) partnership existed between a suburban, state-supported, research university and a large, urban, K–12 charter district. What is unique is that it encompassed many projects that were generated for multiple purposes. For example, faculty consulted with teachers and administrators on choice of curricular materials, best practices, content objectives, and generating a sustainable learning community; the university offered on-site courses and extended PD to meet the needs of the teachers; practicing teachers hosted and mentored elementary teacher candidates during early fieldwork experiences; and, faculty used this ripe context to conduct research in the areas of teacher development, mathematics education, and models of PD. Our collaborative embodied elements of many organizational types, making it a distinctive and rich partnership.

## PROJECT ELEMENTS

The university partner housed approximately 17,000 students, and the district partner, comprised of two campuses (K–5, 6–12), served approximately 2,600 students (99.8% African American; most considered underprivileged, according to government free and reduced lunch records). The two partners had an existing relationship, as the university was the authorizer for the charter district. However, the collaboration discussed here was formed outside and beyond the charge of this existing, regulatory relationship, in a genuine attempt by both school and university administrators to make improvements (Benken & Brown, 2007).

The area of greatest concern was mathematics. Early in the partnership, over 75% of its students were unable to pass the standardized, state-level mathematics assessment, with scores having declined since 1999. This situation was exacerbated by high teacher turnover (40%), common to urban schools (Guin, 2004). Aware of the acute high-stakes testing situation, this school had made a proactive attempt to improve scores through isolated inservice, with no documented or visible results. Isolated and short-term staff development has proven inadequate for effective school reform and improved student achievement (Darling-Hammond, 1999). Teachers often report these one-shot workshops to be irrelevant and they forget most (~90%) of what they believe to have learned (Miller, 1998). Our initial conversations with teachers and administrators indicated that they were concerned about their students' learning and interested in ongoing PD to improve what they labeled as the *dire* situation. In an effort to understand the low math scores in this district, the university sent us (at the request of district administration) as consultants. We examined current curricula, approach to and previous attempts at PD, and overall program relative to K–12 mathematics.

By the second year of this collaboration new dimensions were added. The primary focus of this second year was on-site, blended courses in mathematics and pedagogy for the high school mathematics teachers; these teachers needed coursework to complete initial certification. In the third year efforts moved to projects on the K–5 campus; for example, teachers participated in PD in many content areas and worked toward building a learning community. Formal contracts delineating the partnership were never drawn, thus making this collaborative different from a traditional professional development school.

Over the 5-year period, monetary support was provided by the university initially through faculty consulting stipends, then expanded to release time and internal grants that covered supplies for research and teachers' classrooms, food, travel, stipends for teachers to participate in courses, and course materials. Additionally, faculty involved in the partnership received additional administrative support on campus from staff in the School of Education. The district provided support through allocation of teachers' PD time and the cooperation and time of building administrators. Both partners were committed to the effort and contributed time and resources.

## Underlying Conceptual Framework

The following tenets guided both our conceptualization and ongoing development of all partnership components: (a) emphasis on teachers' understanding of mathematics and knowledge of content for teaching (Ball, Lubienski, & Mewborn, 2001); (b) parallel emphasis on contextually embedded general pedagogy, leading to pedagogical content knowledge (Benken & Brown, 2008a); (c) incorporation of challenging, conceptual content activities; (d) discussions grounded in teachers' practice; (e) focus on teachers' conceptual understandings, growth, and independence; (f) design that integrates teachers' beliefs, prior knowledge, and autobiography; (g) modeling of effective, reform-oriented practices; (h) generation of a learning community that cultivates interdependence and mentoring (e.g., Lave & Wenger, 1991; Palincsar, Magnusson, Marano, Ford, & Brown, 1998); and (i) acknowledgment and attention to the realities of the teachers' school context and teachers' perceptions of that context (Sleeter, 2008). Whereas all of these aspects of the program were essential to the learning of all members of this community, those that aided the community in building a working relationship based on mutual respect and understanding (e.g., d, f, i) were most critical and necessary to achieve more content-driven goals.

## Mutuality Level and Resistance Sources

Representatives from both organizations entered into the partnership with aspirations to improve the academic situation within the district. Thus, all members of the newly-forming community had a common, overarching goal, which remained intact and central throughout the 5-year period. Furthermore, constituents also held more individualized goals, which were both altruistic and pragmatic in nature. Faculty were interested in expanding teachers' content and pedagogical understandings to enhance their ability to improve student learning; they also were eager to use the partnership as an urban fieldwork placement for teacher candidates and a context for research. Teachers wanted to improve their ability to use instructional materials and design lessons; they were also motivated by university credit that could be used toward certification and stipends for hosting teacher candidates. District administrators desired to improve teachers' pedagogy, students' achievement, and the working relationship with their university-authorizer; it was also critical that they made progress toward state and federal mandates. The fact that all constituents held both community-minded and more individualized goals was not necessarily a cause for concern; all objectives contributed to the mutually held, overarching goal and the partnership was both beneficial and necessary to all.

Research suggests that, within such an elaborate, partnership model, power struggles are anticipated (e.g., Monroe & Obidah, 2004); our collaborative was no exception. Dimensions of resistance stemmed from multiple constituents: teachers, school administrators, on-site faculty, teacher candidates, and university administrators. Throughout the period of the project, the power dynamic seemed to manifest in three different phases. The first phase began immediately when we (faculty) entered the district as consultants. The roles were clear and the power relationship was transparent and mutually agreed upon—we were professors from the university in the building to provide expertise and our observations of current practice. Although the nature of this new relationship was predefined, we expanded the formal boundaries; we were welcomed into the community and trusted as allies in its school improvement mission. Whereas it is not often discussed in professional literature, personality plays a central role in the development of partnerships (Gendlin, 1964). Our outgoing personalities afforded smooth entry and generation of a friendly, working relationship. Additionally, our prior experience as teachers and administrators in urban schools allowed us to be easily enculturated into the school's norms and environment.

As our role expanded in the second year, when we began working with teachers and administrators more collaboratively, we entered a new phase. In this phase, fear and mistrust of intention motivated power struggles and began circumventing community goals. Whereas we were invited into this community, it was impossible to miss the fact that we did not look like others in the building and had agendas (e.g., research) other than improving this district that simply made us different. Teachers involved as participants in the research project initially perceived us to be highly educated white women, who were likely passing judgment and there to tell them the *correct way*. Although many may find this observation obvious, findings from our experiences with the partnership suggest that teachers' unspoken perceptions must be explicitly and overtly attended to in the planning and implementation of research and/or PD efforts (Brown & Benken, 2009). Until genuine relationships were generated based on newly developed community norms and an understanding of and respect for what each member brought forward (House & Kahn, 1985), conversations were somewhat superficial and motivated by administrative advocacy and external factors.

Race and other differences (e.g., level of education, teaching experience) must be examined up front and therefore, hopefully, circumvent any possible negative effects that naively ignoring difference can bring. Our experience has taught us that goals, both public and private, should remain at the forefront of the project; power dynamics, which can impede progress, must be counterbalanced. It became important that we prove to these teachers that we held our own "war stories," could empathize with their stories, and were committed to helping them move forward in ways that made a difference for these teachers in *their* context.

Surprisingly, in this second year, an additional source of resistance surfaced—teachers resisted learning content. Specifically, the high school mathematics teachers' anxiety (Hembree, 1990) and professional identities prevented them from engaging in learning mathematics (Brown & Benken, 2009). These teachers were also very concerned about many of their students' nonacademic needs and, as a result, often came to our course meetings unable to focus on mathematics and how to teach mathematics. To move forward with the PD we needed to meet them where they were in their thinking about teaching mathematics within their school. We used pedagogical and student-centered discussions as a vehicle through which to explore content.

By the third year of the collaborative we entered a new phase in the power dynamic when we moved onto the K–5 campus and began working with elementary teachers and administrators. We found this transition to be seamless, as we had already laid the necessary groundwork; we had built a respected, informal, personal working relationship (Benken & Brown, 2008b). The upper-school teachers had "spread the word" that we could be trusted as both people and partners, and were committed to their goals and concerns for their students.

## SUCCESSES, LIMITATIONS, AND ESSENTIAL CONSIDERATION

Overall, our collaborative partnership proved to successfully foster goals for all constituents. For example, the partnership facilitated the district in making progress toward its community goals—improved student achievement on standardized assessments, teacher learning and progress toward certification, administrator growth in the areas of PD and curriculum integration, and a community of learners that could continue to develop independently of the university. Additionally, faculty involved with the project learned how to better facilitate teacher development in urban communities. Urban settings pose an added layer of complexity to the formation of a partnership (Anderson & Olson, 2006). Faculty also learned how to structure university–school partnerships in ways that are honest and respective of context and participants. Finally, university administrators gained insight into effective oversight of, and support for, charter districts, as well as what is needed to support elaborate, long-term partnerships. The humanizing process that encompassed building a trust relationship among all constituents emerged as the central foundation for all of these positive outcomes.

Limitations to sustaining this type of partnership include monetary support and continued involvement of essential community members (e.g., faculty, administrators). One impediment to this collaboration continuing beyond Year 5 was diminished funding for PD. In spite of this reality, some aspects of the partnership continue (e.g., preservice field placements, friendship among members of the community, on-site learning community). The second primary impediment was members finding balance between personal and community goals. For example, after 4 years faculty had to pull out and attend to obligations on campus. Similarly, district administrators could no longer devote as much time and attention to the partnership; other challenges took priority.

## Essential Considerations for University–School Partnerships

1. Content must be central.
2. Context must be examined and integrated—urban settings unique, visible, and included.
3. All participants' community and personal needs must be understood, and included.
4. Resistances, power, and personality must be addressed.
5. Authentic working relationship based on genuine buy-in, mutual respect, and understanding of difference needs to be developed at the beginning.
6. On-going reflection and reassessment is critical to progress.
7. Goals for the partnership must not be circumvented and overshadowed by personal needs.
8. Financial, administrative, and community support are needed to sustain the partnership.

To begin the journey of creating a successful, long-term partnership that has multiple constituents, we found it critical to acknowledge the human aspect of the experience. Ideally, a working relationship should be created prior to formal components (e.g., professional development) of the partnership beginning.

# REFERENCES

Anderson, L., & Olson, B. (2006). Investigating early career urban teachers' perspectives on and experiences in professional development. *Journal of Teacher Education, 57*(4), 359–377.

Ball, D., Lubienski, S., & Mewborn, D. (2001). Mathematics. In V. Richardson (Ed.), *Handbook of research on teaching* (4th ed., pp. 433–456). Washington, DC: American Educational Research Association.

Benken, B. M., & Brown, N. (Fall, 2007). Capitalizing an underutilized relationship: The case of one university as authorizer. *Charter School Review, 1*(2), 36–42.

Benken, B. M., & Brown, N. (2008a, January). Integrating teacher candidates' conceptions of mathematics, teaching, and learning: A cross-university collaboration. *Issues in the undergraduate mathematics preparation of school teachers: The Journal, Vol. 1.*

Benken, B. M., & Brown, N. (2008b). Moving beyond the barriers: A re-defined, multi-leveled partnership approach to mathematics teacher education. *Issues in Teacher Education, 17*(2), 63–82.

Borko, H., & Putnam, R. T. (1996). Learning to teach. In D. C. Berliner & R. C. Calfee (Eds.), *Handbook of educational psychology* (pp. 673–708). New York: Simon & Schuster Macmillan.

Brown, N., & Benken, B. M. (2009). So when do we teach mathematics? An exploration into vital elements of professional development for high school mathematics teachers in an urban context. *Teacher Education Quarterly, 36*(3), 55–73.

Darling-Hammond, L. (1999). *Teacher quality and student achievement: A review of state policy evidence.* Seattle: University of Washington: Center of Teaching and Policy.

Gendlin, E. T. (1964). A theory of personality change. In P. Worchel & D. Byrne (Eds.), *Personality change* (pp. 1–38). New York: John Wiley & Sons.

Guin, K. (2004). Chronic teacher turnover in urban elementary schools. *Education Policy Analysis Archives, 12*(42), 1–30. Retrieved October 12, 2008, from http://epaa.asu.edu/epaa/v12n42/

Hembree, R. (1990). The nature, effects, and relief of mathematics anxiety. *Journal for Research in Mathematics Education, 21*, 33–46.

House, J. S., & Kahn, R. L. (1985). Measures and concepts in social support. In S. Cohen & S. L. Syme (Eds.), *Social support and health* (pp. 83–108). New York: Academic Press.

Lave, J., & Wenger, E. (1991). *Situated learning: Legitimate peripheral participation.* New York: Cambridge University Press.

Miller, E. (1998). The old model of staff development survives in a world where everything else has changed. In R. Tovey (Ed.), *Professional development, Harvard Education Letter focus series*, No. 4 (pp. 1–3). Cambridge, MA: Harvard Education Letter.

Monroe, C. R., & Obidah, J. E. (2004). The influence of cultural synchronization on a teacher's perceptions of disruption: A case study of an African American middle school classroom. *Journal of Teacher Education, 55*(3), 256–268.

Palincsar, A., Magnusson, S., Marano, N., Ford, D., & Brown, N. (1998). Designing a community of practice: Principles and practices of the GIsML community. *Teaching and Teacher Education, 14*(1), 5–19.

Sleeter, C. E. (2008). Preparing White teachers for diverse students. In M. Cochran, S. Feiman-Nemser, & J. McIntyre (Eds.), *Handbook of research in teacher education: Enduring issues in changing contexts* (3rd ed., pp. 559–582). New York: Routledge.

# 10 A System's Perspective for Professional Development in Science and Mathematics Education

## The Texas Regional Collaboratives

*James P. Barufaldi and Linda L.G. Brown*

Our experiences of educational collaboratives spanning more than 17 years has involved universities; local, state, and national businesses and corporations; state and federal educational agencies; school districts; and individual campuses. Examples from the Texas Regional Collaboratives (TRC) for Excellence in Science and Mathematics Teaching are provided.

The TRC is an organizational, dynamic, and integrated system that unites research, theory, and best practice directly into classroom applications through professional development programs (PD) in science and mathematics education. The purpose of the chapter is to describe the collaborative methodology, research, and networking process of the TRC.

## ORGANIZATIONAL INVOLVEMENT

The TRC program is an outreach component of the Center for Science and Mathematics Education (CSME). Its administrative office is headquartered at the CSME at the University of Texas at Austin. The TRC has created a network of 36 local regional science collaboratives and 24 local regional mathematics collaboratives throughout Texas.

During the 2007–2008 school year, the science collaboratives served 7,894 teachers, and 497,322 students. The collaboratives in mathematics served 8,033 teachers and 433,782 students. The 60 regional collaboratives partner with 46 institutions of higher education universities (public and private) and community colleges across Texas. The 20 Education Service Centers in Texas and many school districts that serve unique populations of students form collegial relationships with the TRC network.

## ORGANIZATIONAL MATRIX

Each collaborative site includes a project director and Instructional Team Members (ITMs) who deliver 75–105 contact hours of instruction to approximately 25 teachers annually. In addition, the TRC has partnered with the National Science Teachers Association (NSTA) to provide 900 science teachers across the state of Texas with access to the NSTA Online Learning Center. The instructional teams include master teachers, mathematicians, scientists, instructional specialists, and science and mathematics educators. Each collaborative is autonomous; yet, they must subscribe to important common elements of PD such as: (a) commitment to collaboration, high standards, alternative assessment, experiential learning, and constructivism; (b) the philosophy of bringing the real world into the classroom; and (c) integrating instructional and communication technology into their educational programs.

The TRC provides Texas teachers of science and mathematics a support system of scientifically researched, sustained, and high intensity PD and mentoring for implementing the state standards. The TRC community operates from a system's perspective and the program has initiated crucial and timely change in delivering exemplary PD opportunities to teachers. Activities are designed to improve students' scientific thinking, their mathematical and technological literacy, and interest to pursue science, technology, engineering, and mathematics (STEM) related careers. The activities are structured to reflect the needs and concerns of teachers and stakeholders in the community.

The TRC requires ongoing financial and human resources. Obtaining support is needed to implement programs; therefore, partners work together by cost-sharing, and in-kind contributions to develop and sustain a high quality PD. Major funders include the Texas Education Agency (TEA), the National Science Foundation, AT&T Foundation, Toyota USA Foundation, Shell Oil Company, El Paso Corporation, and The Cynthia and George Mitchell Foundation. The ultimate goal is improvement in STEM through collaboration. Darling-Hammond and Richardson (2009) state: "Because effective collaboration requires much more than bringing teachers together, we need to learn how schools can form and support teacher learning communities that engage in joint work" (p. 48). This statement reflects the essence of the TRC. Extensive research and evaluation have been conducted to ascertain the effectiveness of the TRC. Research supports PD initiatives in collaboration, sustained over time to improve teacher's knowledge and skills, and provides opportunities for hand-on, minds-on learning (Barufaldi, 2007).

Pedagogy, rigor, and accountability permeate the TRC statewide system. The structure of the program is based on design principles of Guskey (2000), Loucks-Horsley, Styles, and Hewson (2003), and Darling-Hammond and Richardson (2009). Four primary activities are offered through the TRC network, including PD Academies (PDAs), PD Programs (PDPs), Honoring the Teachers events, and an Annual Meeting.

PDAs are provided to ITMs who then conduct workshops and courses within their regions for teacher mentors to initiate the *train-the-trainer* cycle. PDPs are designed by ITMs at each regional collaborative and provide 75 to 105 contact hours of standards-based PD in content and pedagogy to prepare teachers to become Science Teacher Mentors (STMs), or Mathematics Teacher Mentors (MTMs). Once the STMs and MTMs are adequately prepared, they share their knowledge with teachers on their campuses.

Honoring the Teachers events, conducted by local regional collaboratives, honor teachers who have completed the program. The Annual Meeting brings together members from higher education, policy makers, teachers, campus administrators, and local regional collaborative sponsors to share and network with others in the TRC "family."

The connections of the TRC system occur *between* and *among* ITMs, teachers, mentors, and students to develop and retain beginning teachers while rejuvenating experienced master teachers. One teacher mentor and five cadre members can potentially impact 100–750 students.

Addressing pedagogy and rigor through science and mathematics PD has direct, positive influence on accountability. The TRC PD work is part of a dynamic system, Dynamic PD System (DPDS). Figure 10.1 illustrates the various components of the system—the PD program, facilitator, and teacher—intersect at the student level. The TRC is cognizant of the sensitivity of the model to social, political, and economic forces that may possibly impact the system.

The DPDS model illustrates the importance of collaboration in developing a highly integrated network of teachers, facilitators, and stakeholders. Due to the collaborative network of the regional collaboratives, the sustainability of an integrated program is achievable, and is demonstrated each new school year regardless of personnel changes or district policy.

Formal contractual agreements are annually signed with the local regional collaboratives and based on competitive applications to redistribute funds from the U.S. Department of Education's Mathematics and Science Partnerships (MSP). Research and operational funds are solicited from multiple organizations. Numerous evaluation and analysis activities for statewide initiatives evolve as requested from local and state agencies. Informal arrangements occur with agencies as museums, aquaria, zoos, and observatories. Many informal contracts are arranged by local regional collaboratives within close proximity whereas others provide weeklong programs during intense summer PD.

Teachers embrace networking that collaboration supports and nurtures because many may be the only science or advanced mathematics teacher in the school, or at times, district. Meyer (2003) investigated sustained PD in science teacher renewal and retention and identified six factors; building confidence in teaching ability, creating professional environments, providing classroom materials, providing current information on statewide issues, providing leadership opportunities, and providing networking opportunities.

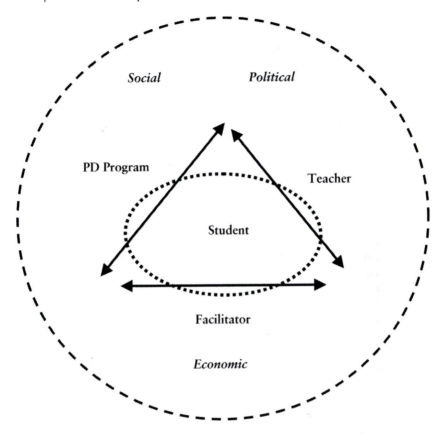

*Figure 10.1*   Components of a dynamic professional development system.

The TRC is responsive to the concerns, recommendations, and interests of its stakeholders and seeks new ways to deliver quality instruction. For example, recent innovations in the TRC system include uses of the Internet through the TRC Podcast Network, Webcasts, and the TRC Online Learning Community: Community Building for STEM Educators.

## RESOURCES

Funding received is distributed to local regional collaboratives to support classroom teachers. Annually, each regional collaborative submits budget requests for the annual competitive grant process. A majority of universities and community colleges offer tuition incentives for teacher participants, and subsidize the program with access to classrooms, laboratories, professors, and other instructors.

Funding varies for each regional collaborative and is dependent on student needs determined by state mandated standardized exams and local collaboratives. Grants, faculty assignments, school and university in-kind contributions are typical supporting funds. Many regional collaboratives are supported by local agencies regarding office and building costs. The regional collaboratives have been successful in attracting supplemental funds from more than 50 local and community partners.

The complexity of developing and maintaining a successful collaboration requires and demands extraordinary efforts of power, personal, public networking activities, and commitment. Years of cyclic project management in planning, negotiation, implementation, adjusting, and analysis of "lessons learned" as program ends and new programs begin are required. As the TRC scaled-up, its ability to reach teachers throughout the state can be attributed to professional trust and responsibility. These values, "We serve the teachers and students of Texas," "We treasure our people," "We operate with integrity," "We reward our partners", and "We contribute to systemic reform and to the community," form the fabric upon which the TRC operates. TRCs tenure of designing and implementing exemplary PD, implementing scientifically-based research models, materials, and best practices equip teachers with necessary knowledge and skills in a constructivist-driven instructional model.

## WHAT MAKES THE TRC EFFECTIVE?

The TRC, situated in a tier one-research institution, is a well-designed model. The designers were cognizant of the educational system and addressed the model from a system's perspective. The model is sensitive to the social, political, and economic pressures. Research continues to inform the organization and operations.

The operation of the TRC is based on soft money. Ongoing, sustained support requires intense efforts for new funding. Although the TRC is successful in attracting financial and human resources, seeking funding is a highly intense and time-consuming activity. The TRC continues to have major buy-in, commitment, and support from its stakeholders.

Collaboration is the synergy to meet the challenge of developing and implementing successful PD programs in STEM education (Barufaldi & Reinhartz, 2001). The TRC strongly supports the position that experiences for teachers must encourage and support efforts to collaborate. The authors further note that members functioning in collaborative groups share an understanding and respect for each other and their respective organizations in the way they operate as well as for cultural norms and values, limitations, and expectations of the organization. Collaborating partners are able to compromise, are flexible, open to suggestions, and acknowledge that conflict is good and it is acceptable to agree or disagree (Mattessich & Monsey,

1992). Tinoca (2004) studied factors within PD programs that affect student learning. His research finds one major outcome of PD is student learning with program focus on partnerships and sustained collaboration.

Reflecting on the process of building the TRC organizational system, the following lessons were realized:

1. Collaboration, working together, can produce very beneficial results.
2. Collaboration is a learned process. It takes time, perseverance, and patience
3. Incentives and rewards are imperative to sustain meaningful collaboration.
4. Support and encouragement are necessary to create linkages among the partners, and to help them realize that all can learn from others.
5. All partners will not contribute equally; recognize the strengths and weaknesses of each partner; remember that all members should have equal opportunity to contribute.
6. The collaborative unit must have an adequate, consistent financial base to support its activities.
7. It is important to focus on the shared vision. The vision should be the "guiding light" to direct and modify your course of action, if necessary.
8. A collaborative relationship requires short-term and long-term planning and well-defined channels of communication that support all levels of the collaborative process.

## RESPONDING TO CHALLENGES WITHIN THE SYSTEM

Curriculum and graduation requirements for students in Texas have changed rather dramatically. For example, a student entering Grade 9 beginning in the 2007–2008 school year, must take four science credits and four credits in mathematics, prior to graduating in 2011–2012. This new graduation requirement has initiated concern among school districts to provide highly qualified teachers to teach the courses. In 2005–2006, approximately 40% of science teachers in Texas in the lowest-performing schools were assigned out-of-field and 40% failed their science certification examination once. School districts are concerned about the lack of instructional materials, equipment, and laboratory space to offer the courses.

The TRC has encountered numerous economic, social and political issues, and challenges. Because the TRC relies on soft money, attracting financial resources for PD activities is challenging. Frequently, when school districts experience an economic down turn, the first budget item deleted are those related to the professional growth of teachers. The TRC operational budget remains vulnerable to policy changes at the state level, shifts in state priorities in science and mathematics education, and changes in the political arena. From a system's perspective, the TRC designed and implemented a statewide infrastructure with the capability and resiliency to respond to system changes in a timely manner by competent and quality professional staff at local regional sites and collaborative efforts.

Ensuring PD quality remains an issue dealt with daily. Each year, the TRC collaborates with many school districts and school campuses, project directors and ITMs, and thousands of teachers and students. Over time, the TRC dramatically increased the number of local regional collaboratives and activities. The TRC implemented "checks and balances" processes through extensive documentation from each local regional collaboratives. Each collaborative submit reports of the PD program, evaluations, data on gains in teachers' content understanding, expenditure updates, and other artifacts. Most documentation is submitted electronically via the TRC website. At times, results collected from self-report instruments may lack credibility; therefore, members of the TRC staff conduct site visits to the local collaboratives. The staff visits the ITMs, attends PD programs, honors the teachers' events, and visits classrooms. Classroom observations are imperative to document quality. During visits, staff members document which activities, strategies, and best practices are implemented in the classroom, and present reports and items to the local collaboratives. Quality is also addressed through PD Academies. Project directors and ITMs are invited to attend four to six special workshops a year. Team members are expected to implement information garnered into their PD programs.

Attracting administrators in PD activities continues to be a challenge. Principals represent the power within schools because decisions about budgets, PD, policies, and more face them daily. The "highly qualified classroom teachers," a NCLB requirement for Texas elementary classrooms, is important, as well as supporting elementary school campus principals as Campus Instructional Leaders (CIL). It is their job to encourage teachers' attendance at sustained science education PD programs, and implement what is learned. Brown (2009) found that the impact of elementary campus principals' support of elementary teachers' PD through the TRC–PD correlates with fifth-grade elementary students' performance on state mandated standardized tests. Unfortunately, elementary principals adherence to NCLB "highly qualified classroom teachers" policy, use of data-informed decision making, PD, and CIL to support science education did not occur at every elementary campus in Texas. The data revealed that some principals do not value the importance of science education for student learning or for teachers' learning of science concepts. The long-term impact of these curricular choices may be disastrous for these children.

## SUMMARY

*Rising Above the Gathering Storm* (Committee on Science, Engineering, and Public Policy, 2007) calls for recommendations and action items to enrich the teaching and learning of STEM education and increase America's talent pool by vastly improving K–12 mathematics and science education. The authors of this chapter believe that quality professional development is the key to enrich STEM education. According to the White House Education Agenda, monies will be available to recruit mathematics and science degree graduates into teaching professions. Support will be provided for teachers to learn from professionals. It is anticipated that the focus will ensure all students have access to quality curriculum in science and mathematics education at all grade levels. The TRC's mission and goals are closely aligned with the White House Education Agenda and other national reports.

The TRC is effective because it operates from an organizational system's perspective, shares common vision among partners, subscribes to research-based design principles, focuses on best practices, requires sustained collaboration, provides human and financial resources, and disseminates outcomes. These attributes are paramount to ensure that the aforementioned goals are attained.

## REFERENCES

Barufaldi, J. (2007). *A research-based professional development model in science education.* Paper presented at the Fourteenth International Conference on Learning, University of the Witwatersrand, Johannesburg, South Africa.

Barufaldi, J. P., & Reinhartz, J. (2001). The dynamics of collaboration in a statewide professional development program for science teachers, models of science teacher preparation. In D. R. Lavoie, & W. Roth (Eds.), *Models of science teacher preparation—Theory into Practice* (pp. 89–104). Dordrecht, The Netherlands: Kluwer Academic.

Brown, L. L. G. (2009). *Opening Pandora's Box: Texas elementary campus administrators use of educational policy through data-informed decisions for science education.* Unpublished dissertation. The University of Texas at Austin, Austin. TX.

Committee on Science, Engineering, and Public Policy (2007). *Rising above the gathering storm: Energizing and employing America for a brighter economic future.* Washington, DC: The National Academies Press.

Darling-Hammond, L., & Richardson, R. (2009). Teacher learning: What matters? *Educational Leadership, 66(2),* 46–53.

Guskey, T. (2000). *Evaluating professional development.* Thousand Oaks, CA: Corwin Press.

Loucks-Horsley, S., Styles, K., & Hewson, P. (2003). *Designing professional development for teachers of science and mathematics.* Thousand Oaks, CA: Corwin Press.

Mattessich, P. W., & Monsey, B. R. (1992). *Collaboration: What makes it work.* St. Paul, MN: Wilder Foundation.

Meyer, J. (2003). *The role of sustained professional development in science teacher renewal and retention.* Unpublished dissertation. Austin, Texas: The University of Texas at Austin.

Tinoca, L. (2004). *From professional development for science teachers to student learning in science.* Unpublished dissertation. Austin, Texas.

# 11 Conducting Research that Practitioners Think is Relevant
## Metropolitan Educational Research Consortium (MERC)

*R. Martin Reardon and James McMillan*

The phrase "school–university partnerships" is often used to connote agreements that facilitate teaching practice arrangements for students in teacher education programs, but school–university partnerships are far from one-dimensional (Barnett, Hall, Berg, & Camarena, 1999; Callahan & Martin, 2007; Ravid & Handler, 2001; Slater, 1996). For example, Teitel (1999) claimed that there were three themes beyond the preparation of educators which could be delineated among school–university partnerships: improvement of student learning, professional development of educators, and research and inquiry into improving practice.

This paper describes a school–university partnership with a direct focus on the conduct of research. From a different perspective, this research initiative incorporates the second and third of Teitel's (1999) themes, with an overarching goal of positively impacting student learning.

## ORGANIZATIONAL INVOLVEMENT

This partnership, known as the Metropolitan Educational Research Consortium (MERC), is among seven school districts in the Greater Richmond area in Virginia (Chesterfield County, Colonial Heights City, Hanover County, Henrico County, Hopewell City, Powhatan County, and Richmond City), and the School of Education (SOE) at Virginia Commonwealth University (VCU). MERC unobtrusively marked its 15th year of operation in 2006. The initial school district members of MERC are all still committed to it, which, in itself, is a testament to the value accorded to MERC by its participants and to the soundness of its organizational structure.

## FORMAL/INFORMAL

MERC is a formal collaboration among the participants. The superintendents of the participating school districts sign a formal agreement with MERC, which lays out the aims of the collaboration, and stipulates the level of support which each of the participants will provide. The participating school district superintendents, their research directors, school board members, and designated VCU faculty collectively constitute the MERC Policy and Planning Council (PPC), which meets twice a semester. The position of chair of the PPC rotates biannually among the superintendents from the member districts.

The dean of the SOE attends the PPC meetings and shares perspectives on important aspects of educational policy and practice. The MERC director serves as the designee of the dean of the SOE, and attends to the day-to-day leadership of the collaboration, in dialog with the Steering Committee of the PPC.

## PURPOSE

The stated aim of MERC is "to conduct research practitioners think is relevant, and transfer it into schools and classrooms" (MERC, 2009a, ¶2). This concise statement is rephrased later on the MERC webpage, where the founding members of MERC are characterized as wishing to "provide timely information to help resolve educational problems identified by practicing professional educators" (MERC, 2009a, ¶4).

Bransford, Brown, and Cocking (2000) suggested that the "influence of research on the four mediating arenas (between research and practice)—educational materials, pre-service and in-service teacher and administrator programs, public policy, and public opinion and the media—has typically been weak" (p. 248). The comprehensive nature of the mediating arenas depicted by Bransford et al. lends substance to McClintock's (2007) outspoken critique that "educational research accumulates in great, growing bulk, with all manner of contradictory findings, and no leverage by which to affect practice in any significant way" (p. 1).

MERC's strongly pragmatic rationale—encapsulated in its declaration on its website that "research has value, primarily when it is utilized to improve school programs and professional practice" (MERC, 2009b, ¶1)—stands in contrast to McClintock's (2007) assertion. Aside from this unmistakably pragmatic emphasis, MERC did not grow out of any particular theoretical paradigm.

## RESOURCES AND FUNDING SUPPORT

### Personnel/Space

MERC was established on August 29, 1991, by John Pisapia, the then-chair of the Division of Educational Studies in the School of Education (SOE) at Virginia Commonwealth University (VCU). Upon the retirement of John

Pisapia in 1996, the MERC directorship passed to James McMillan, who, in 2000, succeeded his former chair to what became the Foundations of Education Department. Consequently, MERC has had a history of strong academic leadership.

Since its inception, the day-to-day administration of MERC has been delegated to a managing director (Gwen Hipp), who works from office space provided in the SOE at VCU. The managing director is possessed of encyclopedic "local knowledge," and the extent of her "network" enables her to be very effective in organizing meetings and arranging schedules.

The MERC office is housed in one faculty-sized office on the fourth (top) floor of the SOE at VCU, adjacent to the office of the MERC director, who, as noted above, is also the chair of the Foundations of Education Department in the SOE. Thus, even the physical positioning of the MERC office is in consonance with the profile of MERC as a high-quality collaborative venture.

## Access

Access to most MERC information and past research is available online (MERC, 2009c), and the MERC website as a whole is accessed on a regular basis. For example, a recent audit by the SOE webmaster found that the MERC site received the third highest number of visits of any SOE site, with more than 146,000 unique visits and over 161,000 page views in 2008 (M. Frontiero, personal communication, February 18, 2009). Frontiero found that one PowerPoint presentation from the MERC research conference in 2006 (see later for discussion of the context of the MERC research conference) concerning effective strategies for classroom management, registered 4,800 hits in January, 2009 (M. Frontiero, personal communication, February 17, 2009).

The MERC office is staffed 40 hours per week and has its own email address, phone, and fax. It is physically accessible at the times and in the manner that accords with the usual arrangements for a VCU building.

## Supplies

The MERC office shares the photocopying facilities and general office supplies of the SOE at VCU. In addition, the managing director accesses an off-site printing facility for high-quality printing.

## Incentives

The MERC PPC develops research topics itself or endorses research proposals submitted to it on an annual basis by VCU faculty or MERC school districts. SOE faculty members (and occasionally other VCU faculty members) with relevant expertise are commissioned by the MERC director to assume the role of principal investigator (PI) on "full" MERC studies. Historically, the PI on a "full" study can opt either to be paid a stipend or take a one-semester course release—in which case the participatory stipend goes to defray the cost of an adjunct to teach the released course. "Full" studies are also staffed by a half-time graduate assistant.

The PI of a "full" study leads a study team consisting of the half-time graduate assistant, and approximately 10 school district personnel, nominated by the school district superintendents. The study team is expected to meet once a month (or as needed) throughout the study.

The PI on a "full" study submits the IRB documentation and conducts the study, while keeping the PPC updated on progress. Issues that arise along the way may result in modifications to the original plan, and such modifications are ratified through the PPC. Upon completion, the PI presents the findings of the study to the PPC which then votes on the release of the findings. Provided the vote is in favor of release of the findings, the PI submits an electronic copy of the study findings, writes a research brief, and arranges through the managing director to conduct a 2-hour inservice seminar (which also carries "Continuing Education Unit" credit for participants) for MERC district personnel. The inservice is advertised widely through the MERC districts, and the inservice is generally held at VCU (which is a central location). On completion of all the aspects of a "full" study, the PI receives an honorarium equivalent to the stipend, regardless of which of the two participatory options (stipend or time release) he or she chose initially. MERC also commissions "half" studies (which attract no course release time and half the honorarium), along with literature reviews and best practice reviews on designated topics.

The participating school districts agree to provide per-pupil funding to maintain the MERC office and the faculty incentives. The VCU SOE provides the office space, the "indirects," and graduate student assistantships to work on the full studies.

## MUTUALITY LEVEL

MERC is strongly collegial. The SOE dean and the MERC director dialog on a regular basis and as necessary to ensure VCU adequately supports the collaboration. The director is well-known within the MERC community as an academician and colleague, and his perspective is respected among equals in the PPC environment. The director exercises his leadership by being supportive of the wishes of the superintendents and ensuring that the lines of communication remain open outside of the official meetings.

MERC is highly visible within both the VCU and the Richmond educational communities. MERC was recently designated as one of the 40 organizational units in VCU that contribute most substantially to the Greater Richmond community.

As mentioned above, MERC has held its own research conference (at which many of the sessions are presented by teachers from MERC districts) for the past six years. The PowerPoint presentations from some of the conference sessions have been found to be valuable resources.

## RESISTANCE SOURCES

There is certainly awareness among the school district that participation in MERC requires the allocation of financial resources that are in short-supply. Whereas all the charter members of MERC are still actively engaged with it, the cost of membership has been mentioned as a disincentive for some potential members from within the Greater Richmond areas.

There is a degree of reserve among individuals within the participating districts about sharing data at the school and even from the central office level, and some MERC studies have been impeded by (among other factors) the reluctance of individuals and sometimes individual school leadership teams to embrace a particular MERC study—despite the endorsement of the district superintendent. These sources of resistance are not particularly directed against MERC, but arguably stem from a desire not to cast "my" school or school district in a poor light in comparison with some neighboring schools or school districts. As a basic tenet, MERC never publishes any data that compares the participating schools or school districts, but because all the MERC districts are in the Greater Richmond area, participants in studies wish to avoid even the possibility of potentially unfavorable comparisons.

Another source of impedance for classroom studies stems from the recognition among teachers and school leadership teams that classroom research requires siphoning off some time that could be used for instructional purposes. Even though conducting a study under the auspices of MERC goes a long way to ensuring that appropriate data will be procurable, it is by no means a guarantee of unhindered access.

## POSITIVES

The positive aspects of the MERC collaboration are laid out forthrightly in the MERC website. As far as the MERC school districts are concerned, they "benefit from an organizational structure that enhances their capacity for a strong program of research by directly addressing issues and problems they face" (MERC, 2009a, ¶ 4). On the other hand, VCU benefits by fulfilling part of its mission to be immersed in the educational issues that affect the social environment in which it exists. As the MERC website declares, VCU "benefits by fulfilling a broad range of research, evaluation, and public service objectives" (MERC, 2009a, ¶ 4). Finally, the MERC districts and VCU "jointly benefit by positioning themselves to compete for grants which require a school division/university partnership, and for evaluation projects in the schools as well as VCU" (MERC, 2009a, ¶ 4).

## LIMITATIONS

To active researchers, it will come as no surprise that, whereas MERC is unquestionably a well-run collaborative venture, it has some limitations. The major limitation is that PIs are coming from outside the school district. This objective, outsider status is part of their strength as researchers, but it can make ready acceptance of the PI problematic—with implications for the data collection process. In the same vein, members of study teams can be reluctant to share "house secrets" with PIs, or, conversely, take the opportunity to "vent," providing far more detail than is useful and amplifying relatively minor issues. On occasions, reluctant study team members tend not to do their "homework," and detract from the effectiveness of the study team.

## CONCLUSION

The word *impedance* was used above to describe the sources of resistance in the MERC collaboration. This terminological substitution (impedance instead of resistance) was chosen deliberately. In the study of electricity, impedance is subtly different from resistance. Whereas resistance is a property associated with direct (notionally one-way) current, impedance is associated with alternating current (notionally, a flow of electrons first in one direction and then in the other in a conductor). Impedance is dependant not only on the amplitude of the voltage, but also the phase of the current. The consequence of impedance is that electrical energy is expended just moving electrons around.

Without excessively laboring this metaphor, there are a number of points of comparison between the way that MERC operates and impedance. In a positive sense, there is an active two-way "alternating current" of information between the member school districts and MERC administrative personnel (as well as among the school districts themselves at the MERC PPC meetings). MERC operates at the highest levels of school district administration with school district financial support (high voltage).

At the same time, there is a tendency for the energy generated by MERC studies to be dissipated quickly when it comes to moving information between MERC and the schools. This impedance results in the outcomes of some MERC projects being projected on small screens. In concert with Ravid and Handler (2001), MERC is predicated on the belief that "the results of each project should benefit all educators" (p. 237) at least, the educators in the MERC districts. For example, the first co-author recently conducted an inservice seminar signifying the completion of a full MERC study. Although extensively advertised by broadcast digital fliers, and repeated emails to specific individuals in the MERC districts, only four people (three guidance counselors and one assistant principal) attended the seminar. Of course, an individual instance of a poorly attended seminar should not be taken out of context, and the figures cited above indicating the popularity of the MERC website are strong indicators of the value placed on MERC research. However, toward the end of the seminar, the four attendees (none of whom were newcomers to the area) discussed why they had never heard of MERC before. One of the guidance counselors was mystified that in her case she was currently working in her second MERC district. All were surprised and pleased to know that they could access MERC articles online, and arrange for presentations in their school districts on the MERC topics. Clearly there is a need for MERC to continue to develop its lines of communication with the end-users of its research.

Slater's (1996) metaphor for university/school district collaboration—in what the series editors called her "bureaucratic hermeneutics" (p. vii) of such a venture—referred to a nuclear arms control negotiation scenario in which the Russian and U.S. negotiators were involved in "the quest for the appearance for the quest for peace" (p. xxiii)—not true peace itself. In the case of MERC, the inherent complexity of the impedance metaphor that was chosen here to describe the university/school interaction tempers snap judgments. As Slater went on to suggest, the research orientation of the university-based PI must be respectful of the practical wisdom of the school district regarding the best way to use (or not use) MERC research findings. As Slater counseled, "success is measurable in many ways and should not be restricted to the signs of success of one organization over another, by one set of beliefs and values over the other" (p. 24).

In short, MERC's longevity as a university/school district collaboration speaks to the ongoing relevance to practitioners of the research it conducts. MERC thrives today because of the financial support and the strong commitment of time and resources it receives from its collaborative partners. The university researchers commissioned by MERC to conduct studies have strong incentives and appropriate support for their activities. From this perspective, the extent to which PIs can negotiate the complexities of the collaboration that is MERC is one measure of their ability to conduct research that practitioners think is relevant.

# REFERENCES

Barnett, B. G., Hall, G. E., Berg, J. H., & Camarena, M. M. (1999). A typology of partnerships for promoting innovation. *Journal of School Leadership*, 9(6), 484–510.

Bransford, J. D., Brown, A. L., & Cocking, R. R. (Eds.). (2000). *How people learn: Brain, mind, experience, and school*. Washington, DC: National Academy Press.

Callahan, J. L., & Martin, D. (2007). The spectrum of school–university partnerships: A typology of organizational learning systems. *Teaching and Teacher Education, 23,* 136–145.

McClintock, R. (2007, March 28). Educational research. *Teacher's College Record.* Retrieved from http://www.tcrecord.org/content.asp?contentid=13956.

Metropolitan Educational Research Consortium (MERC). (2009a). *About us.* Retrieved February 23, 2009, from http://www.soe.vcu.edu/merc/aboutus.htm

Metropolitan Educational Research Consortium (MERC). (2009b). *MERC.* Retrieved February 23, 2009, from http://www.soe.vcu.edu/merc/index.htm

Metropolitan Educational Research Consortium (MERC). (2009c). *Research & Publications*. Retrieved February 23, 2009, from http://www.soe.vcu.edu/merc/research.htm

Ravid, R., & Handler, M. G. (Eds.). (2001). *The many faces of school–university collaboration: Characteristics of successful partnerships*. Englewood, CO: Teacher Ideas Press.

Slater, J. J. (1996). *Anatomy of a collaboration: Study of a college of education/public school partnership*. New York: Garland.

Teitel, L. (1999). Looking toward the future by understanding the past: The historical context of professional development schools. *Peabody Journal of Education, 74*(3 & 4), 6–20.

# 12 A Miracle in Process

## What it Takes to Make an Educational Partnership a True Collaboration

*Kathleen Shinners*

## INTRODUCTION

What should we know about partnerships that can be called educational collaborations? Experience and research reveal that they can be as cacophonous as a symphony tuning or as raucous as a New England town meeting. Ultimately, however, for them to be successful, partners must, like the orchestra, achieve harmony, and, like the town citizens, plan together toward common goals. Perhaps the most apt metaphor at the moment to describe educational collaboration is "Miracle on the Hudson." When U.S. Airways Fight 1549, carrying 155 people, crashed-landed in the Hudson River in February 2009, credit was given to the various state and federal agencies that deployed a flotilla of rescue vessels to save the passengers from the icy waters. The crew, particularly the captain, was praised for their flight experience, command of the aircraft, adherence to protocol and procedure, and exceptional leadership (Wald, 2009, p. A25; Wilson & Baker, 2009, p. A1). The diverse group of passengers, largely strangers, became enmeshed in a human drama during this "orderly mess" to save lives (Wilson & Buettner, 2009, p. A1).

How, then, can the Flight 1549 experience symbolize and inform the work of educational collaborations? These partnerships function with defined leadership roles and established hierarchy, but they must also be flexible enough to encourage leadership among partner-teams to avoid or overcome a potential "orderly mess" and work toward project goals. Partner-teams must also develop strategies to utilize in a positive way all external influences on the partnerships to gain project support, while also mitigating external stresses on distractions that can undermine a partnership's success. Thus, much like the flight crew on the plane, an educational collaboration partnership directs—yet also depends on—the decisions and behaviors of the population for which it is responsible.

In this chapter, I analyze a National Science Foundation (NSF) grant-funded University of Rhode Island (URI) Marine and Environmental Grades Kindergarten–12 (GK–12) Fellows Program within the context of a "Multiple Configuration," a collaboration type listed in Slater's School/

University Collaboration Matrix. The GK–12 Project is defined within Slater's model by exploring this type of collaboration relative to its own characteristics—namely, organizational involvement, level of formality, purpose, resources, level of mutuality, resistance sources, positives, and limitations. Further, the chapter addresses lessons learned and the level of success the partnership achieved in meeting its stated goals, relative to its characteristics as a "Multiple Configuration."

## DEFINING THE PROJECT STRUCTURE AND GOALS

The URI Office partnered with six districts in the state of Rhode Island to provide teaching experience to graduate Fellows and professional development to public school teachers, and to enrich the lives of students with science literacy. For each year of the 6-year project, approximately 12 classroom sites, 12 Fellows, 12 teachers, and 12 faculty mentors participated in the program.

The partnership, primarily because of its funding and structure, was formal, and established clear channels of communication and reporting as well as defined roles and attention to hierarchy within and among institutions. For example, URI was required to provide annual progress reports to NSF; agreements with URI and school districts were established with memorandums of understandings (MOU's); Fellows, as well as teachers, were given a formal list of expectations; and regular Fellow meetings with URI staff were held monthly (Shinners, 2002).

The project's stated goals, as summarized in their NSF grant proposal, are summarized as follows:

1. Enable faculty, graduate Fellows, teachers, and their colleagues to bring researched-based science content and practices into classrooms.
2. Familiarize Fellows and teachers with differentiated teaching methods, including inquiry-based pedagogy and field-based activities, and introduce them to a wide range of innovative pedagogy.
3. Improve students' science literacy and motivate them with knowledge of global concerns, while helping them to make informed, responsible decisions about their lifestyles and the policies that will affect them.

The project goals set by the university, addressed participants' desired behavioral changes. For example, Fellows and teachers were expected to adopt inquiry-based teaching practices informed by research, and students were intended to become more informed about their lifestyles and the policies that impact them. The project scope was broad in that it set goals for participants across institutional boundaries in both university and school settings.

Extending behavioral expectations across institutional boundaries is a trademark of "Multiple Configurations," given that they are essentially collaborative and therefore must address how individuals and groups "mobilize themselves" to act in organizations (Hord, 1986). In a "Multiple Configuration," as they co-write a grant, one or more institutions can cooperate on goal development and logical structural considerations, such as establishing formal communication channels. However, in the case of URI, as in many grant-funded projects, the university had not identified its partners when the Project Investigator wrote the grant and, therefore, drafted expectations for teachers and students based on the university's perspective. "Multiple Configuration" thus brings previously separate organizations into a new structure fully committed to a common mission. Then, when project planning is complete and creates a true structure around shared goals, a higher level of mutuality among project partners can result (Mattessich & Monsey, 1992; Shinners, 2002).

## LESSON LEARNED

When pilots file a flight plan, they inform air traffic control of their destination and expect that pertinent information be disseminated to all relevant personnel in order to ensure a safe landing. Working back from that expectation, airline and airport personnel are trained to work collaboratively to achieve that goal. Likewise, when universities set broad project goals that address participant behavior across institutions, they need to:

- Test the feasibility of those expectations by conducting research on other similar projects; analyze the hierarchy of potential partnering organizations
- Create a semi-autonomous structure for the "Multiple Configuration" that enables cross-project communication and sets accountability requirements for participants

## MUTUALITY LEVEL: EVERYONE IS ON THE SAME "PLANE"

Understanding how mutuality works is essential in attempting to understand collaborative behavior (Axlerod, 1984). In analyzing the URI GK–12 project through the lens of mutuality, then, how much structural consideration was given to the university as well as the public schools in the areas of risk taken, rewards given, roles assigned, and formal levels of communication?

## FLIGHT PLAN: SHARED VISION/COMMON
## NEED/PROJECT DESIGN

The GK–12 project pointed the university and public schools toward a common direction by providing a much valued service to the public school community. When the project was created, Rhode Island public schools had a great need for professional development (PD), but scant resources to support it. URI provided science education to schools by delivering PD to teachers at a summer institute, during which a comprehensive science content curriculum was complemented with related field experiences. For example, a talk on salt marshes was followed by a trip to the Galilee, RI, salt marsh, and a session on terrestrial ecology and old growth forests preceded a field exercise on forest ecotypes. In this way, URI was able to combine attainment of grant objectives to familiarize Fellows and teachers with differentiated teaching methods while at the same time meeting a real school-based need (professional development). After the second year of the project and acting on the evaluator's recommendation, URI included one session on forming successful teacher–Fellow partnerships responding to participants' insufficient understanding of their roles. The training focused on their common goals and on how their assigned roles contributed to those goals (Shinners, 2002).

## ONE CAPTAIN, ONE CREW: POWER HIERARCHY AND PROJECT STRUCTURE

Like the airplane captain, the URI drove the project. The university provided project resources, such as stipends for graduate Fellows, summer training for Fellows, and course stipends for teachers. It also created the project structure and managed project operations by selecting participating districts. However, URI did not have direct control over the partnering institutions—Rhode Island public schools—which, like many public schools everywhere, are bureaucratic organizations strongly invested in their hierarchy. Schools sought advantages related to project participation, such as rich PD opportunities for their teachers and diverse instructional opportunities for their students, and they also participated within the confines of their governance structure. For example, principals controlled issues critical to project success, such as teacher release time and field trip opportunities. How were teacher/Fellow teams able to navigate between project requirements and school control? The answer partially lies in how participants used both formal and informal networks and communication channels to move through project challenges resistance and factors.

## LESSON LEARNED

When designing a "Multiple Configuration" partnership, project organizers should require that teachers self-select for the project and be approved by their administration, rather than being assigned by principals. In short, prior to program commencement, as part of project planning, senior staff need to establish formal regular communication channels among teachers and project staff to assure consistent expectations.

## TURBULENCE AHEAD: RESISTANCE FACTORS

Feedback from Fellows and teachers during the early years of the project indicated that tensions existed among project participants. A few teachers indicated that the graduate Fellows, following university-set vacation schedules, had interrupted the continuity of their classroom teaching, and that their research-related projects did not always align with the state Grade-level Expectations (GLEs). Teachers wanted more communication with project staff and with other teachers and graduate Fellows throughout the school year. Whereas some teachers wanted more time to prepare lessons with the graduate Fellows, they were unable to find common planning time for that purpose. Early in the project, some teachers also complained that graduate Fellows sometimes did not adjust their schedule to meet a critical lesson or test review. Again, early in the project, some teachers were not aligned with project goals and expressed disappointment that the graduate Fellows did not come with more "stuff" like kits and prepared materials for them to use as they resisted project-based, hands-on learning and the shift to real science. Teachers commented that Fellow expectations/roles in the classroom needed to be clearly achieved from the outset. Meanwhile, Fellows were challenged by bell-driven class time limits, lack of common planning time, their own inexperience and expertise at developing standards-based lessons, and time and school-based restrictions on taking students into the field. Sometimes Fellows were not able to present their research because the curriculum could not accommodate it, or the school schedule limited the time required. What action did the university take to address the teachers' interests, which were seen at the time to be of benefit to the project's ultimate success?

## LESSONS LEARNED: ANTICIPATE AREAS OF RESISTANCE AND PLAN ACCORDINGLY

- The University-drafted MOU needs to require principals to provide the teacher/Fellow partnership with sufficient time, scheduling, and field-based opportunities.
- The university needs to train graduate Fellows in public school culture and organizational structure, grounding them in expectations of teachers, as well as students.

## THE UNIVERSITY'S CHALLENGE IN IMPLEMENTING STRATEGIES: TURBULENCE AHEAD

To succeed in its stated project goals and to achieve the potential effect it could have in classrooms, the university was challenged to strengthening role identification and formal communication channels. The university needed to reconsider and better meet teacher and school-based needs and operational culture, which drove the limitations of project success.

After the first 2 years, the senior project staff reviewed the project's structure, protocols, and procedures to create strategies that would enable participants to synchronize their work more closely to meet project goals. They altered the summer institute so that it was used more as a tool for graduate Fellow/teacher bonding and for reinforcing participant roles, goals, and expectations. Staff revised the scope of the training to build partnering skills among participants. Graduate Fellows and teachers met consistently throughout the session to set/report on goals, graduate student and teacher projects, and research topics. Subsequently, by the time the schools were in session in September, the teachers and graduate Fellows had developed a shared language and expectations around a common purpose. By Year 4, URI implemented greater administrative control over its graduate Fellows so that school schedules were respected, and attendance and punctuality in class were more closely monitored. In their monthly sessions with project staff, graduate Fellows were consistently asked to report on the quality of their partner interactions, and common instructional planning time. In making such changes to project structure and protocol, project staff responded to partner needs that had been overlooked during the initial structuring of the project. Changes in summer training were a necessary investment in teacher/Fellow partnerships. These changes empowered the participants, allowing them to assume leadership roles within their partnerships as they worked though their difficulties and took more responsibility for the quality of the relationships within the project (Shinners, 2006).

## PREPARE FOR A SAFE LANDING: PROJECT POSITIVES

Increased university control over the project drove some improvements. By closely monitoring Fellows' classroom schedule and attendance and by holding partners to a common planning time, the university responded more effectively to the limitations imposed on the schools' schedules, thereby creating space for the Fellows' inquiry-based lessons. The university changes, then, enabled teacher/Fellow partners to find systematic ways to work together to better meet project goals. The common planning time, in turn, served to strengthen teacher/Fellow relationships, empowering them to claim classroom-based goals for their students. After 6 years, teachers' comments reflected an awareness of the effectiveness of their partnership with the Fellows. As one teacher said:

> Through this partnership, the students and teachers participate in a learning experience together, which involves inquiry-based activities. Ultimately, they worked together to further the program goal is to help children better understand and appreciate the world of science.

As a result of building stronger partner teams, Fellows could introduce their expertise more easily and incorporate areas of their research into the classroom because of the stronger bonds forged by investing in the partnership earlier in the process and co-planning lesson strategies.

In the last year of the project, teachers commented on students' enjoyment of and benefits to the hands-on approach to science. One teacher's students enjoyed exploring and learning in the "fun labs." In one high school class, a Fellow supplied and supervised a salt water salmon tank and the students felt they were making a difference because they were helping with the salmon population. The project, which brought continuing activity and study to high-school students, encouraged them to understand and value what scientists do. As one said: "I would like to be a marine biologist, chemist, or biologist/any kind of a scientist. I enjoy science because it's all so hands-on."

## CONCLUSION

If the "Miracle on the Hudson" metaphor applies to educational partnerships called collaborations, then how much of a miracle was achieved by the URI GK–12 project? Was a miracle needed for the project to achieve its objectives? Project goals were well defined, like a good flight plan, but behavioral expectations necessary for goal completion did not originally trickle down sufficiently to the passengers or project participants. The university responded quickly by communicating those expectations to Fellows and teachers via clear project communication channels, by delivering increased partnership training, and by requiring greater partner accountability. Such measures helped to avert disaster and ensure a smoother flight. When URI devoted more attention to community building during summer training, teachers and Fellows became empowered. They became vested in stronger interpersonal relationships which, in turn, made for stronger teams. Project structural changes also strengthened teacher/Fellow teams by requiring more site-based accountability from Fellows, teachers, and principals. Stronger teams more consistently understood project goals and roles and were better able to enhance curriculum changes and introduce a hands-on, inquiry-based curriculum practice. For the URI GK–12 Project, this equated to a safe landing.

## FINAL NOTE

What is unique about the collaboration in multiple configurations in comparison to other categories? Because their purposes may be unique to individual projects, and their structures may involve multiple partners from different sectors (public or private, entrepreneurial or bureaucratic),

"Multiple Configurations" may be difficult to configure and unwieldy to control. Multiple locations can lead to inconsistent program administration and site-based results, and participants can have conflicting schedules and different reward systems. However, Slater's School/University Collaborative Matrix provides those who embark on educational partnerships with a roadmap of how the purposes and goals of this partnership can be structured to address such restrictions, enabling project staff to test for areas of the project that need tweaking. Slater's Matrix breaks down the elements of school–university partnerships into essential components, each of which can be analyzed at any time to see if they are contributing to or impeding project success.

## REFERENCES

Axelrod, R. (1984). *Evolution of cooperation*. New York: Basic Books.

Hord, S. M. (1986). A synthesis of research on organizational collaboration. *Education Leadership, 43*(5), 22–26.

Mattesich, P. W., & Monsey, B. R. (1992). *Collaboration: What makes it work. A review of research literature on factors influencing successful collaborations*. St. Paul, MN: Amherst H. Wilder Foundation.

McFadden, R. D. (2009, January 16). All safe as US Airways plane crashes into Hudson River in New York. *The New York Times*, A1.

Shinners, K. D. (2002). *Making a difference: The institutional impact of a grant supported collaboration*. Paper presented at the annual meeting of the American Association of Educational Research, New Orleans, LA.

Shinners, K. D. (2006). Follow the leader: Project structure and leadership roles in a grant-supported collaboration. *The International Journal of Educational Management, 20*(3), 206–214.

Wald, M. (2009, January 16). Plane crew is credited for nimble reaction. *The New York Times*, A25.

Wilson, M., & Baker, A. (2009, January 16). A quick rescue kept death toll at Zero. *The New York Times*, A1.

Wilson, M., & Buettner, R. (2009, January 17). After splash, nerves, heroics, and comedy. *The New York Times*, A1.

# 13 Collaboration and Equitable Reform in Australian Schools
## Beyond the Rhetoric

*Joanne Deppeler and David Huggins*

## INTRODUCTION

The aim of this chapter is to highlight a number of issues that are considered important in shaping thinking about university–school and school-system collaboration. It draws on our work in the *Learning Improves in Networking Communities* (LINC) projects that involved a number of organizations including the Faculty of Education, Monash University, the Catholic Education Office, Melbourne (CEOM), national research institutions, and a number of Catholic secondary schools in Melbourne and regional Victoria, Australia, from 2001 to the present time. We use Slater's Matrix to describe and critically discuss the complex dynamics of the multi-levels of collaboration within these projects over the past decade.

## PURPOSE

Consistent with the international trends, accountability for the academic outcomes of students is a fundamental feature of current educational reform policy in Australia. The intention is that the learning progress of educationally disadvantaged students will match those of other students over time and be free from negative effects of discrimination (MCEETYA, 2008). There are particular challenges for Australia in achieving this agenda. Compared with higher performing countries, such as Canada and Finland, the indigenous and social backgrounds of students in Australia have a greater influence on their educational outcomes (McGraw, 2007). There are wide gaps between the highest and lowest levels of achievement, and a significant proportion of young people disengaging from school and achieving only minimal standards of education (Masters, 2007).

We share a strong commitment to the principles of inclusive education and designed LINC projects with the goal of redressing some of the educational inequities in mainstream Catholic schools. Thus, we attempted to connect the imperative of accountability to building collective capacity for generating and using evidence to investigate conditions in classrooms and schools. The overall design was predicated on research and practices that connect school improvement with teacher professional learning (PL; Mulford, 2008; Timperley & Alton-Lee, 2008) and connect assessment with student learning (William & Thompson, 2008).

These approaches emphasize that both professional collaboration and inquiry are critical to being informed about practice rather than simply using routines and structures "that work." *Collaborative Inquiry* (CI) involves articulating and sharing evidence and practices in a PL community (Stoll & Seashore Louis, 2007) which in turn builds, clarifies, and extends knowledge construction in the process of improving practice. Within each school our intention was to empower a team of teachers and leaders to work together as researchers toward positive change in areas that they had identified as important to their school. We expected that this process would be more likely to connect the mutual understandings of the participants with their responses and to highlight the value and importance of collective responsibility for *all* students (Deppeler, 2007).

## ORGANIZATIONAL INVOLVEMENT, RESOURCES, MUTUALITY & POSITIVES

LINC was purposefully designed to involve multiple levels of organizational collaboration that were both formal and informal, elaborated for a range of specific purposes, and with substantive resources and positives across levels. University collaboration with CEOM was formalized in contracts for: (a) teacher professional development; and (b) research supported by an Australian Research Council (ARC) grant to document changes and evaluate effectiveness. Schools with interested teachers volunteered for the project and were provided with support resources (tuition, teacher release, school-based academic & CEOM expertise, research knowledge). Teachers collaborate in knowledge production with colleagues in their school, within a school network, and with university and the CEOM educators. Teacher's individual work is assessed and over 2 academic years culminates in a master of education degree.

At each level, collaboration includes a formally defined and jointly developed structure and set of goals, shared authority, responsibility, and accountability for the work. We believe it is these features along with the long-term provision of substantive knowledge resources connected with each school context that contributed to the generally high level of mutuality across the multiple levels and led to some powerful benefits for the participants.

Internal and external evaluations informed by a range of quantitative and qualitative research evidence have demonstrated that the approach fostered teachers' PL and accountability, generating significant positive changes in teacher knowledge, practice, and efficacy, and lead to improvement in students' literacy achievement with a greater parity of outcomes across all groups of students (Deppeler, 2007; Dick, 2005; Meiers & Ingvarson, 2005), and positive organizational changes within and across schools (Deppeler, 2006; Deppeler & Huggins, 2007; Dick, 2005).

Despite these positives, evolving conditions in the collaborating organizations have created tensions and resistance challenges for the collaboration. In individual contexts there were common and less visible patterns of power that have varied over time and on a number of levels. We argue that collaboration is highly complex and dynamic and is enhanced by long-term commitment to CI processes. Of critical importance were leaders who were committed and found innovative solutions to obstacles, tensions, and ongoing changes in the organizations.

## BUILDING RELATIONSHIPS: THE DYNAMICS OF POWER AND VOICE

Risk-taking was a feature of the collaboration and was closely intertwined with a judgment of the trustworthiness of the others in the relationship. At the outset, the innovative nature of the project meant that our level of professional risk was equally high in terms of the institutional and financial resources we each had committed and in terms of our professional reputations should our approach prove unsuccessful. Professional risk was also high because CEOM applies the principle of *subsidiarity* that assumes that central authority should have a subsidiary function (power) and therefore does not decide matters, which can be handled at school level. Thus, any initial decisions we made at university and school-system levels would be impossible to achieve should principals decide not to participate.

Our level of risk was, however, balanced by an equally high level of potentially mutual benefits and the deep professional trust we had built through previous projects. For principals, the potential risk of creating change and discomfort for teachers was off-set by the perceived value of additional resources and potential benefits for school reform. Similarly, teachers who were unsure of the long-term risk of increased and unmanageable work-load demands were initially willing to engage because of the perceived positives: high quality, school-based professional development, funded by the CEOM and credentialed by the university.

Our democratic and participatory approach meant that we expected teachers to have equal opportunities to contribute critical discussion of evidence, to pose questions, and to determine investigative responses. This did not, however, mean that all of the teachers contributed equally or had equal power in voicing arguments and decision making. Unavoidably, relationships among researchers, educators, teachers, and principals were confronted by the dynamics of being *outsiders* or *insiders* in relation to the specific issue being considered at the time, and the perceived value of the issue, their authority, power and responsibilities, and the established level of trust.

Whereas mutual trust was integral to the processes of CI, it was not easily established without a struggle. Building trustful relationships between university educators and teachers depended upon respect for teachers' professional knowledge, experience, and concerns and their context. However, our early attempts to discuss evidence about teaching and the learning of diverse students highlighted the differences in our teaching and research perspectives. Many of the binaries described by others (e.g., Carlone & Webb, 2005; Labaree, 2003) were evident in the transcripts of our early conversations. Teachers typically placed a higher value on normative understandings and action-based solutions focused on short-term outcomes. In contrast, university perspective emphasized a wider research lens and analytical and critical reflection to understand long-term processes. Despite our emphasis on non-hierarchical patterns of decision making, early teacher expectations were that university educators should use their authority to take responsibility for any decisions regarding research. We provided access to useful data and research evidence to empower teachers to build inquiry and analysis into their pedagogical practice.

Collaboration focused on research inquiry has advantages for confronting competing perspectives because it involves the explicit articulation of beliefs and assumptions that arise from critically examining evidence. However, CI also depended upon teachers' willingness to expose themselves to critique and their sensitivity to any vulnerability created for colleagues. Despite the use of protocols for enhancing collaborative discussion, at least one teacher withdrew from each team and one team from each project, citing their discomfort with collaborative processes. Encouraging teachers to express their ideas and opinions was, in some cases, very different from the school's usual operational style. It was therefore, sometimes easier to maintain the status quo than to critically examine evidence about effectiveness and then to change practices.

Teachers most likely to influence collaborative discussion were those in leadership positions with visible authority to enact changes in their school. Collaborative discussion influenced the specific direction of teacher projects and some members had a greater influence in determining what issue was worthy of discussion. There was an initial tendency for members to agree quickly on a solution rather than examining issues more critically and for individual leaders to make the final decisions. As teachers built capacity to understand and use research processes so did they build confidence in their authority to voice arguments and influence change. Extended opportunities to discuss evidence about teaching and learning was believed by teachers to have strengthened relationships and built understanding for the professional differences among the team members, which in turn allowed shifts in power such that there was a greater parity among team members and instances of genuine collaboration. In some contexts, teachers' power and position arose from their membership in the LINC team and its associated successes and from their collective access to authority and expertise. Collective power to influence classroom and school-wide changes also arose from participating in the distinctive pedagogy developed through the process. At all levels, the status and authority of participants were enhanced when the evidence of success they had demonstrated at one level was confirmed by evidence collected at a higher level of authority (e.g., individual teacher success confirmed by the team; team success by the network/university; LINC successes confirmed by external research evaluation).

## NEGOTIATING PATHWAYS BETWEEN THE INDIVIDUAL AND THE COLLECTIVE

Collaboration across multiple levels was highly complex and produced various sources of tension in negotiating pathways between the *individual* and the *collective* visions of the participants. We believed that as project leaders our responsibility was to create spaces for collaboration among teachers and schools. To achieve this aim and to be consistent with the principle of subsidiarity, our operational stance was characterized by respect and openness and intention to support each school team and individual teacher to determine what was important. We did not, therefore, have preconceived ideas concerning the format or direction each conversation would take or what its outcome would be. Our obligation was to empower *individuals* to reframe identified issues and create solutions to address them. Simultaneously, we needed to maintain the integrity of the project's intent for the *collective* and to sustain the collaboration.

Our success with nationally competitive funding had, in part, been due to the congruence of our approach with national policy that visibly supports university collaboration for school reform. This view, however, appeared to be restricted to collaboration focused on narrowly defined goals of academic achievement and overlooked some of the important connections between educational and other social problems. This challenged us to negotiate alternative pathways. For example, one team responded to inequities in their school by reframing identified issues to focus on improving health and well-being and developed innovative partnerships with local businesses and indigenous community. Schools with alternative reform priorities used alternative measures to demonstrate evidence of success (e.g., improved attendance or engagement) and did not always meet the restricted literacy improvement targets, particularly in the short term. Restricting the perceived *value* of the collaboration to academic criteria limited our collective authority to voice their *successes*. This has implications for power in determining whose voices will be heard in academic and other publications and ultimately who will receive resources to sustain collaborations. In a similar way, the educative obligation and responsibilities of the university educator toward individual teachers was in tension with participating as an authentic collaborating member of the school team and ensuring parity of contribution among the participants. Ethical dilemmas were created in determining the boundary between an individual's and the collaborating colleague's contributions to work submitted for academic assessment (Deppeler, 2007). Teams confronted similar challenges in their attempts to make collaborative decisions and build collective responsibility while simultaneously individuating teacher contributions and responsibilities and respecting individual autonomy.

## MANAGING CHANGE AND RESISTANCE

Across multiple organizational levels collaborative environments have been established and incrementally built, dealing with resistance, implementing changes, and achieving positive outcomes for the participants. Whereas each environment has unique characteristics and has created individual solutions, there are common management features that appear to support these processes. At all levels there were examples of strong commitment for the work and a refusal to allow organizational structures or other forms of resistance to impede progress or administration and resistance to dominate the process. The rigid regulatory and bureaucratic structures of our respective organizations were ordered around function, routine, and hierarchy. Logistical limitations, such as lack of time and resources, acted to lessen opportunities for active collaboration. Consequently, timely responses to practical problems were often critical for maintaining teachers' engagement. Timely responses were often dependent upon a creative solution or influencing those in positions of higher authority (e.g., to extend university assignment submission deadlines [university educator]; to mobilize professional expertise or funds for teacher release [school-system leader]; and to schedule time and spaces for team meetings [principal/school leader]).

Making successes visible beyond those directly involved in the collaboration was another highly effective and ongoing means of managing change and resistance. At the school-system and university level this meant we shared project outcomes within our institutions, national educational authorities, and at academic conferences. At the school level, school-wide PD, professional publications and conferences provided opportunities for building momentum and meeting some of the challenges of sustainability.

## LESSONS LEARNED

Using the Slater Matrix we have described the form and purpose of our collaboration, including the resources and positives that contributed to the generally high level of mutuality across multiple levels. Collaboration did not occur without resistance and it created tensions and challenges for those involved. Our approach has enabled the incorporation of diverse perspectives to construct educational knowledge relevant to social justice in a range of contexts. There have been examples of genuine collaboration where teachers and academics were able to act outside the traditional roles associated with their positions and collaborate in authentic ways to advance their practice. Although relationships and power among participants varied over time, the processes appear to have supported a shift toward collective understanding and away from individual authority. However, these changes appear to be isolated to participants with limited benefits to the wider school or system.

A major limitation of this form of collaboration is that it depends on the long-term commitment of partners. In considering the benefits of our long-term involvement we therefore acknowledge that the shape of our collaboration has changed substantively over time in response to changes in our respective institutions. For example, incongruent policy and provision between Australian national and state authority and the Catholic education system and local schools has resulted in competing curricular agendas and increased accountability. Our partnership has been robust to the various internal structural and regulatory challenges that these changes posed. The impact of these issues creates questions about the nature of collaboration and the way it is played out in PL and change processes in schools. CI is not simply about using evidence to determine what works to improve student learning but is also about collaborating to determine what is important. If school-system and university partners are to play a full part in school change processes then they will need to be given opportunities by their respective institutions and by government to work beyond forms of collaboration restricted to narrowly defined goals and to empower schools to determine what is relevant for their context. This may involve educators and other professionals in collaboration with a wider range of community organizations. Engaging with these issues using the Slater Matrix has also challenged us to rethink how we might better structure university/school system collaboration as part of our respective institutional planning.

## REFERENCES

Carlone, H. B., & Webb, S. M. (2006). On (not) overcoming our history of hierarchy: Complexities of university/school collaboration. *Science Education, 90*(3), 544–568.

Deppeler, J. (2006). Improving inclusive practices in Australian schools: Creating conditions for university-school collaboration in inquiry [Special issue]. *European Journal of Psychology of Education, 21*(3), 347–360.

Deppeler, J. (2007). Collaborative inquiry for professional learning. In A. Berry, A. Clemens, & A. Kostogriz (Eds.), *Dimensions of professional learning* (pp. 73–87). Rotterdam, Netherlands: Sense.

Deppeler, J. (in press). Professional learning as collaborative inquiry: Working together for impact. In C. Forlin (Ed.), *Teacher education for inclusion: Changing paradigms and innovative approaches*. London: Routledge.

Deppler, J., & Huggins, D. (2007, July). *Linking research, professional learning and policy decision-making: A school system perspective*. Paper presented at the colloquium: Addressing Marginalization in Education: Inclusive Education Reform: The Seventh International Conference on Diversity in Organizations, Communities and Nations. Amersterdam, The Netherlands.

Dick, W. (2005). Learning Improves in Networking Communities (LINC). In M. Meirers & L. Ingvarson (Eds.), *Investigating the links between teacher professional development and student learning outcomes: Volume 2,* (pp. 4–28), Commonwealth of Australia.

Labaree, D. F. (2003). The peculiar problems of preparing educational researcher. *Educational Researcher, 32*(4), 13–22.

Masters, G. (2007). Restoring our edge in education. *Research Developments in Education, 18,* 6–9. Retrieved November 27, 2009, from http://www.acer.edu.au/documents/RD18_Summer07.pdf

Meiers, M., & Ingvarson, L. (2005). *Australian Government Quality Teacher Programme: Investigating the links between teacher professional development and student learning outcomes: Volume 1*. Commonwealth of Australia.

MCEETYA (2008). *Melbourne Declaration on Educational Goals for Young Australians*. Retrieved March 30, 2009, from http://www.mceetya.edu.au/mceetya/melbourne_declaration,25979.html

McGaw, B. (2007). Crisis? The real challenges for Australian education. *Independent Education, 37*(2), 21–23.

Mulford, B. (2008). *The leadership challenge: Improving learning in schools*. Camberwell, Australia: Australian Council for Educational Research.

Stoll, L., & Seashore Louis, K. (2007). *Professional learning communities*. Berkshire, UK: Open University Press.

Timperley, H., & Alton-Lee, A. (2008). Reframing teacher professional learning: An alternative policy approach to strengthening valued outcomes for diverse learners. *Review of Research in Education, 32,* 328–369.

William, D., & Thompson, M. (2008). Integrating assessment with learning. In C. A. Dwyer (Ed.), *The future of assessment: Shaping teaching and learning* (pp. 53–82). New York: Lawrence Erlbaum.

# 14 Benefits, Challenges, and Lessons of Longitudinal Research Collaborations

*Elizabeth A. Sloat, Joan F. Beswick, and J. Douglas Willms*

We describe an early literacy monitoring system designed in collaboration with multiple education stakeholders aimed at redressing low literacy rates among children in Kindergarten to Grade 2. We first describe the monitoring system and how the need and design for the system evolved through an extensive consultation with our research partners. Then we discuss the more significant benefits of engaging in large-scale and longitudinal study collaborations. The chapter concludes by examining critical challenges and lessons learned about developing, implementing, and sustaining a long-term innovation aimed at modifying practice at the K–2 grade levels.

## DEVELOPING THE EARLY LITERACY MONITORING SYSTEM

The Early Literacy Monitoring Project began following the 2001 release of the Organization for Economic Cooperation and Development's (OECD) Programme for International Student Achievement survey that examined how well education programs in each country in the international survey had developed the literacy, mathematics, and science skills of 15-year-olds (OECD, 2001). When the Canadian data were extracted from international results, our region scored the lowest in all three domains, a result consistent with past local, national, and international studies (Human Resources Development Canada, 2001). As researchers, we were concerned about the alarmingly low literacy rates in this rural part of Canada, and wanted to determine whether we could help address the situation. We first met with government officials and school boards to explore the idea of working together, and eventually agreed that a collaborative effort had potential for making a difference. Given the research on the importance of a successful start in reading for long-term academic success, we agreed that our efforts would target the primary grades with an emphasis on literacy development.

Five school boards were eventually selected to participate in a study to design, implement, and test a strategy for targeting K–2 literacy skill development. Our aim was to create a mechanism for ensuring children succeeded in learning to read during the primary years so they could meet added reading-to-learn demands during the elementary grades. The monitoring project ultimately involved our institute, 5 school boards, 26 schools distributed across each board jurisdiction (including 6 federally funded First Nations schools), and approximately 200 K–2 teachers and 3,000 students in a 5-year research collaboration.

The monitoring system's design emerged during an extensive 1-year consultation with boards and schools. Two members of the project team first met with collaborators to seek their input on what they needed in a targeted early literacy development strategy. Reliable and thus standardized data to guide policy and program planning along with informing individualized instruction emerged as the most important feature. Teachers wanted instructionally relevant, benchmarked information so they could identify and intervene early with struggling learners. Administrators wanted aggregate data to evaluate existing interventions and to guide further program and policy development. Following initial partner consultations, researchers convened to design a monitoring system that was then vetted with boards and schools. This partner-informed consultative process continued all year until we had an assessment-led, data-driven early literacy monitoring system for targeting reading skill development.

Monitoring entailed the use of three early literacy skills-based assessments that generated concise, incremental, and ongoing data on specific dimensions of each student's reading ability (e. g., phonemic awareness, alphabet knowledge, and fluency). Teachers then had each child's raw assessment scores to guide individualized instruction. At the same time, scores were sent to our institute where they were consolidated into a report issued twice annually to teachers, principals, and superintendents. These reports set out each child's skill level on every assessment administered such that educators had both an individual and whole class reading profile for September to December, and September to May. Data could also be aggregated by schools and boards to assess aspects of programming like remedial intervention effects.

Given the large and longitudinal design of our study, the project mobilized substantial human and financial resources with all partners carrying equally weighty sets of tasks. These were divided into the three general domains of schools, boards, and researchers. First and foremost, teachers carried a tremendous burden of responsibility. They were trained to administer two of the three data collection monitoring measures and were then tasked with carrying out the assessments accurately and on time during the year, submitting results to our institute, and working with results to refine teaching and learning practices. Administrators were also tasked with finding substitute teachers, locating school space to conduct the assessments, liaising with school boards, and leading school-level intervention responses to the data.

To facilitate information flow and task responsibilities, a school board designate was identified to liaise between the university and each board's participating schools. These designates also assumed a tremendous amount of responsibility because they were charged with ensuring the monitoring was conducted accurately each year. They also received training and subsequently trained teachers on how to administer each of the measures, and further ensured schools had all materials and supports necessary for carrying out the project. Designates also carried much of the responsibility for working with schools to develop intervention strategies based on data results.

Designates were also instrumental in shaping policies about how the project would be administered, such as determining specific criteria for excluding some high-needs students from the project. As issues arose, information flowed from the university to designates, typically via a group email, who then consulted with their board superintendent, teachers, and principals. Responses flowed back to the university where information was consolidated and again vetted with designates for reaching a final decision.

As researchers, we carried the leadership responsibility for designing the monitoring system to meet collaborators' needs and approval, implementing and maintaining a yearly project timeline, providing all project materials, organizing the training for teachers to administer the assessments, and organizing and overseeing the data gathering process. Developing and maintaining a concise data base for generating feedback reports was a particularly important responsibility given the implications of data findings for students. We were also responsible for funding the entire effort and costs were substantial.

Substitute teachers were required five times a year for completing one instrument alone, and we also hired and trained 25 retired primary teachers to administer another of the three measures in the fall of each year. We also funded all assessment tools, and covered the salary and material costs associated with generating and couriering the feedback reports to schools and board offices twice each year.

## BENEFITS OF THE COLLABORATIVE RESEARCH

As our 5-year research collaboration evolved, several key benefits emerged toward strengthening the teaching and learning process. First and most importantly, the monitoring served as a proactive and protective mechanism for identifying children at risk of early failure that allowed schools to intervene before reading difficulties became entrenched. The use of standardized measures drastically reduced the amount of guesswork for teachers in assessing individual strengths and limitations, and further ensured that quieter struggling learners did not go undetected. The monitoring also mitigated the harmful effects of misdiagnosing competent readers as learning disabled due to factors like behavioral challenges, and ensured that able learners had materials in keeping with their competency levels.

Participants received the kind of concrete, individualized, and standardized data they said they needed to guide instructional planning at the class, school, and district levels. The data also facilitated multiple forms of teacher collaboration both for students' learning, and for teachers' professional development. Teachers' knowledge and skills were also fostered through their application of assessment-led instruction and needs-based learning principles. The data served to augment teachers' observational assessments of students' performance and increased their confidence in their judgments about daily instructional practices. Teachers particularly found the data helpful for communicating with parents and identifying areas for home-based support. The concentrated focus on early reading also served to define and strengthen administrative leadership at the primary level.

## COLLABORATIVE RESEARCH CHALLENGES AND LESSONS LEARNED

We learned several lessons from our large-scale and longitudinal research collaboration that ranged from pragmatic administrative tasks to more abstract philosophical and theoretical issues. For example, our government–university agreement went through several iterations before we received written confirmation for the study to proceed. At the same time, there was much discussion about the merits and limitations of administering standardized assessments to primary school children.

Administrative and pragmatic issues aside, there were a number of weightier lessons learned. We have already noted the 1-year consultative effort required to consolidate many voices, perspectives, and even emotions under the auspices of a single research enterprise. Engaging all partners in an extensive consultation was important for fostering practitioners' engagement in the research, and for enabling researchers to gain a deeper understanding of and appreciation for the professional lives of teachers. We have also acknowledged previously the heavy financial demands of a large-scale collaborative study. Even with committed long-term funding from government and funding agencies, the magnitude of costs for administration alone meant that there were limited resources for additional elements like researcher-led professional development programs for teachers and adding further research questions to the study.

Three additional challenges and lessons emerged as our school–university collaboration evolved that highlight the complexities of research partnerships. For us, the most important challenge was the capacity to initiate and sustain an authentic spirit of collaboration with our partners. Ideals of equity and sharing rest at the heart of the collaborative enterprise in the sense that researchers and practitioners collectively negotiate and thus share the same view of a particular problem. They then collaborate to develop a resolution so there is a shared set of project goals along with a shared commitment to fostering meaningful change. Project implementation and intervention responses require equal contributions to the tasks and responsibilities of the research-to-practice endeavor.

We sought from the outset to establish a climate and culture of mutuality, balance, and equity in terms of the project's purposes and goals, and in the distribution of power among all stakeholders. Yet variations in power and autonomy remained within the university–board–school configuration. Differing degrees of autonomy are inherent within these groups because, technically, researchers are not accountable to either boards or schools, but schools are accountable to their boards. At the same time, researchers depended on boards and schools to ensure the project was conducted accurately and on time, and to see the project through to the end of the study's 5-year timeline. It was thus crucial that participants maintained an open mind and a willingness to try the monitoring for determining the efficacy of the model as a universal intervention.

As one might expect, perceptions governing a lack of authority and self-determination were most keenly felt among some classroom teachers. Whereas most assumed an identity of equity and mutuality in terms of our goals and efforts, a viewpoint we wanted partners to embrace, others perceived the initiative from a perspective of power that emanated from the top-down, and thus teachers felt they had little say in or control over the research enterprise. This perception was, in part, fueled by the addition of specific research objectives to the study's purpose and design. As researchers, we wanted a comprehensive data base that showed a precise and incremental development of early literacy fundamentals (e.g., phonemic awareness) so we could examine factors like age and summer drop-off in relation to reading development. As such, participants were asked to complete one of the individualized assessment measures five times a year rather than the three times typically followed with the instrument.

We were clear from the beginning that a few additional objectives like this were being added to the goals articulated by schools and boards so our partners knew why we wanted to collect this data, and most agreed they added value to the study. Yet even with efforts to assure participants that agendas were compatible rather than competing, some perceived that the work was for university research purposes and little else.

Still others felt that the project forced them to compromise their personal teaching philosophies. Those who did not believe in the use of standardized assessments or the need for direct instruction in specific skills like phonemic awareness resisted using the data to inform teaching and learning. Others resisted and even seemed afraid of what they saw as extreme scrutiny and hence a covert accountability measure based on what the data revealed about their professional knowledge and teaching abilities. In all cases, these resistances rested mostly with individuals and in one case an entire school. Researchers and district designates dialogued extensively with participants until a resolution was reached, though in some cases this took time to achieve.

Workload demands placed on teachers emerged as a second significant challenge in fulfilling the goals of the school-based collaborative research enterprise. Most educational change efforts have the greatest impact on teachers because they are both "the subject and the agent of change" at one and the same time in most school-based studies (Sikes, 1992, p. 36). Our project placed added demands on teachers in both the amount of time spent on their job along with significant intellectual challenges, particularly in terms of analyzing data findings and adopting new strategies to respond to assessment results. Some held the view that they already knew their students' strengths, limitations, and needs, and hence the assessments and data generated only served to add an element of redundancy to an already demanding workload.

General research frustrations and a sense of fatigue emerged as a third area of note in terms of the challenges and lessons of large-scale and longitudinal collaborative research investigations There were several factors that engendered these feelings, key of which was the ongoing implementation of new policies and programs by boards and government during the pilot-study. When research collaborations are longitudinal, the combined effects of the research along with negotiating mandated change not only risks placing too many burdens on practitioners, but can also impede schools and boards from maintaining a priority focus on the research effort. A key question from teachers during our year-long consultation was whether the funds were in fact in place to guarantee that the project would be sustained over the forecasted 5-year time period. Many teachers conveyed their general frustration and fatigue with undertaking the work needed to implement any program change, only to have new initiatives abandoned or replaced after just a short period of time.

There was at the same time a somewhat contradictory frustration from teachers and school board designates in terms of wondering whether the research program would be widely adopted. Some elected to reserve their fuller investment in the project until they could know for certain the extent to which the monitoring system would be adopted permanently. Frustrations governing the universal implementation of the system extended to include the pace at which even minor recommendations emanating from the study were adopted. As one example, teachers in nearly all pilot schools identified erosion in the roles of school-based literacy mentors as a particular concern. These positions are staffed by teachers tasked with helping schools provide targeted literacy interventions for children at risk of early failure. Providing direct instruction is only one part of their mandate and thus they do not have homeroom responsibilities.

Increasing demands for literacy mentors to provide targeted instruction to greater numbers of struggling learners fostered concerns that these positions risked eroding to a point where mentors became regular classroom teachers of students requiring intensive intervention. Schools recommended that mentors be allowed to retain their focus as support personnel and shift part of their efforts from teaching to mentoring other teachers. This would then facilitate a classroom-based professional development model, which teachers strongly stated they needed and preferred, so they could deliver differentiated and assessment-led instruction more effectively. Even though researchers pursued this suggestion with boards and government, and the idea met with a positive response initially, in the end, the recommended course of action was not pursued.

Finally, it is worth acknowledging that waiting for overall study findings to emerge also influences a sense of research fatigue. In the case of our study, determining the monitoring system's overall efficacy as a preventive literacy intervention involves comparative analyses of measures like the government's Grade 3 literacy assessment between pilot school children with those not in the study. School-level data collection has only just been completed so time is needed to prepare the data for analysis and to obtain data from our government partner.

## SUMMING UP

As researchers focusing on issues of social policy and practice, we believe that the best pathway for progressing from research to practice is through an equitable partnering with educators. For now, it is the most effective investigative model we have for bridging the divide between researchers and practitioners, and research and practice. Such collaborations teach researchers about the life and reality of classrooms and schools, and they influence the way that educators think about and enact practice. Most importantly, research-to-practice collaborations can renew and strengthen a collective commitment to students and their success, those who should be our first and most important concern.

We do need to be mindful, however, of the faults and limitations of collaborative research and take steps to mitigate their effects. A central challenge lies in establishing and maintaining the full spirit of partnership among all educators so a true sense of equity and ownership lasts for the duration of the collaborative effort. Whereas it may seem idealistic to think that solutions exist for all areas of resistance, it is an ideal worth striving for in creating the kind of collaboration that genuinely yields improved outcomes for learners.

## REFERENCES

Human Resources Development Canada. (2001). *Measuring up: The performance of Canada's youth in reading, mathematics and science*. Ottawa: Statistics Canada.

Organisation for Economic Co-operation and Development. (2001). *Knowledge and skills for life: First results from the OECD Programme for International Student Assessment (PISA) 2000*. Paris, OECD.

Sikes, P. (1992). Imposed change and the experienced teacher. In M. Fullan & A. Hargreaves (Eds.), *Teacher development and educational change* (pp. 36–55). London: Falmer.

# Part V

# Postsecondary

The category postsecondary school–university collaboration refers to a formal or informal arrangement among two or more institutions, usually involving a university, community college or university, and a community group or school district which has special interest in access to higher education. The special interest group is often concerned with minority or disadvantaged representation and alternative access to special programs leading to full matriculation and ultimately graduation from the higher education institution. Many times it concerns teacher training to serve these special populations.

Resources to support a postsecondary partnership often come from grants and foundations that provide a myriad of support to underserved population. The sources of the monies can be initiated from the community group or school district, but in the case of government grants and foundation monies, are usually signed off by the higher education institution as a condition of funding. Mutuality is in question here because the flow of funds is to the higher education institution to pay for the services provided to the prospective students often in the form of tuition. The power struggle for these funds is at the institutional level, because often this form of partnership is enacted for community college/university entrance rather than students going directly into university environments.

Problems associated with this type of collaboration are that the boundaries of outreach are to the specified parameters of the funding agency. Casting a wider net to attract more students, or altering the population served is restricted, yet, these programs clearly benefit minority and disadvantaged students who would certainly not have the opportunity for higher education without them, or trains teachers to serve them more effectively in order to raise student achievement levels.

We offer three examples of postsecondary collaboration. Flores and Claeys's chapter concerns access to higher education for prospective teachers who are Latino. Nakama and Cooper's chapter focuses on women leaders in community colleges who are mandated to collaborate to produce a career pathway system for secondary student entrance and success in higher education. The last selection is the Penner-Williams, Perez, Herrera,

Worthen, and Murry chapter, involving six different states that adopted a successful professional development model to train and certify teachers for culturally and linguistically diverse student teaching.

Flores and Claeys describe a top-down (university, community college, school district) formal agreement collaboration to recruit, prepare, and retain Latino and minority low-income college students into teaching. Through government Title V funds and foundation scholarships, the participants try to address the teaching shortage and increase representation for this population.

The authors candidly consider the low mutuality that exists in this project which they ascribe to a lack of participants being bound to the contractual agreement. As such, there is a concomitant lack of power and influence in the school system that agrees to hire interns from the project pool but retain autonomy by not guaranteeing hires, and instead follow the norm of their own traditional administration policies. Meanwhile, the community college remains self-governing and separate from the university. Thus, the resulting resistance concerns macro institutional policies and micro interpersonal relationships for each organization. The novice teachers blame outside factors for their lack of success, the community college entrenched bureaucracy thwarts goals, and the school district resistance to alternative certification is apparent in their description of the project.

With this in mind, the success of this project is evident in several ways: (a) the expanded representation and participation in decision making, a must for collaboration; (b) a "reciprocal and bidirectional" need recognized for the advisory board; (c) a subtle yet increasingly effective altercation of the hiring process of the school district; and (d) a sharing of data for research. In fact, the community college has institutionalized the program and as long as funding can be sustained, there is a real attempt at "reciprocity in collaboration" that is evident in this program.

Nakama and Cooper describe the role of women leaders in a mandated collaboration involving community colleges. The socially-constructed knowledge base employed by the participants is the milieu of women's work as they share the processes of alliance and coalition building in this project. Similar to the first project in this section, the goal is to prepare secondary students for higher education with the lofty goal of a well educated and skilled workforce. Federal monies flow to the state through a legislated collaboration to produce a career pathway via a top-down and decentralized power structure.

The task of these women was to share and leverage resources across boundaries and the vehicle they designed was a shared decision-making model among participants. As a result of the contractual power flow to the school, resistance and politics influence the project, yet the women's leadership style created a situation where individuals, not policies, diffused the conflict between central and local control and focused on individuals coming together for a common goal.

The women developed a system-wide initiative with councils at the community college to come up with creative ways to navigate across organizational contexts and form alliances and coalitions; they shared power and dissipated some of the resistance to the project. This collective human interaction is the natural way women work. Real collaboration requires trust, networking, resiliency, and knowledge sharing in small communities in order for projects such as this to be successful.

The last example in this section is the Penner-Williams, Perez, Herrera, Worthen, and Murry collaboration involving the dissemination of a model of inservice teacher preparation for English language learners. Expansion of a successful professional development model to six universities in other states was formal in that it used an existing model that was replicated, and informal and voluntary with regard to the relationship of each higher education institution and its established and respected contacts with the school systems that are the gatekeepers to teachers and training.

Using federal grants to pay for university tuition, fees, and supplies, as well as project directors, staff, and evaluators, each site adapted the model to fit their circumstance. Another positive was that because of this decentralization, power was not held only by one entity.

Mutuality was high for the university and the school system that shared research on students and presented at conferences, but the commitment was extensive for each. Whereas universities made a 5-year commitment, and teachers committed to 5 semesters of coursework, resistance was evident as one school district hired other consultants outside of the program and other fast-track alternative certification models were always present to compete for enrollment. Those in the program established professional learning communities and trust was established among all participants in this project. In order to sustain the work, the authors focus on funding, personnel, and time commitment for all participants which are common limitations for all collaborative projects.

This chapter is a good example of the power and advantages of university-to-university collaboration (among several universities across states), university-to-district collaboration, and collaboration within districts to establish learning communities.

# 15 Reciprocity in Collaboration
## Academy for Teacher Excellence's Partnerships

*Belinda Bustos Flores and Lorena Claeys*

We examine in this chapter the Academy for Teacher Excellence (ATE), at a Hispanic serving institution, in creating collaborative partnerships with primary stakeholders to enhance college access for minorities and low income students, specifically Latinos pursuing the teaching profession.

## ORGANIZATIONAL INVOLVEMENT

ATE, housed in the College of Education and Human Development, at the University of Texas at San Antonio (UTSA), collaborates with six school districts, a charter school, two community colleges, and colleges and programs within UTSA. This essay focuses on our primary partners: school districts and community colleges. School districts are experiencing severe shortages in the critical teaching areas and are considered "high need" serving mostly low-income and minority students. Community colleges, with a high transfer rate to UTSA, serve a predominately Latino college population.

## FORMAL/INFORMAL CONFIGURATION

At the onset, ATE's formal collaboration configuration was from the top down based on a goal to create a collaborative partnership. While we initiated the process, we did have a desire to change and had an idea of the direction we wanted to undertake, both of which Slater (1996) indicates are required to work collectively toward a goal. In an effort to change the top-down dynamics, we held semiannual meetings with our partners. We maintained contact and sent event information through phone and email communiqués.

## PURPOSES OF THE COLLABORATION

ATE's goals are based on a strong theoretical and conceptual framework drawn from the literature on minority student college success (Rendón,

1994; Padilla, 1999; Tinto, 1997) and minority teacher candidate recruitment and retention (Flores, Clark, Claeys, & Villarreal, 2007; Flores, Claeys, & Wallis, 2006). Given the under representation of minority teachers, one of ATE's goals is recruiting, preparing, and retaining Latino, other minority, and low-income college students into the teaching profession, specifically the critical shortage areas of bilingual, mathematics, science, and special education.

## RESOURCES

ATE's resources are externally supported through government and private funding. ATE was established in 2003 through a Title V grant for Hispanic Serving Institutions from the US Department of Education (USDOE). The UTSA is supportive of ATE's goals providing an office suite on both campuses and two work-study students.

Over the past 6 years, ATE has acquired additional funding to support activities to continue the recruitment, preparation, and retention efforts of teachers in preparation programs. To date, three *Transition to Teaching and a College Cost Reduction and Access Act USDOE* grants have been awarded. Additional funding includes an award from the Texas Higher Education Coordinating Board with the goal of exploring teacher retention and success. The Long Foundation provides scholarship funds to financially needy student teachers. The Greater Texas Foundation funds the development, implementation, and research of a pilot induction year support program. ATE is under the leadership and direction of Belinda Flores, principal investigator, and Lorena Claeys, executive director.

## MUTUALITY LEVEL

ATE's mutuality level is low given that not all partners are bound to a contractual agreement, and thereby the organization cannot wield its perceived power to effect change. As Slater (1996) suggests: "The presence of elements of boundary maintenance, whether cohesive or not, is an element of power wielding and solidarity within the organization" (p. 16). Further, its visibility is moderate to high dependent on the individual partner. Hence a discussion is pertinent to describe these relationships.

### School Districts

Although school district administrators readily concede that they considered university faculty the experts, they do not necessarily forfeit their independence. School districts provide letters of support and in general support ATE's goals of increasing the number of highly qualified teachers; however, they are not contractually bound to hire teacher interns. Moreover, school districts expect that ATE complete initial screening and only recommend highly qualified teacher interns. School districts maintain their autonomy in determining hiring practices.

## Community College

As per a Title V grant, there was a contractual agreement with San Antonio College (SAC) to create an ATE Teacher Academy Learning Community (TALC) to support teacher candidates. Some aspects of TALC were institutionalized at SAC, but goals were modified to meet institutional needs. These actions serve to remind us that community colleges are self-governing entities and are not the university's sovereigns.

## RESISTANCE SOURCES

Given that each organization wants to assert its legitimacy (Slater, 1996), resistance likely occurs. In examining resistance sources, we noted that these existed both at the macro- and micro-level. Macro-level resistance included institutional policies and practices. Micro-level resistance was found in individualistic and interpersonal relationships.

## School Districts

As part of hiring policy, school districts have two formal levels of hiring. An initial screening and hiring is conducted by school district central office personnel; hired applicants are then recommended to school principals. Principals are then free to interview and officially hire the applicant. To better understand the process and the hiring delays, we conducted a survey with participating school districts. Analysis revealed that critical barriers to hiring qualified teachers include: (a) salary and budget constraints; (b) school facilities and technology equipment; (c) attraction to higher performing schools; (d) proximity to home neighborhood; (e) bureaucratic overload (excessive paperwork, criminal background checks); and (f) personal reasons. Perplexingly, only two reasons—(a) salary and budget constraints, and (b) bureaucratic overload—are directly related to hiring practices within school districts' control. All other barriers are external and beyond districts' control. One would assume that streamlining the hiring process so that teachers could be hired early and quickly would reduce competition with other more attractive school districts.

We identified micro-level resistors in the school district personnel and novice teachers. Initially, school district human resources personnel and principals were resistant to consider participants prior to completion of their entire district screening process even though they were aware of ATE's screening process. School district personnel were also leery because of their prior experiences with non-university alternative certification programs.

Initially novice teachers were resistant to induction support even though they faced the challenge of managing personal and emotional needs with workplace demands. Novice teachers tended to blame outside sources (peers, media, community, culture) for their inability to be successful teachers. Due to emphasis on high stakes state mandated exams, teachers assigned culpability to state and school district testing policies which required periodic benchmarking. Teachers felt that testing consumed their teaching opportunities. Novice teachers' inability to accept responsibility for daily teaching practices further exacerbates resistance to innovative practices creating a *habitus* (Slater, 1996) of mind.

## Community College

With the community college, we noted macro- and micro-level resistance. Bureaucracy and entrenched practices often deterred the fulfillment of project goals. Initially the project was housed under the education department. Upon the dean's retirement, the project was moved to a center. This resulted in personnel change and a setback in terms of project goals. Newly-assigned personnel needed to be acclimated to the project and goals. However, new personnel had their own agenda. Slater (1996) reminds us that these actions serve to inhibit the progression of project goals and stifle the partnership.

## POSITIVES

Positive outcomes have resulted from the collaborative partnership. These positive outcomes can act as catalysts for change. As a result of partnership meetings, we realized that to build effective relationships for collaboration, we should ask our partners for recommendations. They suggested that we build a collaborative partnership by including representatives from: human resources, parent liaisons, community, business, community colleges, college students, as well as other universities within the community. This broadened our thinking that a partnership to be truly collaborative includes other stakeholders not previously considered.

Another outcome was the formation of the Partnership Advisory Leadership Stakeholder (PALS) board. During PALS meetings, participants suggested that there be greater dialogue for identifying agenda and action items. By mutually agreeing on discussion topics, the formal partnership becomes reciprocal and bidirectional rather than being top-down. We surmised that when we dialogue across partners, we learn and build on each others' strengths while increasing ownership and accountability for minority college access and retention into the teaching profession.

## School Districts

In the case of school districts, a positive outcome is that school principals that hire faculty have noted the quality of the teacher interns; not only do they continue hiring other candidates, these principals serve as program emissaries. For example, if principals interview several applicants and can only hire one, they will take the initiative to call a fellow principal and recommend the others. Proactive principals also will explain to colleagues the positive benefits (e.g., induction and networking support) of hiring ATE teacher interns that differ from other teacher preparation routes.

Resulting from this collaboration, ATE has prepared over 60 mathematics and science culturally efficacious, qualified teachers—mostly Latino (50%) and women (80%), who have been hired by school districts. These teachers serve over 7,500 students in high-need schools with a majority (90%) Latino population.

The high satisfaction among principals that hire staff has resulted in change in school district hiring practices. Partner school districts are willing to pre-hire teacher candidates within the first semester of enrollment in the program. Proactive principals are calling ATE staff inquiring about potential participants, rather than waiting for participants to submit a formal application with the school district. By formally partnering with ATE, school districts have made a commitment to analyze their own hiring practices, study PALS proposed recommendations, and implement recommendations that are within their economic means.

In the case of ATE, a mutual benefit is that collaborative school districts provide ATE personnel access to their campuses and value their input on personnel matters. Partner school districts are willing to share data that can be used for research projects.

## Community College

The SAC partnership resulted in the institutionalization of ATE-Teacher Academy Learning Community. This enhanced the navigation process for transferring students. Consequentially, another area community college approached ATE to strengthen, expand, and further formalize our partnership. We had anticipated serving a total of 330 students, but surpassed our goal. Inevitably, ATE served over 800 first-generation undergraduates, mostly Latina teacher candidates. Of these, the majority (70%) have been transfer students.

An overall outcome of the collaboration is that research has been generated, disseminated at professional conferences, and published. An article specifically outlines the university and community college partnership (Flores et al., 2006). Another manuscript describes the recruitment, retention, and preparation of Latino teacher candidates (Flores et al., 2007).

## Limitations

Recruitment and retention of qualified applicants are a great challenge. At the undergraduate level, transfer students often did not have the grade point average (GPA) to be admitted to the teacher certification program. In addition, whereas some transfer students met GPA requirement and had completed associates degrees, they lacked the lower division course requirements needed to pursue mathematics or science teaching areas.

In the case of recruited mid-career individuals, the challenge was that some had degrees in mathematics or science, whereas others only had degrees in related fields. We realized that applicants lacking upper-division mathematics or science content hours were likely not to pass the teacher content exit exams. Our screening process also revealed that others were not suited for the teaching profession because of preconceived notions. Discernible negativity was expressed about the teaching profession, minority populations, and/or school districts serving low-income or minority students. Some applicants revealed naïve ideas about the demands, knowledge, and skills required of the profession. These individuals were not selected for the project, thus reducing our potential pool.

Another challenge faced is ingrained policies and procedures within the school districts which resulted in slow changes within the school districts' hiring process. Often our teacher candidates became frustrated and discouraged because of entrenched bureaucracy. Slater (1996) conveys that individuals protect their existence within the organization and their actions become inhibitors of change. Thus, policies are given perpetual existence beyond their usefulness.

A major limitation is that ATE is externally funded. Institutional interpretation of federal regulations also limits ATE's capacity to leverage resources across various funding streams. If external funding is not secured, there will be a threat to the sustainability of ATE and its partnerships. The capacity to influence long-term change is held hostage by retreating to *habitus* of operation (Slater, 1996).

## Lessons Learned for Future Collaborative Endeavors

Using Grobe's (1990) recommendations for effective partnerships, we evaluated our progress. We found we accomplished each of the following practices: (a) develop programs that are grounded in the needs of the community; (b) commit resources that are appropriate and well-timed; (c) provide intensive technical assistance; (d) create formal written agreements; and (e) be patient with the change process and gradually expand the involvement of others. We attempted each of the following practices: (a) involve top-level partnership in decisions; (b) establish clear roles and responsibilities of each partner; (c) ensure that shared decision making and local ownership occur; and (d) provide shared recognition and credit for all personnel involved. Certainly, the collaborative efforts demonstrated by the Academy for

Teacher Excellence serve as promising practices. A critical lesson learned in ATE is "reciprocity in collaboration." Whereas research abounds about the importance of collaborative partnerships across different institutions, in addition to diligence, passion, and commitment, reciprocity in collaboration requires: (a) listening to each other; (b) creating a plan of action toward goals; (c) recognizing and countering entrenched bureaucracies and resistance; (d) assuring that efforts lead to policies; and (e) examining policies' outcomes. Although universities may be considered the experts, we must not operate in isolation or from an authoritarian stance. In involving stakeholders in decision making, it is vital to be inclusive in membership and decision making from the onset. "The giving and taking of information and the awareness of the source of positioning of members of each group are critical components in implementing a change effort" (Slater, 1996, p. 86). Thereby, decisions require collective input, monitoring, and outcome; we must capture and capitalize on collective strengths to achieve goals.

## REFERENCES

Flores, B. B., Claeys, L., & Wallis, D. (2006). Academy for Teacher Excellence: Extending the dialogue in university and community college partnerships. *Journal of Learning Communities Research, 1*(1), 29–51.

Flores, B. B., Clark, E. R., Claeys, L., & Villarreal, A. (2007). Academy for Teacher Excellence: Recruiting, preparing, and retaining Latino teachers though learning communities. *Teacher Education Quarterly, 34*(4), 53–69.

Grobe, T. (1990). *Synthesis of existing knowledge and practice in the field of educational partnerships*. Washington, DC: Office of Educational Research and Improvement.

Padilla, R. V. (1999). College student retention: Focus on success. *Journal of College Student Retention, Research, Theory & Practice, 1*(2), 131–145.

Rendón, L. I. (1994). Validating culturally diverse students: Toward a new model of learning and student development. *Innovative Higher Education, 19*(1), 23–32.

Slater, J. J. (1996). *Anatomy of collaboration: Study of a college education/public school partnership*. New York: Garland.

Tinto, V. (1997). Classrooms as communities: Exploring the educational character of student persistence. *Journal of Higher Education, 68*(6), 599–623.

# 16 Reconceptualizing Leadership and Power

## The Collaborative Experiences of Women Educational Leaders

*Debra Nakama and Joanne Cooper*

What can we learn from women leaders about the problems of collaboration in complex multi-organizational systems? Do they have something to teach us about how to share leadership and power? These are the questions we address in this study of women who work in schools or community colleges and who collaborate across these settings. Women may be uniquely positioned to think creatively about questions of collaboration and leadership because of their marginalized status in many organizations. As one woman stated: "Our campus is male driven; girls are not allowed to play. We have one female administrator. Is it to say, see we let girls in?"

Because women traditionally have little power in educational organizations, they tend to share it more readily than men and to create innovative ways to collaborate in order to get things done (Himmelman, 1996; Nakama, 2005). As Christine, an educational leader stated: "Power must be shared and it should be shared to serve the school community and the best interests of the students."

Thus, a study of women leaders working in a mandated collaborative situation may provide us with insights and new strategies for collaboration across educational sectors. Bureaucracies have operated to manipulate women and other subordinate groups (Ferguson, 1984). As was stated by Sally, "if you're female, you have much more to prove than if you're male . . . can you do the job?" Ferguson asserted that women are often "feminized" into powerlessness, separating them from others and tying them to roles and rules that deny community. Yet these same forces often push women to create new and innovative strategies for leading and sharing power, from which we have much to learn. Our intention here is to highlight the challenges inherent in today's educational systems and to encourage institutions to critically question their collaborative practices.

## THEORETICAL FRAMEWORK: FEMINIST STANDPOINT THEORY

Feminist theory was used to shed light on previously unrecognized collaborative strategies that may inform current questions in the field. Feminist standpoint theory claims that all knowledge attempts are socially situated, and that these objective social locations are starting points for knowledge (Harding, 2004). Harding asserted that oppressed groups can learn to identify distinctive opportunities to turn oppressive conditions into sources of critical insight about how the dominant society thinks and is structured. This theoretical framework illuminates the distinct elements of postsecondary collaboration that address the reconceptualization of leadership and power.

We conclude this chapter by sharing lessons learned for future postsecondary collaboration, examining ways women navigated their organizational contexts, reconceptualizing leadership and power as shared processes, while forming alliances and coalitions that enhanced their flow of influence. As one educator, Michelle, said: "I've learned a lot about the different stakeholders' positions. . . . I've changed my approach. I understand their challenges and positions so I try to structure any position to be win-win."

## ELEMENTS OF THE POSTSECONDARY COLLABORATION

This chapter is drawn from a study of women leaders in Hawai'i who were part of an initiative focused on the transition of secondary students to postsecondary institutions and involved collaboration between Hawai'i's land grant university, the community colleges, the public school system, department of labor, community, unions and businesses. The goal was the preparation of a well-educated and skilled workforce for the state.

Data were collected from institutional documents, and through interviews and observations of participants. Women leaders of collaborative initiatives implemented between 1994 and 2004, were selected through purposive or criterion-based sampling. These women (a) were from high school or community college institutions; (b) held a campus, district, or state administrative role; and (c) participated in a district wide and/or statewide collaborative initiative. Participants were initially identified through researchers' knowledge and experience. Then, snowball or chain sample techniques were employed (Marshall & Rossman, 2006) to select participants. The study included 10 women leaders, 5 from the Department of Education (DOE) and 5 from the University of Hawai'i Community Colleges (UHCC).

### Organizational Involvement

This postsecondary collaboration involved many partners, including federal and state governments, the state's flagship university, the state's community colleges, and public schools system. For this initiative, the agency in Hawai'i that received funding from an array of federal sources was the State Board for Career and Technical Education, a subcommittee of the University of Hawai'i Board of Regents, which appoints the state director for career and technical education.

## Formal Configuration

The UHCC, DOE and Hawai'i Department of Labor signed formal memoranda of agreement. These agreements assured postsecondary collaboration among the university, the community colleges, the K–12 school system, and labor in order to improve workforce development in Hawai'i.

The DOE and UHCC were also mandated by legislation of the 2000 Hawai'i State legislature to develop a task group to initiate a collaborative partnership that improved services for adults and expanded opportunities for high school students resulting in measurable outcomes for both. The task group, DOE/ UHCC Coordinating Council, was designed to have substantial decision-making power and implementation control over actions by both institutions.

## Purpose

The purpose of the memoranda of agreement was to establish a career pathway system through articulated programs of study, career guidance, and counseiing services. Federal policies guiding the postsecondary collaboration facilitated the reconceptualization of leadership as a process needed to build an integrated system that is open to change. This type of leadership is different from leadership needed to control people to comply with traditional roles in an educational system (Nakama, 2005). The policy directions also mandated that power be redefined as a combined "top-down and decentralized" strategy. Substantial decision-making power was to be shared by institutions, councils, and committees.

## Resources

The State of Hawai'i has two large bureaucratic educational systems: one statewide secondary system, the Hawai'i DOE; and one statewide postsecondary system, the University of Hawai'i system, which includes the UHCC. As interdependencies developed between and among the many partners involved, leadership and power became redefined in ways that facilitated the sharing and leveraging of resources across organizational boundaries. In our study, women leaders were asked questions about their funding: "Are you able to share funds across the system?" Michelle explained: "With difficulty, through Memoranda of Agreement (MOA), foundations, and temporary contracts we were able to transfer funds."

## Mutuality Level

The collaborators who were fairly visible in the system worked across educational sectors (e.g., secondary and postsecondary). Whereas the mutuality level would seem to be high because the work was contracted through formal agreements and the power flowed one way to the schools, there was often resistance to change by the partners. Documents revealed that ongoing politics and structural differences fragmented educational institutions. Specifically, conflict between centralized and local control caused mutuality to remain low with collaboration dependent upon individuals involved, rather than on established policies.

## Resistance Sources

The collaboration aimed to create change. Resistance arose within and among members throughout the two educational systems. The secondary schools were preoccupied with traditional academics and pressures to increase test scores in the current assessment environment. Higher education distanced itself from the relatively low status of career and technical education, forcing it to drift uncontested or be consumed by turf wars. Resistance also came in the efforts to create teacher change, both at the community college and the public secondary school levels. This resistance was partly due to the tradition of academic freedom that permeates institutions of higher education and partly due to the difficulties in changing any large bureaucratic system, such as the state department of education.

The women leaders had to assimilate, internalize, and make conscious choices in order to collaborate successfully. They spoke of how their institution used unspoken rules of conduct to dominate and control interaction among people. As Sally stated: "there is an unspoken thing of men being more powerful." To circumvent hierarchical resistance and institute change, these women developed a system-wide faculty driven initiative with the Program Coordinating Councils (PCC) at the community colleges.

## Positives

This initiative provided support to change the status quo to significantly increase student learning. It also created opportunities for curricular and collaborative innovations that resulted in Hawai'i's present career pathway system. The women in this study developed creative ways to navigate across organizational contexts, forming unique alliances and coalitions. They embraced a new understanding and practiced leadership and power as shared processes that value all stakeholders. It was clear that these women conceptualized leadership through relationships with the people they led. As Therese stated: "You're not a leader if nobody is following you."

## Limitations

Funding and the difficulty of sharing funds limited the work of this collaboration over time. Because Hawai'i is a state of islands, outreach efforts were complicated. Organizational boundaries also limited the work.

For example, whereas the federal government mandated the sharing of resources, individual fiscal systems disallowed this.

The bureaucratic nature of organizations, along with male-dominated conceptions of leadership and power, combined to influence the work of women and their efforts to work across educational systems, as well as with other agencies. Women leaders used the term "micromanaging," to describe an institutional strategy used predominately by men in their organizations in which they wielded power, intimidating the women, and thwarting their efforts to work together. It was a way to sabotage the collaborative intent of women leaders. Michelle's former female administrator shared power but did not last. Michelle reflected on the situation: "It was the soldiers under her who were control freaks that got her in trouble. These males under her were opposites (micromanagers)."

## LESSONS FOR FUTURE POSTSECONDARY COLLABORATION

Women leaders in this study used their "outsider-within" (Collins, 1993) status to survive and to advance postsecondary collaboration. The lessons for future postsecondary collaborations underscore five core themes.

The first theme illuminated the ways in which women leaders reconceptualized both power and leadership as non-hierarchical concepts that resided throughout their organizations and across institutional borders. Power was reconceputalized as a process of human interaction. Leadership was redefined as a collective process, developing empowering relationships or interactions with people within smaller communities. Leadership continually evolved and moved toward a vision that included service. As Christine stated: "When you share power, know what leadership style to use." Because these two concepts are interdependent, it is important to understand how each influences the other.

The second theme in this study reveals the ways in which power and leadership intersected through collaboration. These two elements aligned the energy associated with power and leadership to realize all human potential, allowing concepts to exist as a whole instead of as fragments. Doris described how she worked through the fragmented nature of bureaucracies: "Identify the pieces, pull the pieces together . . . allow everyone to make their own connections, then the picture gets bigger and clearer."

The third major theme in this study illustrated how women leaders learned about stakeholders' interests/values and developed relationships to find common ground, and to seek or leverage shared resources. They learned to lead across educational sectors while understanding that this learning takes time. As one leader stated: "Collaboration needs trust . . . it's a journey."

The fourth significant theme exposed women leaders' navigational strategies. Networking, gaining new knowledge, and utilizing personal resiliency were employed to initiate change across the educational sectors. To survive, the women leaders had to find their way through institutional administrative processes to create partnerships. "The hardest thing is that each agency has its own politics, culture, and problems . . . we must focus on the students' needs" (Michelle).

The fifth significant theme revealed how women leaders created smaller communities to achieve team goals: forming teams of stakeholders; developing trust; empowering through professional and resource development activities; and integrating outside institutions in support of the team's purpose. As Sally stated: "We're just learning how to talk to each other; we have our own set jargon and ways."

In summary, collaboration challenges existing practices of power, wealth, and control that substantially contribute to growing class, race, gender, and other inequities in many societies (Himmelman, 1996). Paradoxically, postsecondary collaboration offered the possibility to change existing practices of leadership and power. Within this collaboration, women leaders "claimed their right to have their own part matter and function as influential agents of change" (Cooper, 1995).

## CONCLUSIONS

Whereas the women in this study have much to teach us about collaboration and how they negotiate leadership and power, Gill (1995) asserted it is important to avoid stereotyping. These women lead in a variety of ways. Perhaps most remarkable is their ability to not only survive, but create new, more effective collaborative processes across educational sectors and within the context of large, often inflexible educational bureaucracies. Regan and Brooks (1995) created a double helix model as a metaphor to identify and explore the essence of leadership grounded in women's experience and to develop the concept of relational leadership. It is this concept of relational leadership that seems most effective in collaborative efforts. Michelle in our study stated the importance of honoring each agency's "politics, culture, and problems." Without this, relational leadership is very difficult. However, Michelle sees a clever solution in the efforts to find common ground: "We must focus on the students' needs." It is our hope that this research can serve to assist others in their struggle to collaborate across educational sectors and within the confines of large, bureaucratic, often patriarchal systems. The barriers are formidable but so are the women leaders working to make a difference for students.

## REFERENCES

Collins, P. H. (1993). Learning from the outsider within: The sociological significance of black feminist thought. In C. Conrad, A. Neumann, J. G. Haworth, & P. Scott (Eds.), *Qualitative research in higher education: Experiencing alternative perspectives and approaches ASHE reader series* (pp. 111–130). Needham Heights, MA: Ginn.

Cooper, J. (1995). Administrative women in their writing: Reproduction and resistance in bureaucracies. In D. M. Dunlap & P. A. Schmuck (Eds.), *Women leading in education* (pp. 235–246). Albany, NY: State University of New York Press.

Ferguson, K. (1984). *The feminist case against bureaucracy.* Philadelphia, PA: Temple University.

Gill, B. A. (1995, October). *Educators and visionaries: Women educational leaders in action.* Paper presented at the Conference of Atlantic Educators, St. John's, Newfoundland, Canada.

Harding, S. (Ed.). (2004). *The feminist standpoint theory reader: Intellectual & political controversies.* New York: Routledge.

Himmelman, A. T. (1996). On the theory and practice of transformational collaboration: From social service to social justice. In C. Huxham (Ed.), *Creating collaborative advantage* (pp. 19–43). London: SAGE.

Marshall, C., & Rossman, G. B. (2006). *Designing qualitative research* (4th ed.). Thousand Oaks, CA: SAGE.

Nakama, D. (2005). *Leadership, power, and collaboration: Understanding women educational leaders' experiences through a feminist lens.* Unpublished doctoral dissertation. Ann Arbor, MI: UMI Company (UMI Microform No. 3171062).

Regan, H., & Brooks, G. (1995). *Out of women's experience: Creating relational leadership.* Thousand Oaks, CA: Corwin Press.

# 17  A CLASSIC © Approach to Collaboration

## Documenting a Multi-State University and Multi-School District Partnership

*Janet Penner-Williams, Della Perez, Diana Gonzales Worthen, Socorro Herrera, and Kevin Murry*

The student population in the United States currently represents one of the richest tapestries of linguistic and cultural diversity this country has ever seen. Given this emerging diversity, it is projected that by the year 2020, culturally and linguistically diverse (CLD) students will represent over half of the student population enrolled in public schools across the U.S. (Kindler, 2002). As a result, institutions of higher education have been challenged to create professional development programs that prepare educators to meet the specific linguistic, academic needs of English Language Learners (ELL; Wong-Fillmore & Snow, 2002).

This project documents a postsecondary collaboration between six universities in the following states: Kansas, New Mexico, Arkansas, Iowa, North Carolina, and Pennsylvania. This collaboration stemmed from the work being done at the Center for Intercultural and Multilingual Advocacy (CIMA) at Kansas State University (KSU). The CLASSIC © Professional Development Model, developed at KSU, is a research-based hybrid and flexible form of distance education that uses on-site professional learning communities and provides targeted, long-term professional development for inservice content-area teachers working with ELL student populations (Murry & Herrera, 1999). CLASSIC © has been in existence for over a decade as evidenced in the endorsement of over 1,500 inservice educators K–12 in English as a Second Language (ESL) within the state of Kansas.

Given the proven research-base of this program model, Eastern New Mexico University began to successfully replicate CLASSIC © in Fall 2000 and has endorsed over 500 K–12 educators. The University of Arkansas, East Carolina University, Morningside College, and Penn State joined forces with KSU to collaborate in the replication of CLASSIC © in Fall 2007, driven by the knowledge that what can be accomplished collaboratively is more than that which is produced separately (Slater, 1996). This multi-state collaboration has provided a unique opportunity for each participating university to replicate CLASSIC © while simultaneously creating the site-specific professional development conditions and practices within the model that meet the needs of their individual partner districts and teachers.

## A CONSTRUCTIVIST APPROACH TO COLLABORATION

Although the collaboration among the participating universities in this project would be defined as *formal,* all the institutions involved worked together driven by the knowledge of ELL student and teacher needs. Formally, the university-to-university partnership is structured so that each of the five partnering universities has access to the CLASSIC © course materials developed by KSU for up to five ESL graduate level courses. All six universities come together for bi-annual training in the CLASSIC © Professional Development Model. These bi-annual trainings facilitate a successful partnership as they are based on a core intellectual agenda and shared decision making which has allow all members to participate in the collective formulation of how the program model will be applied to reflect their site-specific needs (Stevenson, 2001).

Each university partner collaborates with one or more local school districts to implement the CLASSIC © Professional Development Model. Each of the university-to-school district/schools partnerships is informal. Entry into the school district and schools was gained by each university through district and school gatekeepers with whom trusting relationships were established (Creswell, 2006). Epitomizing these trusting relationships were the inservice teachers working with ELL students in the participating rural and urban school districts who voluntarily enter the 2.5 year program.

As part of the partnership, ongoing data collection is formally undertaken for research and dissemination purposes. This focused approach to data collection is driven by the fact that districts and school leaders are increasingly looking for professional development models that provide concrete evidence that the program contributes to improved teacher practice and student learning outcomes (Borko, 2004; Fishman, Marx, Best, & Tal, 2003). An example of the formal data collected are the pre-assessments and post-assessments administered at the beginning and end of every course which enable each university to monitor participants' growth and impact on professional practice. Ongoing data collection on student learning outcomes is also a focus of this collaborative partnership. Preliminary data analysis (both quantitative and qualitative), indicate improved test scores on state benchmark exams, and greater numbers of schools meeting annual yearly progress (AYP).

## A COMMON PURPOSE: SUSTAINED LONG-TERM PROFESSIONAL DEVELOPMENT

The purpose of this collaboration is to implement a research-based professional development model that provides coherent and sustained long-term professional development for content-based teachers working with ELL student populations via the CLASSIC© Program Model. Professional development for teachers in this collaboration is based on adult learning theory and is aligned with the following standards: the National Staff Development Council standards, National Teachers of English to Speakers of Other Languages (TESOL) standards, and the National Board for Professional Teaching Standards (Murry & Herrera, 1999).

## RESOURCES AND FUNDING: APPLYING THE PROFESSIONAL DEVELOPMENT PROGRAM

Resources for the majority of the partnering universities come from federally-funded grants. With this funding, partner universities are able to pay for graduate-level tuition, fees, textbooks, and supplies for participating teachers. A project director, project investigator, and project evaluator are funded through the grant with the university providing office space for personnel. District schools provide space for the participants to meet. As an incentive, the graduate hours earned by the teachers may lead to advancement on the district salary scale.

## COLLECTIVE PARTICIPATION

Moving beyond the "ivory tower" syndrome in which universities believe that programming must begin and remain within the institution, this collaborative partnership demonstrates how universities across the United States can participate in a collective formulation and site-specific application of a pre-existing program model. The success of this partnership lies in the fact that the power relationships among the participating universities are decentralized; no one entity has all the power or influence. The demographics and complexity of participation is shown in Table 17.1.

Although each university is engaged in specific research initiatives based on their site-specific needs and district partnerships, a high level of mutuality exists between the university partners. For example, participating universities share potential research questions they plan to pursue and get valuable feedback and insights from the other universities. There is also a high level of mutuality between the university and their partner school district(s). In offering additional ESL endorsement models, this project supported district efforts by increasing the number of teachers qualified to teach ELL students (Kindler, 2002; Wong-Fillmore & Snow, 2002).

Additional positive outcomes of this collaboration have been the co-submission and acceptance of national conferences proposals, co-authoring of journal article submissions, and collaborations for future funding proposals at the federal level. This collaboration has also yielded rich data sources that can be compared across universities. Finally, the varied experience levels and cultural backgrounds of the faculty and staff at each university provide the backdrop for dialogue about creative research efforts.

*Table 17.1*   Summary of Demographics for Six Collaborating Universities

| | Kansas | Arkansas | Iowa | East Carolina | New Mexico | Pennsylvania |
|---|---|---|---|---|---|---|
| No. of Districts Served | 20 | 1 | 5 | 2 | 10 | 1 |
| No. of Schools Served | 40 | 8 | 10 | 5 | 20 | 10 |
| Grade Levels Served | Pre K–12 | 6–12 | Pre K–12 | Pre K–12 | Pre K–12 | Pre K–12 |
| No. of Teachers in Program | 400 | 48 | 70 | 35 | 200 | 50 |
| Research Interest(s) | Theory into Practice: Reflection, Critical Conversation, and Coaching | Coaching and Strategy Implementation | Accessing Rural Educators to Enhance Professional Development | Collaborative Technology-Mediated Learning | Multidimensional Professional Development for Rural Educators | Urban Focus: Targeting One District's High-Need Student Population |

## CRITICAL CONSIDERATIONS

Research on professional development indicates that long-term professional development is more likely to contain the kinds of learning opportunities necessary for teachers to integrate new knowledge into practice (Brown, 2004). One of the cornerstones of CLASSIC © Program Model is the fact that it is a long-term professional development model. At the university level, implementation of CLASSIC © entailed a 5-year commitment. For participating teachers at the district level, a 2.5 year time commitment is required as only one course can be taken per semester. The fact that the coursework is offered each semester via a hybrid distance education model, allowing each professional learning community to independently select the time they meet each week, provides participating teachers with some flexibility. However, it still requires a commitment of 3 hours weekly on the part of the teachers to complete the required coursework outside of school time, which could be a potential point of resistance.

Other professional development opportunities can also create sources of resistance. For example, given that districts are not involved in designing the program and with the push to "do something now" to prepare *all* teachers for working with ELLs, one district partner has brought in other consultants to conduct district-wide workshops in ELL strategies. Alternative endorsement programs offered by other universities in the participating states, which promise a fast track approach to getting an ESL endorsement, have also resulted in some teachers questioning the time commitment required to complete the CLASSIC © Program.

## MEETING THE NEEDS OF ELL STUDENTS

The collective participation of all partners in the university-to-university collaboration has created a symbiotic relationship in which faculty from multiple universities have come together as a collective whole to address a need to provide teacher training for educators who were previously unprepared to support their ELL students in the classroom. This collaboration has also demonstrated that the CLASSIC © Program Model can be successfully duplicated in multiple states, in a range of rural and urban settings, with consistent and positive effects on teacher practice and student learning. The number of universities collaborating in this partnership has also provided a large data sample from which the impact on teacher learning and student achievement can be analyzed across states.

Additional positive outcomes have resulted from the site-specific university-to-public school collaborations. Research on teacher collaboration has documented the positive impact of professional learning communities on promoting the implementation of new learning (Bryk & Schneider, 2002). The teacher-to-teacher relationships that have developed as part of the professional learning communities created in the CLASSIC © Program Model have helped to create collegial interactions within the schools that previously did not exist. The application of strategies that the teachers learn through the professional development program have also had a positive impact on teacher practice as demonstrated by the increased student-to-student collaboration, teacher-to-student collaboration, and preliminary reports on standardized assessments.

## IF WE ONLY HAD MORE . . .

Limitations of the project are largely due to money, personnel, and time. First, each university-funded grant provides coursework for a total of 100 teachers over a 5-year period. Increased funding would allow for more teachers to participate by paying for additional teachers' tuition and fees along with the supplies needed for the professional development. Second, because each federally funded project traditionally only provides one project manager, participants must be located in a neighboring districts.

If additional project managers were provided, more districts might be able to participate. Third, given the time commitment teachers are required to make, some teachers are hesitant to participate in the program. This time commitment could be overcome if school districts were willing to support three hours per week of release time for teachers' participation in the project.

## LESSONS LEARNED FOR FUTURE COLLABORATIVE ENDEAVORS

Institutions of higher education are being called upon to create partnerships in which educational research is a distributed activity, shared among multiple institutions of higher education (Lagemann, 2008). In order for such partnerships to be successful, we have learned that *trust* within the university-to-university collaboration is central, which goes against the grain of tradition. This is in large part due to the unwritten rule that institutions of higher education must develop their "own" work and not duplicate that of others. This same *trust* is also critical when establishing university-to-district partnerships. To establish this trust with the districts, each university had to gain entry into the district and demonstrate that the CLASSIC © Program Model was not something that was going to be done *to them*, but be done *with them*. Finally, trust between the teachers in each professional learning community, which contradicts the traditional "egg carton" structure of schools where teachers do not collaborate, was central. The sharing of common challenges, concerns, and frustrations that were previously unspoken within the professional learning communities served as the catalyst from which these trusting relationships were built.

Finally, this partnership has demonstrated to school educators and their educational systems the value of *long-term, course-based, professional development*. Research indicates that long-term professional development is more likely to contain the kinds of learning opportunities necessary for teachers to integrate new knowledge into practice (Brown, 2004). Within CLASSIC ©, teachers are given the time they need to apply theory into practice and the results appear in increased teacher and student capacity.

## REFERENCES

Borko, H. (2004). Professional development and teacher learning: Mapping the terrain. *Educational Researcher, 33*(8), 3–15.

Brown, J. L. (2004). *Making the most of understanding by design*. Washington, DC: Association for Supervision and Curriculum Development.

Bryk, A. S., & Schneider, B. (2002). *Trust in schools: A core resource for improvement*. New York: Russell Sage.

Creswell, J. W. (2006). *Qualitative inquiry and research design: Choosing among five approaches* (2nd ed.). Thousand Oaks, CA: Sage.

Fishman, B. J., Marx, R. W., Best, S., & Tal, R. (2003). Linking teacher and student learning to improve professional development in systemic reform. *Teaching and Teacher Education, 19*(6), 643–658.

Kindler, A. (2002). *Survey of the states' limited English proficient students and available educational programs and services, 2000–2001 summary report.* National Clearinghouse for English Language Acquisition & Language Instruction Educational Programs. Washington, DC: George Washington University.

Lagemann, E. C. (2008). Education research as a distributed activity across universities. *Educational Researcher, 37*(7), 424–428.

Murry, K., & Herrera, S. (1999). CLASSIC impacts: A qualitative study of ESL/ BLED programming. *Educational Considerations, 26*(2), 11–18.

Slater, J. J. (1996). *Anatomy of a collaboration: Study of a college of education/ public school partnership.* New York: Garland.

Stevenson, R. (2001). Shared decision-making and core school values: A case study of organizational learning. *International Journal of Educational Management, 15*(2), 103–121.

Wong-Fillmore, L., & Snow, C. E. (2002). What teachers need to know about language. In C.T., Adger, C. E. Snow, & D. Christian (Eds.), *What teachers need to know about language.* Washington, DC: ERIC Clearinghouse on Languages and Linguistics.

# Part VI

# Technology Projects

Technology projects are multi-institutional endeavors that can involve many partnership combinations among which are schools, university, business, government, and/or research centers. Usually more formal in terms of agreement, they infer that the workforce of the future needs to have specifically skilled personnel, therefore schools should take part in the preparation of students for this work environment. In doing so, some form of hi-tech equipment is necessary to aid in the training/teaching, thereby increasing student academic achievement.

Funds needed for technology projects are high; consequently, grants, foundations, and often hi-tech businesses themselves contribute to the top-down flow of monies to schools. These are innovative projects that aim to make a change in the curriculum that teachers deliver to students and in the way they teach. Maintaining funding, sustaining training, and providing support over time is critical for a successful technological collaboration.

Risberg and Borthwick describe a technology project whose target population is two third-grade teachers and their students in a public school setting. The collaboration team included one of the teachers, a university faculty member, and a parent, a software engineer. The collaboration was not formally contractual, but was funded by a grant. Evaluation of student progress in using Palm Pilots for mathematics instruction was the impetus for university involvement as a research opportunity independent from the institution. The school itself bought the software used in the project, and adaptation for a specific purpose was provided by the parent.

Whereas mutuality among the three primary participants was high, problems surfaced at the school site itself due to tensions, disruption, and the traditional power hierarchy reinforced by the principal and other resistant teachers who chose not to participate. This pressure caused one of the teachers to drop out of the project prior to the beginning of the second year, even though her students experienced success.

It is interesting to note that any innovation that is contained in a sea of bureaucratic and personnel restraint is difficult to sustain unless the participants do what is necessary to garnish support or choose to use the innovation as a catalyst for widespread institutional change. As Risberg and Borthwick describe, this did not happen in this project and there was an active attempt to stifle it and limit dissemination of the good work that was occurring.

Another element in this project and others in this volume is that the habitus of the school perpetuates distrust of outsiders and without innovative, forward looking leadership, there is little to sustain even grant-supported projects which find themselves short lived. The climate must be amenable and have leadership and vision of the benefits of the project and communicate positive support to the rest of the faculty in order for them to buy in to the innovation.

For collaborations to sustain themselves, besides administrative and faculty support, they may require an agent of change who can organize and disseminate information so that those not directly involved buy in to the change in operation. Therefore, Risberg and Borthwick suggest that those embarking on technology collaborations organize into teams, actively disseminate information among all stakeholders, and garner support up front for the adoption of the hi-tech innovation. Most importantly, they actively need to be aware and manage perceptions so that others not directly involved know about and support the project thereby tempering criticism.

Technology projects such as this do show positive results. Student progress was evident, as was collaboration among the participants. The teacher and university faculty member wrote about the project, presented at conferences, and co-taught a credit generating workshop on handheld computer use in the classroom. With technology becoming a more integral part of the curriculum and the teaching–learning process in K–12 education, the lessons shared by Risberg and Borthwick are well worth following.

# 18 School-University Collaboration for Technology Integration

## Resistance, Risk-Taking, and Resilience

*Cathy Risberg and Arlene Borthwick*

In 2001, Cathy, then a third-grade teacher at Westbury (a pseudonym) school, contacted a nearby University in hopes of lining up a research partner to help with the preparation of a grant proposal. Arlene responded, and our collaborative activities have continued ever since.

## PURPOSE OF THE GRANT PROJECT

The grant proposal: *Using Palm Pilots to Differentiate the Math Curriculum*, called for 2 third-grade teachers and their students to work with handheld computers, and was funded through the Palm Education Pioneers Program (Vahey & Crawford, 2002). Cathy prepared the proposal in collaboration with Arlene and Ann Nelson-Burns (pseudonym), a software engineer and parent of two students enrolled at the school. The project was designed to enable teachers to differentiate mathematics activities based on data collected by both teachers and students through the use of handheld computers.

## DESCRIPTION OF THE PARTNERSHIP— FUNDING, SUPPORT, AND RESOURCES

The school was the recipient of the grant and there was no formal contract beyond the grant proposal itself. In essence, the partners in the project were three individuals—a teacher, university faculty member, and parent— rather than three institutions (school, university, business).

The grant provided 40 handheld computers and four days of training for the primary investigator, Cathy. Ann used her own copy of *HanDbase* software to create a custom database aligned with the school's mathematics program and the school provided subsequent funding for the purchase of this software for each handheld. The university approved use of Arlene's service as a research partner and supported transcription of recorded student interviews. Ann volunteered her time to contribute technical support for use of the handhelds and school personnel provided IT network support.

There was a high level of mutuality in the project, with frequent meetings of the teacher, parent, and university researcher, but we operated above an underlying current of school-based tensions that involved a disruption in the hierarchy of power relationships at Westbury. At the beginning of the project, Cathy was aware of these tensions, while Arlene and Ann were not. The original grant proposal was submitted based on behind-the-scenes politics leading to support from the school's Technology Committee and intervention on behalf of the proposal by the head of the Westbury Board; it had only weak support from the School Head. Other than approval of faculty participation by the College Dean, the university paid little attention to the involvement of the individual faculty member in the grant.

## RESISTANCE SOURCES

Elements of school culture were a major source of resistance, in particular leadership style (Reeves, 2006; Spillane, 2006), lack of shared values (Borthwick & Risberg, 2008), and lack of learning community (Senge, 2006).

Resistance to change is a universal experience. It clearly emerged as a major thread in Cathy's efforts to both obtain new technology tools for her students and learn more about the potential of handheld computers in the classroom. This thread of resistance occurred on multiple levels at the school and could be observed from the onset of the grant writing process in 2001 from the administrative leadership team. Over time it manifested itself as a component of the organizational climate and core values and became a reality factor Cathy grew to accept, work around, and utilize as a catalyst for deeper personalized learning.

### Resistance to the Grant Proposal and Risk-Taking

Just days before submitting the grant proposal, Cathy realized that complicated behind-the-scenes politics were being intertwined with her grant and quickly understood that her grant proposal might be becoming a virtual political hot potato for Westbury. When Westbury learned several months later that the grant proposal had been chosen—1 of 87 out of 1200 submitted—Cathy and her team were elated and ready to get started in the fall.

### Resistance during Grant Implementation and Beyond

For Cathy, meetings with school administrators during the grant implementation and the following two years were commonplace. In some of these meetings a common theme emerged that Cathy's efforts would be so much more authentic if she relied solely on herself and her own technological skills and not on her collaborative team.

Administrators even questioned the sincerity of Cathy's grant writing team. While Cathy and Arlene were allowed to share their early findings with the parent and teacher community, administrative support for in-school dissemination disappeared at the end of the second year.

## An End to the Use of Handheld Technologies at Westbury

Hopes of project sustainability were cut short in the fall of 2004, at the very beginning of what would have been the fourth year of handheld use in her classroom. It was just a few weeks into the school year that Cathy was asked to collect the handhelds and take them to the office. The reason for the request, she was told, was her recent receipt of help from the IT direc-tor, distracting him from other priorities.

## RESPONSE TO TEACHER RESISTANCE: UNDERSTANDING AND FLEXIBILITY

During the project's implementation phase, resistance also presented itself in the reluctant participation of a key participant, a third-grade teacher team member who was new to the school. While she participated during the first year of the grant implementation, she openly viewed the use of the handhelds with reluctance, asked not to be included in the process of submitting weekly data and withdrew completely from the project during the second year.

## RESPONSE TO ADMINISTRATIVE RESISTANCE: RESILIENCY

Managing the resistance of the administration involved a three-part strategy. First, the collaborative team kept a steady focus on maintaining the integrity and quality of the project during the yearlong implementation of the grant. Sec-ond, the partnership provided Cathy consistent support and affirmation, scaf-folding the resilience and determination so necessary for the implementation of new technology. Third, the multiple opportunities to write and present their findings provided the project with both a tangible substance and relevance.

## POSITIVE OUTCOMES OF OUR COLLABORATION FOR STUDENTS AND PARTNERS

This project began with a close examination and anticipation of both the benefits and barriers to handheld use in the classroom. Evaluation data con-firmed that students did grow and change in both goal-setting abilities and in their ability to self-assess and self-reflect. We also witnessed the power of class collaboration, including student-to-student and student-to-teacher teaching when introducing new technology. Utilizing student support in this way developed in the students a sense of self-reliance, motivation, responsibility and a heightened sense of engagement, competence, and confidence.

The positive outcomes of the collaboration for Cathy and Arlene were quite evident. For Cathy, the handheld project served to embolden her to explore, learn, and take risks on behalf of her students. She learned not to allow fear to become a barrier for doing what was best for her students.

The grant provided both Cathy and Arlene a handheld computer and the opportunity to explore the use of handheld technology in the classroom. Further, information they collected as part of the grant evaluation provided data for all three team members to synthesize, summarize, and present at state and national conferences. In addition, they developed and co-taught a credit workshop on handheld computers with another faculty member. The project also led to the collaboration of Cathy and Arlene to co-author a chapter on the optimal organizational climate for professional development (Borthwick & Risberg, 2008).

A significant benefit from this collaboration for Cathy was the experience of co-authoring an article with her grant-writing team and finding her voice as an advocate for educational technology to increase access to and acceleration of the curriculum. This interest resulted in Cathy co-presenting at the state level on the topic of digital diversity and pursuing further training to help teachers integrate mobile technology into the curriculum through GoKnow, Inc.'s Train-the-Trainer program.

For Arlene, coming to Westbury to talk with the administrative staff and the technology coordinator, and Cathy's invitation to learn about other new technology being used at the school—a multimedia authoring program called *Blackspace*—was a significant benefit. In 2005, Arlene, the Westbury technology coordinator, and four other area technology coordinators/teachers met to share knowledge about six different multimedia authoring programs and made related presentations at both a state and national conference. As a follow-up, Arlene and one of the technology coordinators published an article comparing features of the various programs.

The benefits to Ann were less tangible; she indicated that she was "captivated" by the proposal. She had a Palm handheld herself but had never written a customized application for it. In joining the collaboration, she became intrigued with learning how the Palm handhelds could be integrated into the classroom curriculum. She presented locally with Cathy and Arlene and agreed to teach Palm basics to Westbury teachers at the end of the first year of the project.

## LIMITATIONS

"The use of new technology tools results in the transfer of "expert power" to teachers—and often even to students. This is seen by some staff and administrators as a disruption of power and a change in. . . . information flow" (Borthwick & Risberg, 2008, p. 43).

While we believed we had an almost perfect collaboration of teacher-researcher-parent to implement new technology, we discovered that to support the use of new technology, an optimal organizational climate needed to be in place. Without school-level technology leadership, vision, and a stakeholder-created technology plan (Byrom & Bingham, 2001), we faced significant limitations to the sustainability of our project. Despite the existence of a technology committee and published strategic goals that included increasing use of technology for teaching, Westbury had no published, detailed technology plan in 2000 that was ever discussed with teachers or parents.

Evidence of a lack of optimal organization climate (Wagner, Kegan, Lahey, Lemons, Garnier, Helsing, et al., 2006) first surfaced with the mixed messages received from the administrative team regarding the grant proposal. These mixed messages later turned into words and actions of disapproval and limited the open sharing of project information within the school. It became clear to our team that there existed a dissonance in the publicly stated goals of increasing the use of technology in the school and the core values that surfaced over a period of years. Certainly Westbury felt it necessary to manage the impression that they were supporting the published strategic goal of increasing technology use while covertly discouraging use of selected technologies. In effect, Cathy, as an innovator, was "launching [a] new idea in the system. . . . playing a gate keeping role in the flow of new ideas into [the] system" from outside the system (Rogers, 2003, p. 283).

Perhaps another limitation to the impact of our collaboration was Westbury's decision to focus in 2004 on Jim Collin's book *Good to Great* as a means to encourage excellence in teaching. In this book, Collins recommended that technology use be limited and quite focused. Therefore, not expanding school focus to include other new technologies could be quite readily justified by referring back to Collins' book.

In hindsight, a major limiting factor to the impact of our collaboration was the lack of attention the partners gave to managing impressions of the project by other stakeholders (administrators, parents) compared to the time spent in implementing the project. The university partner, who helped to evaluate the grant project, had not been hired by the school per se, kept a low profile, and was reluctant to participate as, or be perceived as, a change agent. Our team conversations focused on the success of the handhelds in the classroom, and we shared a year-end report with school administrators based on data collected. While we highlighted anticipated results from expanded uses of the handhelds in other subject areas using a broader set of applications, we did not build in classroom visits by administrators or parents, to inform or influence their perceptions.

## Discussion and Lessons Learned

Questions that arise regarding integration of new technologies in the classroom include essential conditions for adoption and effective use for student learning. Our teacher-parent-researcher collaboration enabled several of these conditions.

## Importance of Collaboration to Support Teacher Change

Apple Classroom of Tomorrow (ACOT) researchers Sandholtz, Ringstaff, and Dwyer (1997) recommended that as teachers proceed with use of new technologies in their classrooms, they *work in teams* including other teachers, mentors, and researchers; and write about and publicly share their experiences. Our work together epitomized this approach as we developed our own small yet powerful learning circle. As in our partnership of parent-teacher-university faculty member, such professional learning communities enable individuals to help one another grow in their knowledge of pedagogy, content, and technology (SIGTE Leadership and NTLS Program Committee, 2008) and the intersection of these three domains known as technological pedagogical content knowledge (TPACK). Our "TPACK Team" included an individual strong in technology (Ann) and one strong in pedagogy and content (Cathy). Arlene stood ready to document our learning right along with student learning, connecting theory to practice.

## Collaboration to Influence School Change, Not Just Individual Change

Change occurs not only through individual learning, but also through a systems approach that addresses organizational learning. Cathy and her students were enthusiastic adopters of technology, yet buy-in from potential local collaborators (other teachers, staff, and the school's administration) was absent in the presence of behind-the-scenes politics. Thus, while a teacher (Cathy, for example) may adopt a new technology for use in her classroom (optional innovation-decision), collective or authority innovation-decisions are required for school or district-wide adoption of new technologies (Rogers, 2003).

## Validation of Project Work through Collaboration

When new technologies are provided through grant funding to an individual within a system, validation of project activities and outcomes will provide reinforcement during the confirmation stage (Rogers, 2003). Reinforcement may come from other project participants (university and community partners), from within the school (teachers, administrators, parents), and/or from grant participants in other school sites.

Cathy indeed experienced conflicting messages, some indicating support for the project and others, especially from administrators, withdrawing support from use of the handhelds at Westbury. This withdrawal of support highlighted the need for "managing" not just the project but *perceptions* of the project by stakeholders by including classroom observations/visits by administrators and parents to share visible results of the project.

## Collaboration to Support Risk Taking

Through her innovation venture, Cathy embarked on a risk-taking effort. In the best of situations, her administrators would have backed her efforts (Borthwick, Hansen, Gray, & Ziemann, 2008). However, in our case, although Cathy may have championed the use of handheld technologies at her school, Rogers (2003) reminds us that innovators are not necessarily respected as opinion leaders in their own system because, in a sense, innovators are "too far ahead of the average individual" (p. 283). This can create a lack of congruency between the system's plan or vision and the innovation, resulting in a sense of uneasiness or a feeling of lack of control by those responsible for the system. Therefore, it was her collaborators who endorsed Cathy's efforts, assuring her resilience even when the handheld program was discontinued at her school. In hindsight, the team could and should have considered additional points and processes for intervention (Bruce, Guion, Horton, Hughes, & Prescott, 2009), to assure the essential conditions for sustaining change at a systems level (Newman, 2008). As it was, none of us felt comfortable in assuming a leadership role (Slater, 1996) to overcome the limitations Cathy was experiencing.

## Conclusion

As we reflect on essential conditions for sustaining our collaboration, both of us can confirm a shared vision (integration of technology to enhance learning of diverse student population), shared resources (knowledge and time), and beneficial outcomes (some at the school and some through presentations and publications) that enhance our continued work together. We hope that the lessons we have learned along the way will increase your chances of successful collaboration for technology integration.

## REFERENCES

Borthwick, A., Hansen, R., Gray, L, & Ziemann, I. (2008). Exploring Essential Conditions: A Commentary on Bull, Thompson, Searson, Garofalo, Park, Young, and Lee. *Contemporary Issues in Technology and Teacher Education, 8*(3). Retrieved February 1, 2008, from http://www.citejournal.org/vol8/iss3/editorial/article2.cfm

Borthwick, A., & Risberg, C. (2008). Establishing an organizational climate for successful professional development: What should we do? In A. Borthwick & M. Pierson (Eds.), *Transforming classroom practice: Professional development strategies in educational technology.* Eugene, OR: International Society for Technology in Education.

Bruce, K.A., Guion, J.M., Horton, L.R., Hughes, J.E., & Prescott, A. (2009, April). *Web. 2.0 for transformative educational change: An interactional model.* Paper presented at the Annual Meeting of the American Educational Research Association, San Diego.

Byrom, E., & Bingham, M. (2001). *Factors influencing the effective use of technology for teaching and learning: Lessons learned from the SEIR\*TEC Intensive Site Schools.* Durham, NC: SouthEast Initiatives Regional Technology in Education Consortium.

Collins, J. (2001.) *Good to great: Why some companies make the leap . . . and others don't.* New York: Harper Collins.

Newman, D.L. (2008). Ensuring integration of teacher changes: What practices will make sure that professional development takes a hold? In A. Borthwick & M. Pierson (Eds.), *Transforming classroom practice: Professional development strategies in educational technology* (pp. 187–203). Eugene, OR: International Society for Technology in Education.

Reeves., D.B. (2006). Of hubs, bridges, and networks. *Educational Leadership, 63*(8), 32–37.

Rogers, E.M. (2003) *Diffusion of innovations* (5th ed.). New York: Free Press.

Sandholtz, J.H., Ringstaff, C., & Dwyer, D.C. (1997). *Teaching with technology.* New York: Teachers College Press.

Senge, P.M. (2006). *The fifth discipline: The art & practice of the learning organization* (2nd ed.). New York: Doubleday.

SIGTE Leadership and NTLS Program Committee (2008). Realizing technology potential through TPACK. *Learning and Leading with Technology, 36*(2), 23–26.

Slater, J. J. (1996). *Anatomy of a collaboration: A study of a college of education/ public school partnership.* New York: Garland.

Spillane, J.P. (2006). *Distributed leadership.* San Francisco: Jossey-Bass.

Vahey, P., & Crawford, V. (2002). *Palm Education Pioneers Program: Final evaluation report.* Palm, Inc. Retrieved December 1, 2008, from http://makingsens.stanford.edu/pubs/PEP_Final_Report.pdf

Wagner, T., Kegan, R., Lahey, L., Lemons, R.W., Garnier, J., Helsing, D., et al. (2006). *Change leadership: A practical guide to transforming our schools.* San Francisco: Jossey-Bass.

# Part VII

# Interagency Collaboration

The type of school–university collaboration termed *interagency* is categorized according to the most complex criteria in the Slater Matrix. It has organizational involvement beyond the university and school, and this involvement can be semi-autonomous and requires a system approach to understand the interrelationship among participants.

The purpose of embarking on such a project is purposeful in that organizational change is a desired end state. Participants look beyond the short term benefits of this collaboration and look toward future evolution of the way they work together that is different from the way they did before the project. Multi-level resources and personnel are necessary for this, and the levels of mutuality among participants are high. The goals are institution building, experimentation, change, and development and production of knowledge that those beyond the institutions involved can use to further their practice. This type of collaboration is a sea change that upsets the status quo of policy and practice in the name of research and systemic development. It is hard work to initiate and sustain such collaboration.

There are four examples provided in this category. Burbank and Hunter's project involves a university, community college, and four school districts whose aim is to diversify the teaching profession with ethnically and culturally diverse members. The second project offered by Gardiner and Kamm involves a university, public school, and educational management company initiative to recruit, prepare, and provide support during induction for teachers in urban education settings. The Leonard and Gonsalves project describes a 40-year commitment by a university, community college, and school district to offer pre-college students access to a variety of dual enrollment, tutoring, and a pre-college program. The university benefit is a research opportunity, professional development delivery for post-service teachers, and graduate course delivery. The final offering in this section is by Sosin, Benin, Linné, and Sosinsky. They describe an education and labor collaborative initiative aimed at increasing teacher and low-income student awareness about the importance of unionism.

Whereas the purposes of each of these examples is different, each talks to the complexity of this multidimensional collaboration involving many partners with competing interests, administrations, and goals, and how they could be organized to achieve success. Most importantly, each talks about the ability to sustain the collaboration and create an environment that engenders institutionalization of the innovation.

Burbank and Hunter's interagency project describes a systemic response to increase the ethnic and culturally underrepresented learner's need to obtain a college degree with the aim to diversity the teaching profession through this university, community college, and multiple school district collaboration. The authors emphasize the disparity of translating the goals of the project with the reality of implementation. The mutuality was high for the stakeholders, and each made contributions to enact this project. The university gave funds, tuition waivers, and book fee waivers, and the community college gave 2-year scholarships. The established governing board was responsible for the process of operation and support, provided counseling, and targeted coursework to be delivered. Yet, problems remained concerning institutional decision making and hierarchical dictated roles and contributions to the project in terms of resources and personnel. Difficulties were also encountered by some of the students in meeting the academic requirements and passing the mandated competency testing that are part of teacher preservice education program. Future funding of the project remains a challenge as well.

It is interesting to note the dichotomy here between the espoused commitment of participants, the theories-in-practice, and the enacted theories-in-use. Whereas the rhetoric was positive, in reality problems arose relating to ownership, communication, and the economic needs of each institution involved. Primarily these involved questions of what constituted support and effective recruitment of candidates, remediation by the community college, formality of the parameters of engagement, and funding.

Power relationships in this type of collaboration are also huge influences. They affect policy and decision making, curriculum decisions, and student selection. The different worldview held by the school-based partners also affects mutuality.

Gardner and Kamm describe an interagency collaboration project between an educational management organization, university, and public school that resulted in an urban teacher education program that is high in mutuality. The main financial resources for the program are provided by the city's public schools and through federal grants. The project's goals are to recruit, prepare, and induct teachers through a teacher training academy as a reform intervention in urban education. Teacher candidates complete their master's level courses in the Academy's schools, guided by their mentors. The program also includes a strong induction program for new teachers. The vision of the educational management organization propelled this project to enactment by creating the urban academies. Ongoing communication among all the stakeholders provides the congruence and feedback for the university designed and delivered content, bridging the gaps between the university and the field, and between theory and practice. In effect, the success of "institutional boundary spanners" created a success far beyond the sum of the parts of the project.

Limitations exist for this project, including: the high costs subject to the political and economic climate; attracting high quality committed people to participate; relevance of university coursework; and the competing demands of a time commitment so evident in projects of this type. Concerns of power imbalance notwithstanding, looking within each institution is an imperative to understanding that the problems addressed in this project are too great for any one partner to solve on their own. Partnership is needed, and hopefully, institutionalizing the innovation will perpetuate the work, cross boundaries, and provide a situation where adaptation to changing demands is made in a responsive, efficient, way to reach the goals of urban teacher education.

Leonard and Gonsalves describe a 40-year-long project that is currently foundation funded, involving a university and three high schools to provide a practicum for graduate students and courses for professional development, pre-college program, dual enrollment of high school students, tutoring, and research opportunities for university faculty. The power structure of the project is both formal and informal. The leadership core is the steering committee, and they have high trust established over many years. They oversee and guide all activities, but there have been changes in the administration of both the university and school system that jeopardize the work of the core and its tacit understanding of the way they operate.

Resistance to the collaboration came from one site who wanted to work independently of the partnership, but continuity is provided by the university and its long-standing stability and history with the project, size of engagement, and power to advocate each school's position with the school district administration by "bridging fractional inter-school disputes."

Limitations of this project are similar to the others presented in this section. Funding sustainability and the shifting nature of grant monies with the temper of the times makes the university a powerful partner as they initiate all grants. Time demands on participants and the distribution of monies to support personnel is another, as is university interests dictating what is promoted in terms of reform and experimentation. High schools compete for spots in the dual enrollment and pre-college spots. The college of education struggles for money and intern placements which are controlled by the school sites.

Finally, participation cannot be mandated. In all the projects in this category, there are huge demands on time and involvement beyond the formal funding guidelines. The benefits have to be personal, professional, and supported by the larger community in order for sustainability to be institutionalized. That is the challenge of interagency collaboration.

Sosin, Benin, Linné, and Sosinsky describe a different kind of interagency collaboration, one that has as its purpose to increase awareness

of unionism, democracy, and social justice, and to revive labor consciousness through education. They state that to reach this goal, it must begin
with the individual and lead to institutional alliances to promote a critical
awareness of the issues of corporate greed, mass media manipulation, and
working environments.

In addition to teacher educators, participants in this project are from
outside of education, representing a broad affiliation of institutions, such as
the UFT, CTF, and AFT, union-based affiliates. This informal arrangement
of voluntary association and personal networking has a growing formal
advisory board, by-laws, and resolution of support that is future oriented
as a change effort to renew labor consciousness and redesign teacher education to enhance activism for social justice in the classroom.

As of the writing of the chapter, forums have been enacted, foundation
monies garnered, some universities have affiliated with this cause, but all
the ties are tenuous. Resistance is strong in corporate circles, and manifests
itself in political traditions that view labor as a special interest group, even
within the labor unions themselves. There is resistance to the educational
mission of the collaborative, as well as resistance to add another responsibility to the busy agenda of classrooms.

For a project such as this, power relationships are important. Whereas
they have generated interest in their cause, and there is now a formal open
forum to discuss the issues, real change, which is the purpose of interagency
collaboration, requires some specific actions that need to be discussed.

Change is not an easy thing to enact. Of all the types of collaboration,
this complex design requires an agent of change, someone or some group
to understand and negotiate, reduce resistance, manage, and lead, so that
the vision for the project can become a reality and can then alter the way
the involved partners work together. The optimal situation is that once the
agent of change manages the outcome, there is an institutional commitment to continue to work together in ways to solve problems in the future.
That is the ultimate goal of collaboration: To realize that communities of
common interest are necessary to solve the problems of education in the
future and that no one can successfully accomplish their goals in isolation.
Collaboration is about community. It is about people "learning together"
as they "work together" toward common goals. In the process, the synergy
creates more than the sum of the parts of the project. It teaches each organization about the culture of the other, and in the process, each becomes
more responsive to the needs of the larger community.

# 19 Project FIRST

## Families, Intercollegiate Collaboration, and Routes to Studying Teaching

*Mary D. Burbank and Rosemarie Hunter*

The profile of American communities is changing. Nationally, nearly one third of school-age children are cultural minorities with 16% of the teaching force from non-majority populations (Gay, Dingus, & Jackson, 2003; National Center for Education Statistics, 2003). Projections for the next 20 years identify dramatic changes in national demographics where 61% of population increases will occur within Hispanic and Asian communities. The Latino college age population, specifically, is projected to reach 25% (Excelencia in Education, 2009; Hodgkinson, 2002; Stanford, 1999). Whereas ethnic and cultural diversity is on the rise, the number of people from linguistically and culturally diverse communities earning college degrees is limited. Efforts to change this trend must be addressed systematically.

Rapid demographic shifts have been particularly dramatic in Salt Lake City (SLC), Utah, where an increase of 117% in its minority population occurred between 1990 and 2000 (Perlich, 2002). Currently, one in three new SLC west side residents is a member of a minority community and more than 60% of residents are people of color compared to only 16% of SLC's total population (Perlich, 2002). Salt Lake's demographic shifts are particularly dramatic within the school-aged population where 53% of students are identified as non-majority (Salt Lake City School District, 2008).

In response to population changes, SLC's education community has actively considered new ways of meeting the needs of its urban school communities. Project FIRST—Families, Intercollegiate Collaboration, and Routes to Studying Teaching—reflects a collaborative effort to diversify the teaching profession through partnerships, networks, and research-based interagency collaboration.

From its inception, project FIRST has been inextricably linked to the partnerships established through the University Neighborhood Partners (UNP) and the College of Education at the University of Utah (U of U), Salt Lake Community College (SLCC), and four local school districts. As an institutional anchor, UNP was created in 2002 to increase representation from Salt Lake City's ethnic minority community at the U of U. Central to UNP's mission are efforts among stakeholders to identify those mechanisms that illuminate pathways to higher education for its community members.

## THE IMPACT OF COLLABORATION ON ENROLLMENT

Bridging the gap to higher education through UNP affiliated projects shows promise. In its biennial *Measuring Up* report (2008), the National Center for Public Policy and Higher Education confirmed that the growing gap of participation in higher education between whites and Latinos in Utah widened to the nation's largest. Since the early 1990s, the number of 19-year-olds in college dropped by 14% and in 1993, less than 1% of the total enrolled students in post-secondary education were Latina/o whereas white students represented 87% of the post-secondary enrollment (Alemán & Rorrer, 2006).

The impact of UNP's efforts reveals improving access trends to the U of U by ethnic minority community members. Since the advent of UNP, the number of U of U ethnic minority graduates from Salt Lake's west side neighborhoods nearly doubled from 45 in 2006 to 71 in 2008. Fall 2009 enrollments indicate over 450 west side residents at the U of U with enrollment at SLCC reflecting a steady increase with 79 west side neighborhood graduates in 2008 (Alemán, 2009).

## BUILDING A TEACHING CORE

Whereas enrollment shifts at the U of U are encouraging, the number of prospective teachers from the west side has remained low. Because access to higher education has been limited for many members of the west side community, researchers examined the factors that may have influenced this trend. A 2004 study by Buendia, Ares, Juarez, and Peercy identified educators' perceptions of west side communities. Many classroom teachers described their students as "the poor," "the non-white," "the non-English speaking," "the uninterested," and "the at-risk" (p. 843). These deficit perspectives set the stage for collective next steps to diversify the teaching core within the community.

In response to a static demographic profile with the teaching community, UNP affiliated educational stakeholders sought efforts to take advantage of the assets held by the west side residents. Teacher education and public education stakeholders identified pathways to higher education to diversify a teaching force committed to culturally and ethnically diverse communities.

Capitalizing on what many consider a "small town" feel within the geographic confines of an urban city, Salt Lake City's K–16 community examined how college could become a reality for a new population of teachers. For many, a sense of *our community* contributed to conversations on access and equity where public goal setting formalized efforts to diversify the teaching profession. Of concern, however, are data that reflect a disparity in the translation of broad goals into specific actions that result in increased access to higher education for traditionally underrepresented students.

## SETTING THE STAGE FOR CURRENT COLLABORATIVE EFFORTS

Collaborative efforts established in the late 1990s provided high school students with a course on teachers work and the foundations necessary for systematic exposure to higher education. The Teaching Professions Academy (TPA) emerged as a university–district partnership where high school students, particularly students of color, experienced teaching as a career option (Burbank, Bertagnole, Carl, Dynak, Longhurst, & Powell, 2005). For stakeholders affiliated with the TPA and UNP, a "grow your own" model provided a springboard for early high school exposure to the teaching profession. As an extension of work in the 1990s, the Families, Intercollegiate Collaboration, and Routes to Studying Teaching (FIRST) project emerged.

In 2006, project FIRST was initiated as a scholarship effort for first generation students and students of color in their higher education pursuits. A unique feature of the partnership is a mutual interdependence where stakeholders extend layered support over time. Project FIRST stakeholders from the U of U, SLCC, and four local school districts committed financial support for 15 high school students to make the dream of a college education more fiscally possible through tuition and book fee waivers. Next, a "passing of the baton" occurs where SLCC provides 2 years of scholarship support for project FIRST students and the U of U provides additional tuition support for those students who matriculate for their final 2 years in a teacher preparation program.

Project FIRST's governing board meets monthly to review student progress, delineate support, and bolster academic success through targeted course work, academic counseling, and peer and faculty mentoring. Through systemic collaboration, a *process* involving communication, goal setting, and reflection takes place. This process identifies and articulates those factors that impact access and success for traditionally underrepresented students. Where the power balance is less defined is in institutional decision making. That is, stakeholders' resources, historical relationships, and institutional hierarchies dictate roles and contributions.

## MORE THAN A SCHOLARSHIP FUND

In addition to providing the necessary financial road map to higher education, project FIRST teacher education stakeholders have begun the process of examining the curriculum and pedagogy used as part of a weekly student support seminar. Data from Year I will inform plans for future curriculum, pedagogy, and student mentoring practices by SLCC and U of U faculty.

Phase I of project FIRST's curriculum examinations included explorations of students' educational histories through narratives of access and success. These stories identified the structures and academic capital that have helped participants reach their current standing as students. Phase I data will inform future recruiting efforts and will highlight the roles of parents and caregivers in supporting their students' post-high school experiences. Phase II, to be instituted, will include caregivers' influence in shaping the direction of family influence on students success over time.

## PUBLIC AGENDAS—PRIVATE GOALS

Since its beginning, project FIRST has shown development. Stakeholders readily espouse a commitment to increasing and diversifying the teaching profession. Stakeholders support efforts to nurture teachers who understand and reflect the life experiences, cultures, and languages of our changing community. Whereas the commitment to project FIRST is robust among project FIRST stakeholders, when pushed to define levels of commitment, nuanced differences surface.

Data gathered through a self-study reveal common goals across project partners. Using an electronic survey format, partners were asked to: (a) identify goals of the first generation and minority scholarship program; and (b) describe how those goals have been met. Next, stakeholders were asked to articulate goals that have yet to be reached. Using a Likert-type scale, stakeholders rated levels of agreement to collaboration, communication, and ownership in project FIRST's success.

Quantitative findings reveal *general* to *strong* agreement in collaboration, ownership, and utility of monthly meetings from seven respondents (i.e., three district representatives, two individuals from higher education, and two community members). In the survey, response options ranged from Agree (5 points) to Disagree (1 point). The results are as follows:

1. Collaboration across stakeholders is strong: mean = 4.43
2. Communication on project FIRST is strong; mean = 4.14
3. My agency/institution feels a sense of ownership in the project: mean = 4.71
4. Monthly meetings are productive: mean= 4.86

Overwhelmingly stakeholders view project FIRST as a valuable step toward cultivating a diverse teaching population. Stakeholders support a weekly seminar and cohort structure as necessary tools to bridge high school and post-secondary education. Targeted recruitment and financial aid for traditionally underrepresented populations remain priorities for stakeholders.

Less consistent are perspectives on what constitutes "support" and effective recruitment. That is, survey and interview data indicate differences in stakeholder perspectives on student eligibility, overall readiness, "motivation," and determination to succeed in college. Communication was identified as an area that could be improved upon slightly.

Six of the seven stakeholders suggested broadening the target audience to students with stronger academic track records. One district stakeholder reported that current financial support for tuition is adequate for "those who will succeed academically." This respondent went on: "For students who really want to succeed, they will find the additional financial support they'll need." This representative does not believe additional funding for books and fees is necessary or realistic given the current financial belt tightening in many school districts.

Whereas strong academic preparation among project FIRST participants is valued, there is variance in stakeholders' definitions for "strong" performance. For example, a second district representative reported: "We have to select the 'right students' and then give them every opportunity to succeed!!" A third district stakeholder echoed this sentiment by clarifying "right" to include the selection of students who are "committed to hard work . . . and who are responsible." She argued that project FIRST policies must clarify expectations for student responsibility in their academic success.

Intuitively, acceptable levels of academic performance appear generic. Less clear is an understanding of whether members hold a common understanding of what constitutes "hard work" and "responsibility." As a collaborative, stakeholders must ensure first-generation college students are provided with the structures to support their academic efforts.

## WHERE WE STAND

In broad terms, periodic self-studies improve the experiences of project participants. Survey and interview data indicate general satisfaction with project FIRST with differences in stakeholders' views on the support necessary for student success; lacking is an understanding of concerted academic support, a culturally responsive curriculum, and the necessary mentoring for first generation students of color.

Current data on project FIRST's success are based primarily on the perspectives of project developers. An equally essential data source is feedback from student participants. Student-generated feedback on their participation in project FIRST will identify the mechanisms students, as consumers, defined as having influenced their personal access and success as project FIRST participants.

## LIMITATIONS

All project FIRST stakeholders have committed scholarships and fee support for students who attend the first 2 years of their teacher education program at SLCC. The U of U has committed an additional 2 years of tuition support through a range of funds, and community and county resources provide peer mentoring and general supervisory guidance. Whereas funding is relatively stable, economic shifts may have a profound impact on the long-term viability of the project. Future scholarships may also be limited.

At present faculty support is provided gratis. Changes in faculty commitment and availability within institutions of higher education may influence opportunities to engage in work traditionally defined as "service."

Beyond the challenges of maintaining ongoing financial support are the realities faced by traditionally underrepresented students. For the majority of FIRST students, academic struggles have been significant. Efforts to meet basic mathematics and reading competencies have required additional course work and general remediation by SLCC faculty and staff. A weekly seminar provides a touch point. Mentoring and tutoring in math and writing are crucial for student success.

In addition to academic support, standardized testing requirements may prove challenging for some FIRST students. Current teacher education admissions requirements mandate a range of testing affiliated with state and national teacher licensure programs. The stipulations of No Child Left Behind's highly qualified standards are prospective barriers for FIRST students and must be considered as part of recruiting, admissions, and long-term support.

Finally, FIRST recruits students from ethnically and linguistically diverse communities. Clearly this population of students is varied. For some students, state mandated background checks may limit eligibility for individuals holding undocumented status.

## MORE THAN GOOD INTENTIONS

In its second year, project FIRST is making progress to diversify the teaching community in Salt Lake City. As one stakeholder noted: "While our goals have yet to be fully achieved, there is no goal we've failed to consider as of this point in time."

As with any collaborative we must expect variability in the execution of our work. It is expected that the financial commitments of stakeholders and levels of participation across stakeholders will vary over time. Further, without evidence of success for the students in project FIRST, the "grow our own" ethos will lose favor with stakeholders and likely put into question, the viability of the project.

The success of project FIRST is dependent upon vigilant reflection by stakeholders. This priority proves challenging. Specifically, our self-evaluation highlights project growth and areas in need of attention including: agreement on students' academic preparation; mentoring support; and a diversified curriculum for student participants. To address our long-term goals we will: alter our teacher education curriculum; secure additional funding for mentoring and academic support; and formalize the U of U's commitment to a "model" program that links the university to the community to broaden community participation on access and success for first-generation, ethnically diverse students. Interagency conversations on immigration status, family support, and plans for ongoing financial commitments are among our future discussion topics.

The continued success of project FIRST will occur if we challenge assumptions and practices that appear inclusive but may be limiting. As one board member noted when commenting on the work of collaborative partnerships: "We must reflect continuously on our collective agendas to make this work a priority." He went on: "As institutions we must have ownership and understand the need for flexibility in decision making."

## POWER BALANCE

A commitment to mutual ownership in Project FIRST is evident in stakeholder feedback. Less evident are the layers of power that influence policy and decision making. For the most part, partners in higher education have adopted a leadership role for funding and project oversight. Whereas school-based partners organize and set the agenda for monthly meetings there is a tendency to hand over discussion topics to those in higher education. This "deference" has determined the direction of the project in several ways. In addition to developing FIRST's curriculum, representatives from higher education have called for greater specificity in student selection criteria. In terms of student support, districts have the final say on student access to the program though individuals from higher education are often the first to critique the selection criteria used by districts.

Whereas differentiated levels of influence are understood inherently, stakeholders must be vigilant in their attention to mutual decision making that reflects a balance of power. As one individual remarked regarding the distribution of power among project FIRST stakeholders: "The model has been a remarkable example of a grass roots collaborative that has held together and gotten better as we have learned from our initial experiences." He continued: "We have a good sense of where our expertise rest, and when we need to turn to others."

Less evident are our understandings of broader issues related to the power held by a predominately white group of stakeholders and their perspectives on how to best serve communities of color. These questions will inform the future work of project FIRST in goal setting, in the identification of the steps necessary for achieving our goals, and as prompts for continued dialogue in our efforts to diversify the teaching community.

## REFERENCES

Alemán, E., & Rorrer, A. (2006). *Closing educational achievement gaps for Latina/o students in Utah: Initiating a policy discourse and framework.* Salt Lake City, UT: Utah Education Policy Center.

Alemán, S. M. (2009). Number of west side graduates doubles in two years. In *University Neighborhood Partners Partnership Report*. Salt Lake City, UT: University of Utah.

Burbank, M. D., Bertagnole, H., Carl, S., Dynak, J., Longhurst, T., & Powell, K. (2005). University–district partnerships and the recruitment of tomorrow's teachers: A grassroots effort for preparing quality educators through teaching academies. *The Teacher Educator, 41*, 54–69.

*Excelencia in Education*. Retrieved February 16, 2009, from www.edexcelencia. org

Gay, G., Dingus, J., & Jackson, C. (2003, March). *The presence and performance of teachers of color in the profession* (a monograph). Washington, DC: Community Teachers Institute.

Hodgkinson, H. (2002). Demographics and teacher education. *Journal of Teacher Education, 53*, 102–105.

National Center for Education Statistics. (2003). *The condition of education*. Washington, DC: Department of Education.

National Report Card on Higher Education. (2008). *Measuring up*. San Jose, CA: National Center for Public Policy and Higher Education.

Perlich, P. (2002). *Utah minorities: The story told by 150 years of census data*. Salt Lake City: Western University.

Salt Lake City School District. (2008). *Statistics*. Retrieved February 16, 2009, from http://www.usoe.k12.ut.us/main/

Stanford, B. (1999). *Tapping the wisdom of positive, persevering teachers: The South Central L.A. study*. Paper presented at the annual meeting of the American Educational Research Association. Montreal, Canada.

# 20 Urban Teacher Residencies

## Collaborating to Reconceptualize Urban Teacher Preparation

*Wendy Gardiner and Carrie Kamm*

The Academy for Urban School Leadership (AUSL), an educational management organization, was founded in 2001 with the specific goal of impacting urban education in Chicago by recruiting, preparing, and providing induction support for a new generation of socially motivated urban educators. To fulfill this goal, AUSL forged partnerships with National-Louis University (NLU) and Chicago Public Schools (CPS) to form the county's first Urban Teacher Residency (UTR) program. By spearheading this interagency collaboration, AUSL brokers the continuum between preservice preparation and urban school renewal.

Currently, there are three established UTRs across the country—in Chicago, Boston, and Denver—and more in development. By demonstrating significant increases in new teacher retention, the profile of UTRs is increasing. At this point Chicago and Boston show a retention rate of 95% and 90%, respectively, after 3 years (Berry, Montgomery, Curtid, Hernandex, Wurtzel, & Snyder, 2008). Indeed, the reauthorization of the federal Higher Education Opportunity Act has earmarked millions of dollars for the development and support of UTRs. Despite a rising profile, UTRs are a relatively new phenomenon. Consequentially, there is a void in the scholarship on this reform initiative.

This chapter seeks to contribute to the developing scholarship on UTRs and educational reform initiatives involving multiple stakeholders. First, we provide an overview of UTRs and describe how AUSL, NLU, and CPS collaborate to provide a more comprehensive and supportive path to urban teaching. Then, we analyze the benefits and limitations of this interagency collaboration. Next, we discuss the imperative of mutuality for the viability and efficacy of UTRs. We conclude by providing insights and lessons learned to guide the process of sustaining collaborative partnerships predicated on mutuality. By providing an in-depth look at the AUSL initiated UTR, we hope to provide insights for those interested in learning more about UTRs, and to those seeking to collaborate in ways that impact educational reform through a more comprehensive path—from recruitment, to preparation, through induction.

## URBAN TEACHER RESIDENCIES: AN OVERVIEW

Urban Teacher Residencies (UTRs) are a recent innovation in teacher preparation specifically designed as a reform intervention for urban education. Current UTRs involve partnerships with not-for-profit organizations that spearhead the collaboration, universities that provide master's level coursework leading to certification, and large urban school districts that are both preparation and induction sites. UTRs go beyond the traditional preparation model to include such distinctive features as: (a) recruiting socially motivated candidates who want to teach in urban schools; (b) fostering collaboration by delivering graduate level coursework in cohort groups; (c) integrating theory and practice through a 1-year "residency" with experienced mentor teachers at "training academies" while residents take coursework; (d) meeting the needs of their partnering school district by recruiting and training prospective teachers and then helping graduates secure teaching positions in the partnering district's high needs, high-poverty schools; (e) providing induction support to program graduates; and (f) providing teacher leadership opportunities for experienced classroom teachers (Berry et al., 2008).

## RECRUITING

AUSL and NLU collaborate to recruit, interview, and select teacher candidates, called *residents*, who are committed to teaching in high poverty, central city schools. An important aspect of recruiting is the financial incentive provided to residents. Funded through CPS and grants, AUSL provides a $32,000 stipend, health benefits, and forgivable loans for tuition on the condition that program graduates teach in CPS's high needs, high-poverty schools for a total of 4 years.

## GRADUATE COURSEWORK IN A COHORT MODEL

NLU and AUSL collaborate to deliver a 1-year graduate level program that culminates with a master of arts in teaching and elementary or secondary certification. The program is a cohort model, to promote collaboration, with an emphasis on culturally relevant teaching—creating an ethos of achievement and a rigorous, multicultural curriculum (Gay, 2000; Ladson-Billings, 2001). University faculty with urban expertise are recruited to teach courses and to work with AUSL personnel to strengthen program coherence.

## ONE-YEAR RESIDENCY

To bridge theory and practice, AUSL and NLU place residents in a 1-year residency in a CPS urban training academy with a skilled CPS mentor teacher. Residents are quickly integrated into the classroom and begin teaching within the first 2 weeks of school. Importantly, residents are eased into classroom instruction as mentors scaffold residents' development through a gradual release of teaching responsibility from mentor teacher to resident teacher. Concurrently, mentors provide coaching and feedback in order to build and support residents' reflection-in-practice (Schon, 1983). To support their role as teacher educators, mentors receive ongoing professional development to enhance their teaching and mentoring skills.

AUSL has recently added a role of Mentor Resident Coaches (MRCs) to provide additional support for mentors and residents, and promote congruence between university and field-based work. MRCs support mentors and residents by observing in classrooms and providing coaching, feedback, and professional development. MRCs also collaborate with university faculty to design courses and deliver content.

## INDUCTION

AUSL hires coaches to provide 2 years of induction support for graduates. Induction Coaches are assigned teachers in clusters of schools where they develop professional relationships with principals and new teachers in order to develop new teachers' practices and mediate principals' expectations. Induction Coaches schedule weekly formal observations, times to meet and debrief, as well as maintain ongoing communication with new teachers. Induction Coaches support new teachers by providing professional resources, modeling lessons, helping teachers set and meet short and long term professional goals, and generally being a source of support and resource for professional growth.

## LEADERSHIP OPPORTUNITIES

UTRs provide differentiated career paths for teachers. UTRs provide an alternative path for experienced teachers to become mentors, Mentor Resident Coaches, and Induction Coaches. In this manner, experienced teachers have a wider range of professional opportunities in which their expertise and experience continues to impact teaching and learning.

## SUPPORTING AND SUPPORT FROM THE SCHOOL DISTRICT

AUSL's executive directors and founder, Mike Koldyke, worked closely with CPS's then-superintendent, Arne Duncan, his advisors, as well as the president of NLU to form this UTR. As such, the partnership was built upon a clear and shared vision for urban reform. Whereas high levels of mutuality exist between partners, CPS bears a high cost burden, but also reaps direct benefits from this preparatory model.

From its inception to today, CPS provides significant financial and material resources. Each of the six training academies are CPS schools and base salaries and benefits for faculty and staff, as well as all books, furniture, and other material and curricular resources are paid for by CPS. CPS also subsidizes residents' training costs by providing $3 million annually. In turn, CPS is infused each year with new, and according to principals, well prepared urban teachers committed to working in high needs urban schools for 4 years. Importantly, in a district known for high levels of attrition, AUSL's retention rate after 3 years is 95% (Berry et al., 2008).

## BENEFITS

One of the clear benefits is that UTRs create a comprehensive process to attract, train, and support those who want to become urban educators through a rigorous process that meets the needs of teacher candidates and urban schools. This process is not streamlined; residents take a year of coursework and have a year in a classroom in order to provide them with optimal theoretical and practical background. To promote collaboration, residents are prepared in cohorts and become teachers of record in clusters of schools. Then, graduates receive 2 years of induction support.

The partnership between AUSL, NLU, and CPS is predicated upon interagency collaboration guided by a shared vision of urban reform. Too often there is a sharp distinction between university and field—be it at the preparation or induction level. UTRs require mutuality and shared vision amongst collaborations at the institutional level (why are we doing this work and to what end?), and between university and field based practitioners (how and why are we doing this work?). The very existence of UTRs requires that institutions reach beyond their walls and engage in problem solving, reflection, and idea generation. Such diversity in membership provides important and differing perspectives and knowledge, and allows members to become institutional boundary spanners (Wenger, 1998) who are capable of generating more expansive perspectives and understandings that could be achieved at the single institutional level.

Ultimately, it is hoped that the collaboration between NLU, AUSL, and CPS will be a source of knowledge generation for how to prepare and induct new teachers for high poverty, high needs schools. Collaboration between university-based faculty, mentors, MRCs, and Induction Coaches can strengthen coherence between theory and practice by providing a base of effective practices from which to theorize, and to theorize effective practices. Such collaboration can also provide a venue for researching effective practices in urban schools and building an intellectual community of learners. Additionally, self-study of collaboration can provide a framework to support UTR development and other interagency collaborations.

## CHALLENGES

UTRs are a financially demanding model. According to AUSL's chief financial officer, it costs approximately $5 million dollars to run the residency program alone. CPS makes a significant contribution of $3 million. The remainder is derived from federal, foundation, and private funds and, therefore, subject to changing political and economic climates. However, given the high cost of teacher attrition, programs that demonstrate high levels of retention in hard-to-staff schools could be considered a wise investment on the front end, and potentially save money in the long run.

As the model spans recruitment, preparation, and induction, so do the costs. In terms of recruitment, primary costs include an advertising budget, staff to recruit candidates and manage acceptance contracts, legal fees for contracts, and travel costs for out-of-state candidates. Primary preparation costs include residents' $32,000 stipends and health insurance, mentor teachers' 20% salary increase, salaries for MRCs, and residents' tuition costs. Induction costs funds salaries and benefits for eight Induction Coaches.

Another challenge is identifying and attracting people who are committed to preparing teachers to be effective in high needs schools and maintaining ongoing collaboration to support program coherence. Exceptional mentor teachers, MRCs, Induction Coaches, and university faculty are needed to provide a continuum of support and professional learning. Mentor teachers and coaches need to be effective teachers as well as have the knowledge, skills, and dispositions to teach in ways that promote student achievement in high needs schools. In order for resident teachers to have congruency between their daily classroom experience and their coursework, it is necessary for university faculty to understand the complexities and demands of high needs, high poverty schools as they provide rigorous, theoretically informed, and culturally responsive graduate level coursework. Whereas finding individuals to fulfill this range of roles can be difficult, the task becomes more complex when realizing that these individuals also need professional support and development.

Finally, ongoing collaboration between university and school-based faculty and coaches is necessary to ensure coherence and congruence from preservice education through inservice induction. Finding time to dialogue, problem solve, and maintain a broad, comprehensive and shared vision is challenging, particularly when individuals are in a range of settings and are responsible for multiple, and sometimes competing, demands.

## THE IMPERATIVE OF MUTUALITY

UTRs are interagency partnerships that are predicated on impacting student achievement through recruiting, preparing, and inducting highly qualified teachers into hard-to-staff schools. Currently, Teacher Quality Enhancement

(TQE) Grants are allocated toward either the development of UTRs or enhanced professional development school models. For UTRs to be effective, or even funded under TQE, a partnership must first be formed and a shared vision of the process from recruitment through induction, derived from a thorough needs assessment, must be articulated. Relationships must be mutual and their vision must be both shared and comprehensive.

Currently, concerns relating to imbalances of power and a lack of comprehensive or shared vision are being raised. For example, if UTRs focus too greatly on the needs of the school system, a reductive form of preparation will take place that only responds to current district needs and prepares candidates for implementing the district's curriculum—essentially, a limited view of practice without a theoretical framework from which to build a comprehensive, responsive teaching practice. Or, if a university does not adapt its curriculum to reflect the sociocultural realities of high needs, high poverty schools and seek out faculty with urban expertise, then teacher candidates will be prepared with a theoretical framework without the ability to translate theory into practice. A shifting balance of power would reduce the voice, experience, and expertise of a partner in a way that would negatively impact the efficacy of the model. We have found that each partner must be willing to ask and address hard questions regarding the intricacies of the partnership, but also about policies, practices, and limitations within their own institutions.

In the case of the AUSL initiated UTR, each partner recognizes that it cannot tackle the problem of recruiting, preparing, and inducting high caliber teachers for high needs schools alone. CPS historically has high teacher attrition rates and low student performance on state wide standardized tests. NLU recognizes that preparing highly effective urban educators requires rethinking the way preservice teachers are prepared. AUSL, in this case, serves as the link that initiated the partnership, brokers ongoing communication, places residents, and pursues grant funding. Yet, without CPS or NLU there would be no preparation or recipient site and no preparation program. Hence, without mutuality and commitment to the joint enterprise, UTRs would not function, or continue to be funded. As UTRs increasingly garner positive national level attention by demonstrating increased new teacher retention rates of highly qualified teachers in hard-to-staff schools, working to build and maintain the relationship is in the best interest of each partner.

## LESSONS LEARNED

The AUSL initiated UTR is in its 8th year. In this time the program has grown and evolved. Whereas UTRs have common features, they exist within local contexts and each will have its own unique stamp. Importantly, UTRs are predicated on sustained collaboration and mutuality.

What follows are some overarching lessons that we hope will guide future collaborative efforts and support mutuality:

- Have a clear, shared vision of an "exceptional urban educator" and backward map what it will take to get there: To this end, there needs to be agreement as to what attributes, backgrounds, and skills predict success in urban teaching as well as what skills, knowledge, and dispositions constitute an effective urban educator. With an end goal in mind, and an understanding of the sociocultural climates in which this work will take place, develop a cohesive and comprehensive program to address UTR features in the local context.
- Commitment: Seek out institutions and individuals who share in the vision and are willing and able to engage in the joint work and critical discourse needed to provide a comprehensive, rigorous, and theoretically/practically relevant program ranging from recruitment through induction.
- Flexibility, reflection, and adaptation are necessary: Improving urban education means rethinking the way teachers have been traditionally prepared and supported. Those working most closely with residents at both preservice and inservice levels must be willing to examine their work, give and receive feedback, and be willing to adapt their practices in order to deliver a high quality, intellectually rigorous, culturally responsive, congruent, and comprehensive program.
- Cross boundaries and communicate: UTRs entail collaborations between three distinct organizations (and many members within these organizations) that have their own cultures, traditions, and bureaucracies. The extent to which UTRs can recruit, train, and sustain urban teachers and maintain its collaborative structure is predicated on a comprehensive understanding of the vision, the model, and the lived realities of those providing and receiving services.

## CONSIDERATIONS

Recruiting, preparing, and retaining high quality urban educators is a great challenge (Oakes, Loef Franke, Hunter Quartz, & Rogers, 2002; Weiner, 2002), one that holds significant impact for the lives of millions of children. UTRs are one means of addressing the problem of attracting, preparing, and sustaining a new generation of urban educators who are simultaneously versed in theory and the social contexts of urban classrooms. Whereas 3-year studies are indicating high retention levels (Berry et al., 2008), UTRs are a high-cost model. As such, a pertinent question becomes: "Is the initial output more expensive than the cost of attrition?" Additionally, since federal dollars are currently earmarked for the expansion of UTRs, what are other ways to raise and allocate the capital required to sustain UTRs?

Given the all too prevalent theory/practice divide, particularly in urban schools, UTRs can become not only a site for inquiry, but also a venue for authentic collaboration. Lessons learned through ongoing research can inform both policy and practice. Additionally, at both the institutional and personal level, UTRs create more opportunities for genuine collaboration. By crossing borders, creating and sustaining a shared vision, and engaging in collaborative work, interagency collaborations such as UTRs can better address the complex issues of teacher preparation and urban reform than what institutions could do individually.

## REFERENCES

Berry, B., Montgomery, D., Curtid, R., Hernandez, M., Wurtzel, J., & Snyder, J. (2008). *Creating and sustaining urban teacher residencies: A new way to recruit, prepare and retain effective teachers in high-needs districts.* The Aspen Institute/ Centern for Teaching Quality. Retrieved January 14, 2009, from http://www.eric .ed.gov:80/ERICDocs/data/ericdocs2sql/content_storage_01/0000019b/80/3e/ b8/0e.pdf

Gay, G. (2000). *Culturally responsive teaching: Theory, research & practice.* New York: Teachers College Press.

Ladson-Billings, G. (2001). *Crossing over to Canaan: The journey of new teachers in diverse classrooms.* San Francisco: Jossey-Bass.

Oakes, J., Loef Franke, M., Hunter Quartz, K., & Rogers, J. (2002). Research for high-quality urban teaching: Defining it, developing it, assessing it. *Journal of Teacher Education, 53*(3), 254–261.

Schon, D. A. (1983). *The reflective practitioner: How professionals think in action.* New York: Basic Books.

Weiner, L. (2002). Evidence and inquiry in teacher education: What's needed for urban schools. *Journal of Teacher Education, 53*(3), 254–261.

Wenger, E. (1998). *Communities of practice: Learning, meaning, and identity.* New York: Cambridge University.

# 21 Sharing Power in an Interagency Collaboration

*Jack Leonard and Lisa Gonsalves*

In this chapter, we discuss a multifaceted partnership between the University of Massachusetts in Boston and the three small high schools of the Dorchester Education Complex. We begin with an overview of the partnership, followed by two colorful stories that better illustrate the challenges of multi-agency collaborations, and conclude with some brief recommendations.

The University of Massachusetts in Boston (UMB), the largest public research institution in Boston, shares a partnership with one of the city's most troubled high schools; the Dorchester Education Complex (DEC) was restructured into three small schools in 2003 after many years of low test scores, a high dropout rate, and a reputation for violence that would not go away. The partnership dates back 40 years and has grown to now include over 20 different programs. The two campuses are four miles apart, connected by public transportation.

## ORGANIZATION

The partnership is now large, complex, and multi-layered. Three different colleges are involved as well as university offices in Student Support and Community Relations. On the high school end, all three small schools participate. Other agencies intersect with the partnership with resources and services, including several foundations (Trefler, National Science, Nellie Mae Educational), a local community college and, of course, the central administration of the Boston Public Schools (BPS).

The partnership includes benefits for students and faculty at both institutions. Graduate students from the Graduate College of Education complete practicum in teaching and counseling; high school students enjoy pre-collegiate programs (such as Upward Bound), dual enrollment courses, summer jobs, ample tutoring, help with the college application process, and even certain health services. For UMB faculty, there are multiple research opportunities and the DEC teachers receive graduate courses and professional development.

## THE BALANCE OF POWER

The relationship between the university and the Complex has formal and informal elements as might be anticipated in such a large partnership. The core relationship is informal in that a few leaders on both ends remain involved regardless of funding; they make quick decisions by email or telephone and operate at a high level of trust. The leaders include DEC principals, a UMB administrator, faculty from both institutions, and a representative from the Trefler Foundation. There seems to be an unspoken understanding that these institutions (university, three high schools, and foundation) are supposed to work together. The leadership core meets every few months as the UMB/DEC Steering Committee to oversee and guide all the multiple partnering activities.

The reliance upon a few key leaders with informal communications is a strength when funds are low, but also a limitation in that program documentation is often lacking and the structure is jeopardized by sudden changes in leadership on either end. For example, from 2002 to 2008 the partnership struggled with a rapid run of three chancellors, five deans at the Graduate College of Education, and five principals among the three high schools. The Steering Committee was at pains to reintroduce the partnership to successive leaders and to remind them of the 40-year university commitment.

The restructuring of Dorchester High in 2003 was a bit of a slap in the face to the partnership and posed possible limitations for future work. One of the three new schools was a Boston pilot school (a school with greater liberties around district and union rules), forcefully moved to Dorchester from a safer location, so the launch was not amicable. Each school was determined to demonstrate its own distinctiveness so there was little interest in group Complex meetings. This resistance to working together limited collaborative learning. Nevertheless, the university made an equitable commitment to all the schools. At first, UMB was forced to meet separately with each school along different agendas, but after a year, new grant funding brought new opportunities and reinvigorated the Steering Committee.

Borthwick notes that partnerships are an "appropriate response to the environmental turbulence and uncertainty of member organizations," because they offer stability and continuity (2001, p. 26). Certainly, UMB was an anchor through the high school reinvention of 2003. The sheer size of their engagement meant they could be a muscular advocate for the small schools in fending off senseless interferences from the central BPS administration and in bridging fractional interschool disputes.

The partnership is not listed as an identifiable item on the regular budgets of any of the participants, so sustainable funding is a limiting problem. Many of the partnership activities listed above are staffed and implemented as grant funding becomes available. Formal agreements are written in conformity with the guidelines of the funders. Grants are invariably written by the university partners, because the high school leaders have little knowledge of available funding or the time to write the proposals. Each grant shifts the mutual balance of power toward the university, because the university is most answerable to funders.

Corrigan (2000) lists time, personnel, and facilities as the three great constrictors in such partnerships. For us, personnel and time are the biggest constraints, whereas facility use is not. The lack of time, particularly on the part of school leaders, is a constant limitation to the partnership. School leaders begrudge the disparate distribution of grant monies; the university uses the extra money to hire staff for implementation and reporting while the high school staff must simply pick up additional responsibilities without assistance.

The university provides teaching and counseling interns, tutors and mentors, faculty who provide dual enrollment classes and professional development, meeting space for various programs, research investigations (often following faculty interests rather than school interests), and a streamlined college admission process for Complex students. The high schools provide office and meeting space, access to the high school students, mentors for the interns plus tiny contributions to pay for office equipment, supplies, snacks, or student incentives.

The arrival of money and the associated programs can stimulate competition for influence and resources. For example, the UMB Student Support Office is well endowed with government-funded pre-collegiate and dual enrollment programs. The three high schools compete to reserve spots in the programs for their students. In 2004, the Student Support Office landed a large 5-year Nellie Mae Educational Foundation grant, which allowed an expansion of formal activities with the Complex, including the employment of a full-time liaison. On the other hand, the Graduate College of Education often struggles to find funding and adequate placements for its interns in the smaller restructured high schools. Tensions escalate as the two divisions both claim ownership of the partnership; this hinders the effectiveness of the Steering Committee.

Ownership of the partnership can be encouraged, but not commanded. In 2005, one Chancellor visited the Dorchester Complex and promptly ordered every university department to "get engaged" with the needy high schools. This proved more difficult than imagined. Nevertheless, the three high schools wrote a "wish list," which served as a guide for development. Numerous activities sprang from this list, including college counseling for seniors, business-related internships, and better alignment of tutoring services. In truth, most university faculty members are probably unaware of the UMB/DEC partnership and over half the students in the three schools have no participation in the activities. Lack of parental involvement is another serious limitation in the partnership.

As large as the partnership may be, the community of the high school is even larger. There are other significant voices, from parents to peer culture to district and state-level governments. We use the ecological systems theory of Urie Bronfenbrenner (1979) to understand the role of partnerships in student development. The university is just one sphere of influence in the life of the developing student and they can either cooperate or compete with other partners.

## TWO STORIES

We offer two stories that further illustrate the subtle tensions of complex partnerships. The first illustrates problems over differences in goals; the second illustrates resistances that arise when programs are quickly assembled in response to a narrow funding window. We acknowledge the tensions, but emphasize that they need not prevent productive work.

The teacher preparation program called Teach Next Year (TNY) was launched by UMB in 1998 with funding from a family foundation run by Pam Trefler. TNY included a year-long internship at Dorchester, graduate classes in the summer and late afternoons, free tuition and a $10,000 stipend, and it proved to be very successful over the next 10 years.

TNY was a formal agreement born out of joint meetings of the university, foundation, and Dorchester faculty, but each institution had different goals for the program. The university and foundation saw TNY as a long-range reform strategy to develop a Professional Development School, which would provide a steady stream of culturally competent teachers, as well as nudge some veteran teachers into better practices by contact. The high school teachers, however, looked to TNY to immediately raise the teacher/student ratio in turbulent classrooms and thereby regain control. Because the high school teachers had the power of refusing to provide mentorships to college interns, they gained some control of TNY. UMB and the foundation retained some ownership in that candidates were dependent for financing, coursework, and final approval for certification. So, the relationship was mutual, with one partner offering academic credentialing and the other offering classroom application.

The differences in goals led to tensions around the selection and placement of interns. The predominantly white Dorchester teachers selected interns with whom they would feel comfortable because they wanted help in their most difficult classrooms; these candidates turned out to be mostly white. UMB was looking for diverse candidates with cultural competence to better address the needs of students. Differences in goals also provoked disagreements around the placement of interns. Dorchester teachers wanted to put the interns in disruptive classrooms where help was needed, whereas UMB faculty wanted to put interns with the best mentors. Dorchester teachers often prevailed for the reasons outlined previously.

The placement decisions were further complicated in that the teachers, with support from UMB, excluded the high school administrators from the decision-making process, arguing that the leadership often "played favorites." Certain teachers partnered independently with the Trefler Foundation, so they gained additional sway over the selection and placement decisions. Other high school teachers often felt excluded from the decision making and benefits of TNY.

In conclusion, simple differences in goals translated into subtle struggles for power between the university and the school and even within the school. However, despite these unresolved tensions, there were numerous positive accomplishments. TNY was central to the reform of the high school. One of the new small schools in 2003 had fully one third of its faculty trained through TNY. The knowledge has flowed in both directions in this partnering activity (Weerts & Sandmann, 2008); UMB still learns from the partnership and regularly tweaks its curriculum in response. Furthermore, TNY became the model for the BPS in-district teacher preparation program.

The second story features the dual enrollment program. For years, UMB offered dual enrollment classes to a select group of DEC through a formal, federally-funded program called Urban Scholars. Students were nominated by their teachers, selected by UMB personnel, and carefully groomed for success to ensure ongoing federal dollars.

New state funding in 2004 prompted the university to offer dual enrollment classes to all DEC students just as registration for the fall classes was closing. The program was expanded "on the fly" in response to the short timeline. The new program was more informal and collaborative but also more vulnerable. The high school teachers' union was skeptical of student success in dual enrollment programs and resisted making major schedule changes so students could substitute a college course for a high school course. Instead, interested students had to pile the dual enrollment course on top of a full load at DEC, which set them up for failure. Furthermore, the high schools were unprepared to offer extra support.

The college placement exams, required for participation in most courses, raised additional problems. UMB faculty scorers resisted the sudden flood of additional tests. Worse, many students failed the exams and UMB was unable to offer the remedial "developmental" courses instead because of strict accreditation standards. These university standards proved to be a limitation; DEC students would not be granted the same supports and privileges as full-time matriculated students.

Students who did proceed with courses faced additional questions: Who would pay for the textbooks and transportation to the campus? The Steering Committee left this up to the schools; some schools found money to help out and others did not. The failure to work out these details in advance increased tensions, competition, and student frustration.

Unfortunately, many students were unable to handle the increased work load and they failed or dropped out. The university questioned the college readiness of the DEC students, so they suggested a minimum grade point average as an entrance requirement. This was promptly challenged by the schools who hoped to offer a "taste of university" to some bright but underachieving students who did not see college in their future. The initial rosy projections of large numbers of dual enrolled students shriveled. A promising opportunity with solid state funding narrowed due to the lack of formal planning that could have addressed the limitations of the high schools and the university.

About this time, the nearby Bunker Hill Community College (BHCC) approached the Complex and offered to work with one of the small schools (Noonan Business Academy, or NBA) on college readiness, because their graduates attended BHCC more than any other college. Funding would come from the same state dual enrollment grant and would be used for testing, tuition, textbooks, and even a full-time liaison who would meet with NBA students weekly.

BHCC found a way to allow high school faculty to administer their college placement exams (Accuplacer) at the high school. The Accuplacer was computer-based, so scoring was automatic and feedback to students was immediate. The initial low scores were a huge wake-up call to students and faculty at NBA but had a positive outcome. Over the next 3 years, high school faculty analyzed this test, comparing it to other benchmark assessments and using it to inform and prepare students. The math teachers were assisted in this work by UMB faculty. An annual test schedule was created and a senior-level prep course was launched. Scores began to increase from the junior to the senior year.

BHCC also offered dual enrollment courses to students. The high school was cautious, but soon learned that students would be able to take remedial courses for free even if they failed to pass the college placement exams, something UMB could not arrange. Most students succeeded and were encouraged to try another class. More than once, NBA shared this model with UMB, hoping they would adopt the Accuplacer and their budget formula, but UMB resisted the modifications and was unable to offer developmental courses.

## CONCLUSION

Ten years of supportive, focused, uncritical, research-based attention has often accomplished in the high schools what broad district policies could not, including improved teacher professionalism and student safety, achievement, and college readiness gains. Some programs, such as TNY and the Accuplacer work, have been duplicated in the district. The benefits to the university are harder to identify. The dual enrollment story illustrates that the culture of the high school is easier to change than that of the university. Certainly the number of Dorchester students matriculating at UMB has increased. Many fruitful research projects have been published. Best of all, the partnership helps substantiate the unique urban mission of the university in this college-rich city.

# RECOMMENDATIONS FOR INTERAGENCY COLLABORATIONS

1. Formal agreements around project work are necessary to satisfy funders, but there is no substitute for informal, high-trust relationships to accelerate the work and sustain it through periods of low funding or institutional change.
2. Timely communication is at the heart of good partnering. More than once, a small school missed out by neglecting emails, telephone calls, or meetings.
3. Inclusiveness for sustainability and streamlined leadership for production are essential and competing goals. Partnering activities are cemented by drawing in students, parents, teachers, and administrators (chancellor, provost, superintendent, and principal). The challenge to institutionalize the partnership never ceases.
4. An impressive number of beneficial partnering activities can result if each activity is developed patiently and separately, then firmly institutionalized and layered with the next activity. Partnerships grow like pearls; they take time.
5. Large funding agencies are better at providing money than offering creative design; some of our best ideas came from the bottom up, from teachers, students, and mid-level administrators.
6. When new funds call for an expansion of the work of partnership, all partners should enjoy the benefits of added staffing to assist with the work, if possible.
7. Good theory promotes good work, such as a good child-centered ecological framework like Bronfenbrenner's (1979) and organizational theory, such as the four frames of Bolman and Deal (2003).
8. Fullan writes that the "moral purpose (the spiritual) gains ascendency" in complex collaborations (1999, p. 40). Partnering invites conflicts, but also calls out the best in each of us. There will be inevitable conflicts in large multi-agency partnerships, but positive outcomes can still occur. It doesn't have to be perfect to move forward.

# REFERENCES

Bolman, L. G., & Deal, T. E. (2003). *Reframing organizations: Artistry, choice, and leadership* (3rd ed.). San Francisco: Jossey-Bass.

Borthwick, A. C. (2001). Dancing in the dark? Learning more about what makes partnerships work. In R. Ravid & M. G. Handler (Eds.), *The many faces of school-university collaboration: Characteristics of successful partnerships* (pp. 23–41). Englewood, CO: Teacher Ideas Press.

Bronfenbrenner, U. (1979). *The ecology of human development: Experiments by nature and design.* Cambridge, MA: Harvard University Press.

Corrigan, D. (2000). The changing role of schools and higher education institutions with respect to community-based interagency collaboration and interprofessional partnerships. *Peabody Journal of Education, 75*(3), 176–195.

Fullan, M. (1999). *Change forces: The sequel.* Philadelphia, PA: Falmer Press.

Weerts, D. J., & Sandmann, L. R. (2008). Building a two-way street: Challenges and opportunities for community engagement at research universities. *The Review of Higher Education, 32*(1), 73–106.

# 22 Collaborating for Labor Consciousness

## The Education & Labor Collaborative

*Adrienne Andi Sosin, Leigh David Benin,*
*Rob Linné, and Joel I. Sosinsky*

This essay describes the Education & Labor Collaborative, an Interagency Collaboration of participants from schools, universities, and labor unions. The collaboration's goals are long-range and multi-faceted: (a) increase teachers' awareness of the specific needs of working-class students; (b) enable teachers to empower their working-class students to act collectively in their own best interests; (c) help schools become better resourced through organized pressure; (d) support parents in their efforts to secure quality education for their children; and (e) help organized labor grow in influence by raising labor consciousness among students and teachers in K–12 schooling.

The collaboration we describe in this essay grew from the premise of our volume of collected essays, *Organizing the Curriculum: Perspectives on Teaching the US Labor Movement* (Linné, Benin, & Sosin, 2009). This premise is that because unionism is essential to a viable economy and healthy democracy, and indispensible as well to the struggle for social justice, reviving labor consciousness through education, especially in view of the current economic collapse, is crucial.

Collaborations in education are between organizations, but they often begin between individuals who have made the decision that they need to address their goals through affiliation with one another. Cooperation on an individual level can ultimately lead to creating institutional alliances able to achieve goals that could not be accomplished by individuals alone. This is why the conceptual foundations for union solidarity compliment the principles of collaboration in this volume.

In this age of neo-liberalism and corporate dominance, there is little doubt that the labor movement's views, issues, and values have been systematically excluded from school curricula, resulting in students who have little knowledge of labor activism and no experience with collective tactics. This abysmal situation is countered by Patrick Finn's (2009b) prescription for "literacy with an attitude." He envisions a paradigm shift in education that would empower working-class students to act in their own collective interests (Finn, 2009a), and he would extend this approach to meeting the real needs of working-class students from the sphere of urban education to the realm teacher education (Finn & Finn, 2007; Finn, Johnson, & Finn, 2005).

The Education & Labor Collaborative (E&LC) grows from our individual commitment to social and economic justice, and from our shared convictions about the theoretical and practical nature of education. Since its formation in 2007, the E&LC steering committee has worked to lay the groundwork for a national movement for substantive and relevant labor studies for youth in public education.

## LABOR EDUCATION AND THE E&LC MISSION

With globalization and the neo-liberal assault on labor unions (Compton & Weiner, 2008), union density, influence, and power have drastically declined. Unions are now too often forced to focus on defending previously won gains and combating union-busting tactics. Unfortunately, this has led too many unions to overlook education as a primary part of their mission. The E&LC is a network of organizations and individuals committed to restructuring the K–16 curriculum to include accounts of past and present labor struggles, emphasizing solidarity and progressive activism to inspire and equip students to advocate for themselves as future workers. The E&LC creates opportunities for unionists and educators to share ideas, develop strategies, and create an expanding network to spread labor consciousness. Whereas members of the Collaborative may disagree about specific labor issues, we are united in advocating worker empowerment through labor organization.

Both *Literacy with an Attitude* (Finn, 2009) and *Organizing the Curriculum* (2009) critique contemporary education, which fails most working-class students. Finn (2009a) explains that the vast majority of working-class students, who know that they are destined for working-class jobs or unemployment, do not value the "school knowledge" that allows only a few to "border cross" into the professional class. Moreover, Finn posits that Freirean educational practices motivate working-class students to want to learn by providing them with the knowledge, values, and skills they need to collectively address the injustices that oppress their communities.

## TEACHER EDUCATION

As founding members of the E&LC, many of us are teacher educators, preparing K–12 teachers who will spend their careers in public schools. The E&LC's position is that teacher educators should present teacher unions as indispensable protectors of teachers' rights. This is not the situation in most schools of education today where little time, if any, is devoted to understanding power relations in education or the necessity for teachers to have union representation. New teachers often take for granted salary step increases, professional status, contractually-defined and defended working conditions, and the due process protections of teacher tenure. They do not recognize that before teachers won collective bargaining rights in the 1960s and 1970s, teaching was a much less secure and remunerative career. In 1933, John Dewey advised teachers to join in a "community of interest of educators with all workers . . . in an alliance in sympathy and in action" (p. 389) in order to combat the economic disaster of the Great Depression—advice that is once again crucial.

Teachers who appreciate the labor movement are better prepared, and more likely to foster labor consciousness in their students. By fostering critical awareness of corporate greed, political mendacity, and mass media manipulation, teachers equip and prepare students to cope with their own future working lives and at the same time create a political environment supportive of unionism. As historian Howard Zinn (1999), advises: "We need to create a generation of students who support teachers and the movement of teachers for their rights" (p. 76).

## FORMATION OF THE EDUCATION & LABOR COLLABORATIVE

The E&LC began with a meeting of five teacher educators at the annual meeting of the American Educational Research Association (AERA) in Chicago in April of 2007. We resolved to have a planning meeting in New York in October of 2007 to launch a collaborative organization of teacher educators, trade unionists, and teachers to promote labor education in the K–12 schools. That planning session led to the creation of the Collaborative, and the development of the following mission statement:

## GOALS OF THE EDUCATION AND LABOR COLLABORATIVE:

- The Education and Labor Collaborative seeks to build working alliances between union workers and teachers, both of whom seek a better deal for working families. Both labor unionists and educators know children fare better when parents are economically secure and able to participate in their children's schooling. Both understand the need for curricular materials and pedagogies that inform students about work, their job rights, the labor movement, and the benefits of collective activism.
- Labor will benefit from a better-educated public, one that understands the role of unionism in a democracy. Imagine how much easier and effective the work of unionists will be when a generation of children graduate from high school understanding their right and duty to be heard, the power of joining together in common cause, and the skill to speak on their own behalf. And imagine how much easier the work of teachers will be when, through unionization, the lives of working

families are improved and the resources they need to support their children's education are widely available.

- Educators, in collaboration with unionists, can break the cycle of reproducing the unjust economic structure through schooling, and change the cultural climate that disrespects poor and working families.

To further these goals, we organized our first Forum at the United Federation of Teachers (UFT) headquarters in New York City in March 2008. Speakers included important labor leaders and distinguished academics, who addressed 150 enthusiastic participants during two days of meetings. At the Forum, UFT Vice President Mike Mulgrew and Fred Glass of the California Federation of Teachers agreed to "support a national K–12 Labor Plan and Conference" at the 2008 American Federation of Teachers (AFT) Convention. Their resolution passed, and as a result, the AFT has now embarked on the path outlined in the Collaborative's mission statement. An advisory board made up of distinguished educators and unionists, including the presenters at the first forum, agreed to guide future endeavors. The second annual E&LC Forum took place in April 2009, with a film festival at Antioch University Los Angeles, and an organizing conference at the United Teachers of Los Angeles headquarters. The Forum connected today's economic crisis to the Great Depression, advocating for a *new* New Deal and reinvigoration of organized labor's struggle for jobs and justice. The second forum gave teachers opportunities to voice their opinions, propose new projects, and expand the Collaborative.

## MATRIX CATEGORIES

The categorization of collaborations in education, as defined by the Slater Matrix in this book, proposes that organizations such as the E&LC are examples of Interagency Collaboration. As members of the E&LC steering committee, we comment here on the applicability of the categories and address the descriptive qualities attributed to this type of collaboration.

### Organizational Involvement

In Slater's Matrix, the Interagency Collaboration category "varies beyond university/school" to encompass organizations not usually considered educational institutions. In the case of the E&LC, closer ties between labor unionists and teachers will open avenues for educational transformation in the interests of social justice. Rather than a concentrated effort by one or even a few organizational entities, E&LC participants constitute a broad and diverse network of affiliated institutions.

## Formal / Informal

Slater's Matrix describes a "semi-autonomous, systems approach" as the defining characteristic of formality in Interagency Collaborations. As a decentralized umbrella organization, the E&LC relies on voluntary participation. Therefore, the E&LC is a mostly informal arrangement, based on the personal networking skills of its participants. As the E&LC develops over time, it grows more formal. An example of the growing formality of the collaborative organization is the constitution of an advisory board and the development of bylaws. Formalization can occur between E&LC participants, as demonstrated by the joint AFT resolution introduced by the California Federation of Teachers and supported by the United Federation of Teachers.

## Purpose

The Slater Matrix attributes characteristics to the collaboration as "future oriented, change efforts, renewal, and redesign of parent institution." The E&LC is most certainly a future oriented change effort, seeking renewal of labor consciousness and redesign of teacher education programs to enhance activism for social justice. By organizing forums that bring together educators, trade unionists, and teachers, the E&LC creates multiple opportunities for promoting labor consciousness.

## Resources, Support, and Funding

Slater's Matrix accurately reflects the multi-level nature of securing resources for the E&LC. As currently constituted, the E&LC is funded by donations from the entities associated with the participants, and all the members voluntarily contribute their time and efforts. Networking by the planning committee members with the New York labor movement led to offers of gratis accommodations by the United Federation of Teachers for the first forum, and from the United Teachers of Los Angeles for the second forum. Support comes from universities affiliated with the E&LC members, who have reached out to their institutions with requests for funding and in-kind support. Unions related to academe and to E&LC members have been generous with donations to defray expenses, time away from work, and in-kind contributions. Whereas these sources of funding are admittedly tenuous, they have been sufficient to launch and thus far maintain the E&LC.

## Mutuality Level and Power Hierarchy

Slater's Matrix notes the characteristics for interagency collaborations as "institution building, experimentation, institution change data, producer of knowledge, and focus on development." In the case of the E&LC,

institution building and institutional change are both evident. The E&LC's mission statement implies that change must occur in schools and in universities that prepare teachers. Within the context of the Collaborative, knowledge workers in the academy, teachers, and trade unionists can learn much from one another about how to enhance labor consciousness. Through selection of its projects, like the Triangle Fire Remembrance Coalition, the E&LC is actively working to provide an impetus to move participating organizations toward expanding labor consciousness and infusing working-class pedagogy into teacher education programs and school curricula.

## Resistance Sources

The corporate bias of textbooks, the designation of labor as a special interest group rather than as an institution essential to democracy, and the American intellectual and political tradition that denies class differences and rejects class-based analysis in favor of a multicultural approach to social justice, ignorance of the labor movement's past and present struggles, and a general lack of knowledge or practice by students and teachers in the use of activist strategies all contribute to resistance. Challenges also come from some labor leaders who are preoccupied with their memberships' problems, hold narrow conceptions of unionism, and are disinclined to reach out to working-class students. As Glass (2009, p. 233) has noted, labor education is "every labor leader's second favorite subject." Slater's Matrix notes that the agenda served by resistance needs to be identified; resistance to the E&LC serves an agenda that promotes unrestrained corporate dominance. As long as the educational system reflects the ethos and addresses the needs of corporate America, resistance to struggles for social justice will be strong and fierce.

## Positives

Slater's Matrix indicates positive attributes for interagency collaboration, including upset to the status quo, innovation, generated knowledge, and advancing the common good. There is no doubt that labor education upsets the status quo. Beyond that, social justice educators create spaces for critical thought and undoubtedly work for the common good. The participants in the E&LC are engaged on a variety of fronts to enact its mission: These include developing labor oriented initiatives in public schools, community colleges, and teacher education programs, and participating in community-based organizations, such as the Triangle Fire Remembrance Coalition, and union-sponsored Youth Brigades. These are real and important activities that involve educators and unionists, who unite in solidarity to accomplish modest yet valuable advances toward empowering working people.

## Limitations

According to Slater, an interagency collaboration is difficult to put together because it requires participating organizations and individuals to change. Despite steadily decreasing union density, which is now alarmingly low, unions ordinarily use their scarce resources to solve immediate problems, support pro-union politicians, and fund current organizing, rather than for long-range organizing through labor education. Additionally, academics confront the ideological orientations of universities, which in spite of their non-profit status are corporate-dominated and consumer-oriented; teachers must deal every day with the stressors of accountability and administrative fiat, and their unions are consequently preoccupied with daily crises. These limitations make the E&LC's work of expanding collaboration among educators and unionists challenging.

## LESSONS LEARNED

If social-justice minded educators and unionists hope to become more than a scattering of voices, they must make deeper and more intense efforts at communication and collaboration. Significant differences between K–12 schoolteachers, labor unionists, and university professors with respect to goals, style, and reward structures both enrich and complicate our collaboration. For example, K–12 teachers typically value the wisdom of classroom practice over the research that is prized by academics; labor leaders often regard research and writing as distractions from representing their members and organizing; and academics are likely to place a higher premium on scholarly writing than on knowledge gained from practical experience in school rooms and union halls. These differences can lead to tensions that impact collaboration, but appreciating individual, professional, and organizational diversity facilitates the communication and compromises needed to negotiate mutual decisions. The most important lessons we have learned are to be attentive to the human and professional needs of all collaborators, and to respect principled differences of opinion. Our forums and other endeavors have already generated a buzz about the Education & Labor Collaborative, leading to expansion of our network in the labor and education communities. Our anticipation of a resurgence of labor consciousness in the new economy, and the vital importance of this development to the ongoing struggle for social justice, makes our continued efforts to grow all the more engaging and worthwhile.

## REFERENCES

Compton, M., & Weiner, L. (2008). The global assault on teaching, teachers and teacher unions. In M. Compton & L. Weiner (Eds.), *The global assault* on teaching, teachers and their unions: Stories for resistance (pp. 3–27). New York: Palgrave Macmillan.

Dewey, J. (1933, April). Education and our present social problems. *Educational Method, 12*(7), 385–390.

Finn, P. J. (2009a). A paradigm shift in the making for teachers of working-class students: From extrinsic motivation and border crossing to Freirean motivation and collective advancement. In R. Linné, L. Benin, & A. Sosin (Eds.), *Organizing the Curriculum: Perspectives on teaching the US Labor Movement* (pp. 75–84). Rotterdam, NV: Sense.

Finn, P. J. (2009b). *Literacy with an attitude: Educating working-class children in their own self-interest* (Rev. ed.). New York: SUNY Press.

Finn, P. J., & Finn, M. E. (2007). *Teacher education with an attitude: Preparing teachers to educate working-class students in their collective self interest.* Albany, NY: SUNY Press.

Finn, P. J., Johnson, L., & Finn, M. E. (2005). *Urban education with an attitude.* Albany, NY: SUNY Press.

Glass, F. (2009). Every labor leader's second favorite subject: A short history of the CFT labor in the schools committee, 1987–2007. In R. Linné, L. Benin, & A. Sosin (Eds.), *Organizing the curriculum: Perspectives on teaching the US Labor Movement* (pp. 233–247). Rotterdam, NV: Sense.

Linné, R., Benin, L., & Sosin, A. (Eds.). (2009). *Organizing the curriculum: Perspectives on teaching the US Labor Movement.* Rotterdam, NV: Sense.

Zinn, H. (1999).Why teachers should know history: An interview with Howard Zinn. In *Transforming teacher unions: Fighting for better schools and social justice* (p. 76). Milwaukee, WI: Rethinking Schools, Ltd.

# Conclusion

*Judith J. Slater*

Collaboration is difficult. It structurally brings together two or more organizations that exhibit different cultural worlds to work on a project of mutual interest and benefit. Representative participants carry with them an organizational outlook and way of working that continues throughout the interactions, negotiations, and implementation process of collaborating. This complicates any human system integration, whether it is organizational collaboration or understanding the political and economic decisions made by other countries or cultures with a point of view other than one's own.

Notwithstanding, the 22 examples in this volume describe the complexity of this work, along with the problems and success authors have had in their work. Many authors acknowledged that it gave them a new way to look at and assess their work. Moreover, the use of the Slater Matrix to organize their discussion gives the editors cause to reflect on some of the overarching themes they have uncovered.

Each of the chapters talks about expectations and changes as a result of the collaborative project. Change is elusive, transient, and frightening. The stronger and more complex the institutional bureaucratic structure, the harder it is to make structural changes in the way they operate. Many of the projects in this volume create smaller changes in people. It is the human dimension that collaboration can most effectively change. People working with people, garnering trust, and sharing expertise and experiences are important indicators of change. In all examples in this volume, regardless of the scale of the project or the number of partners, trust, time, and resources were cited as necessities to make the projects successful and enact change.

From the perspective of the university, the impetus to engage in collaborative work is not strong. It may be mandated by governmental decree, by funding agencies that require an external evaluator or involvement, by mutual agreement between the school administration and the university, or have a mission goal to support the larger community. There is little support monetarily, and the reality of using time for service to a PDS or a consultation project takes away from other more university valued work such as research and teaching. Structurally, the university changes little as a result of collaboration. The school system, on the other hand, whereas it is not structurally affected by the collaboration, often benefits most in that teachers involved gain much skill and expertise as a result of their contact with researchers and support staff that bring new information to them and allow the teachers to make the innovations their own. Whereas they are not interested in the university goals of publishing and reporting results, teachers do take back innovative skills and abilities learned to their students.

Support for collaboration work is important to both problem solving and sustainability. Leadership support is critical to operational momentum, but financial resources often control the parameters of the collaboration. Funding sources wield power by delineating the use of funds. They circumscribe the project in a schema of regulations that require precise documentation to show compliance. Often they describe who does what, when, where, and how. Leadership then moderates the rules, making sure to report back to the funding source. Complex collaboration is dependent on funding and there is always the specter of limited sustainability beyond the project when the funding ends.

The effect of collaboration can be local or more global. The complexity of the type of collaboration determines how global and broad the influence is on participants. Individual benefits that are site specific for participants are important, but equally important is sharing information with a larger community. Dissemination of results is left most often to the university partner, and there must be clarity in what to disseminate so that the elements that are translatable, sustainable, and adaptable will influence others to participate in this type of work.

We are gratified that the Slater Matrix successfully serves as a way to discuss and analyze school/university collaboration by type and that those wishing to engage in collaborative endeavors can look to this as a model for decision making. Knowing the strengths and limitations of each model creates realistic expectations for practitioners. It also gives those working in the field a common language to share and disseminate their work.

Finally, in a time of reduced funding and complexity of economic and political turmoil, collaboration serves as a viable alternative to maximize the potential of the larger community that serves school. Together organizations gain strength and share knowledge and expertise. The synergy is important to bring success to schools, teachers, and students.

# Contributors

EDITORS:

**Judith J. Slater** (slaterjj@earthlink.net) is professor emeritus at Florida International University, in curriculum theory, evaluation and organizational culture. She is the author of *Anatomy of a Collaboration: Study of a College of Education/Public School Partnership* (1996), co-author of *Acts of Alignment* (2000), editor of *Teen Life in Asia* (2004), and co-editor of *The Freirean Legacy: Educating for Social Justice* (2002), *Pedagogy of Place* (2004), *Educating for Democracy in a Changing World: Understanding Freedom in Contemporary America* (2007), *The War Against the Professions: The Impact of Politics and Economics on the Idea of the University* (2008), and *Higher Education and Human Capital: Rethinking the Doctorate in America* (in process).

**Ruth Ravid** (rravid@nl.edu) is a professor at National-Louis University, teaching educational research and assessment. She is the author of *Practical Statistics for Educators* (3rd ed.; 2005); co-author of *Practical Statistics for Business: An Introduction to Business Statistics* (2008); and *Workbook to Accompany Practical Statistics for Educators* (3rd ed.; 2005); and co-editor of *The Many Faces of School-University Collaboration: Characteristics of Successful Partnerships* (2001).

BOOK CONTRIBUTORS:

**James P. Barufaldi** (jamesb@mail.utexas.edu) is Ruben E. Hinojosa Regents Professor in Education and Director, Center for Science and Mathematics Education at The University of Texas at Austin. Barufaldi directed numerous federally funded projects, and is current PI for Texas Regional Collaboratives for Excellence in Science and Mathematics Teaching and NSF Chautauqua-Type Short Courses for College Science Teachers.

**Babette Benken** (bbenken@csulb.edu) is an assistant professor and graduate advisor in the Department of Mathematics and Statistics at California State University, Long Beach. Her research interests include models of mathematics teacher education, how to best facilitate teacher learning, and the role teachers' knowledge, beliefs, and context play in shaping practice.

**Leigh David Benin** (haryo18@gmail.com) is a founding member of the Education & Labor Collaborative. He co-edited *Organizing the Curriculum,* and authored *The New Labor Radicalism and New York City's Garment Industry: Progressive Labor Insurgents in the 1960s* (2000) from Garland.

**Joan F. Beswick** (beswick@unb.ca) specializes in early literacy, transition-to-school, psycho-educational assessment, and programming for students with exceptional learning needs. She is a researcher with the Canadian Research Institute for Social Policy, and the director of a non-profit society working with agencies to enhance young children's developmental and early literacy outcomes

**Arlene Borthwick** (aborthwick@nl.edu) is department chair and professor of integrated studies in teaching, technology, and inquiry at National-Louis University. She has been an active participant-researcher of school-university partnership process since 1990; her collaborative efforts have focused on technology integration, school reform, and teacher advocacy through participation in action research.

**Linda L.G. Brown** (llgbrown@gmail.com) specializes in curriculum studies, science education and educational policy. Her expansive career spans collaborative and cooperative experiences within corporate leadership and project management, science education, state policy, higher education, and research organization and policy implementation.

**Nancy Brown** (n2brown@oakland.edu) is an assistant professor in the School of Education and Human Services, Oakland University. Her research interests include understanding ways teacher identity influences learning and knowledge. She is interested in enabling teachers to teach in ways that promote an equitable and conceptually rigorous education for all students.

**Mary D. Burbank** (mary.burbank@utah.edu), clinical associate professor, is director of secondary education in the College of Education at the University of Utah. She has worked in secondary teacher education and community partnership programs for the past 15 years while at Utah.

**David M. Callejo Pérez** (dmcallej@svsu.edu) is the Carl A. Gerstacker Endowed Chair in Education at Saginaw Valley State University. He has co-edited four books and authored two books. He has written over 30 articles and chapters on race, identity, civil rights, democracy, higher education, and qualitative research.

**Linda A. Catelli** (carlin@aol.com) is a professor at Dowling College and founder/director of two partnerships—Project SCOPE I and II. She holds emeritus status at CUNY and in the 1990s she was one of 56 professors honored nationally as a pioneer in school-university collaboration by the American Association of Higher Education collaboration.

**Lorena Claeys** (lorena.claeys@utsa.edu) is a doctoral student in culture, language, and literacy and the executive director for the Academy for Teacher Excellence at the University of Texas at San Antonio. Her research focus is on teacher candidates and interns' motives for teaching culturally and linguistically diverse students.

**Joanne Cooper** (jcooper@hawaii.edu) is a professor of higher education in the Department of Educational Administration at the University of Hawaii. Her research interests include the study of women and minorities in higher education, narrative and reflection in the academy, and leadership and organizational change.

**Joanne Deppeler** (joanne.deppeler@education.monash.edu.au) is an associate professor, Faculty of Education, Monash University, Australia. Her research focus is teacher professional learning within the context of developing inclusive practices and improving outcomes of schooling for students. She publishes widely and contributes to the professional and policy domains at state, national, and international levels.

**Sebastián R. Díaz** (sebastian.diaz@mail.wvu.edu) teaches at West Virginia University and is president of Diaz Consulting, a firm dedicated to assisting organizations in designing, implementing, and evaluating knowledge systems and educational programs. His research is on developing measures for intellectual capital and knowledge management for organizations.

**Efrat Sara Efron** (sefron@nl.edu) is department chair and professor, educational foundations and inquiry, National-Louis University. Her interests includes moral and democratic education, teacher research, curriculum studies, and Janusz Korczak's legacy. She authored/coauthored articles that appeared in *Journal of Teacher Education*, *Phi Delta Kappan*, *Journal of Curriculum & Pedagogy*, and *Curriculum Inquiry*.

**Belinda Bustos Flores** (Belinda.Flores@utsa.edu) is a professor at The University of Texas at San Antonio. Her research publications focus on minority teacher personal, sociocultural, and professional development, as well as teacher recruitment and retention issues. She also explores the role collaborative partnerships play in teacher development, recruitment, and retention.

**Wendy Gardiner** (wendy.gardiner@nl.edu) is an assistant professor of elementary and middle level teacher education at National-Louis University. Her research and publications are in the areas of urban education, mentoring and induction, and teacher preparation and learning communities.

**Lisa Gonsalves** (lisa.gonsalves@umb.edu) is an associate professor of literacy and assessment at the University of Massachusetts/Boston. Her research covers three broad areas: urban education reform, alternative teacher preparation, and the achievement gap. She is the co-author of *New Hope for Urban Schools: Cultural Reform, Moral Leadership and Community Partnership.*

**Becky Wilson Hawbaker** (Becky.Hawbaker@uni.edu) is the director of the University of Northern Iowa PDS and coordinator of field experiences. She was previously a special education teacher at Malcolm Price Laboratory School at UNI. Other research interests include general education/special education co-teaching, student-led IEPs, self-determination, and teacher work sample methodology

**John E. Henning** (henningj@ohio.edu) is a professor and chair of the Teacher Education Department at Ohio University. His research interests include semiotics in education, teacher collaboration, the teacher work sample, instructional decision-making, and classroom discourse. He was the founding director of the University of Northern Iowa's Professional Development School.

**Socorro Herrera** (sococo@ksu.edu) serves as a professor of elementary education at Kansas State University and directs the Center for Intercultural and Multilingual Advocacy (CIMA). Her research focuses on literacy opportunities with culturally and linguistically diverse children, reading strategies, and teacher preparation.

**David Huggins** (DHuggins@ceo.melb.catholic.edu.au) is assistant director, Catholic Education Office Melbourne, Australia. Huggins has responsibility for providing evidence-based interventions and building capacity for supporting educationally disadvantaged students. He has been actively involved in university/school sector partnerships linking research with professional training and policy initiatives.

**Moira Hulme** (m.hulme@educ.gla.ac.uk) is a research fellow at the Faculty of Education, University of Glasgow. Her research interests include teacher education and teachers' work. She has been involved in a number of research projects commissioned by the Scottish Government, the General Teaching Council for Scotland, and Learning and Teaching Scotland.

**Rosemarie Hunter** (r.hunter@partners.utah.edu) is the special assistant to the president for campus-community partnership at the University of Utah. She is an assistant professor with the College of Social Work and has 30 years of teaching and practice experience in community organizing and development and social work practice.

**Carrie Kamm** (carriekamm@gmail.com) is a mentor-resident coach for AUSL where she provides professional development to mentor teachers and provides professional coaching to mentors and resident teachers. Her research and presentations are in the areas of teacher collaboration and professional learning communities.

**Deirdre Kelly** (Deirdre.Kelly@scotland.gsi.gov.uk) is the research coordinator for Schools of Ambition within the Scottish government. Her research interests include pedagogy, specifically developing online assessment strategies in higher education. Her previous experience includes developing education and skills in an economic development context. A key strength is working across organisational boundaries.

**Debra S. Lee** (leed@waterloo.k12.ia.us ) is secondary curriculum coordinator and part-time professional development associate for the Leadership and Learning Center in the Waterloo community school district. Her experiences include over 30 years as a teacher and administrator in public education, including 15 years teaching internationally.

**Jack Leonard** (Jack.Leonard@umb.edu) was a teacher and principal in the Boston public schools. In 2008, he joined the faculty at University of Massachusetts, Boston, and now teaches courses in urban school leadership. He is the co-author of *New Hope for Urban High Schools: Cultural Reform, Moral Leadership and Community Partnership*.

**Rob Linné** (linne@adelphi.edu) is a founding member of the Education & Labor Collaborative, and co-editor of *Organizing the Curriculum*. He is an associate professor of adolescence education at Adelphi University. Rob's expertise is in language and literacy studies.

**Mary Phillips Manke** (mary.p.manke@uwrf.edu) is associate dean at the University of Wisconsin-River Falls. She has been involved in school–university collaboration for over 10 years. She sees such collaboration as a major obligation of a public university.

**Rachael Marrier** (marrierr@stillwater.k12.mn.us) is supervisor of curriculum and instructional support services for the Stillwater area public schools in Minnesota. Rachael facilitates and leads teachers in the area of mentoring and instructional coaching.

**Cynthia F. McDonald** (mcdonaldc@cedar-falls.k12.ia.us) is director of elementary education for the Cedar Falls school district. Career experiences include classroom teacher, principal, director of teaching and learning, and adjunct in the Educational Leadership Department at the University of Northern Iowa. She has worked extensively with curriculum development, systems change, and assessment.

**James McMillan** (jhmcmill@vcu.edu) is a professor and chair of the Department of Foundations of Education in the School of Education at VCU, Richmond, Virginia. He has been associated with MERC since its inception, and MERC director since 1997. He teaches and publishes extensively on classroom assessment, student motivation, and research methods.

**Ian Menter** (i.menter@educ.gla.ac.uk) is a professor of teacher education and deputy dean of the Faculty of Education, University of Glasgow. His research interests include education policy, comparative studies, and the development of research capacity in education. Menter is the director of research to support Schools of Ambition (2006–2010).

**Maja Miskovic** (maja.miskovic@nl.edu) is an assistant professor in the Department of Educational Foundations and Inquiry at National-Louis University where she teaches qualitative research methods and action research. Her research focuses on social and cultural context of racial and ethnic identity construction utilizing interpretive and critical research paradigms, and teacher education.

**Maria da Graça Nicoletti Mizukami** (maria.graca@pq.cnpq.br) is a professor of the Federal University of São Carlos. She is currently lecturing, supervising, and researching learning and professional development of teacher at the Mackenzie Presbyterian University in São Paulo-SP, Brazil.

**Kevin Murry** (xmas@ksu.edu) is an associate professor of secondary education and the director of research and development at the Center for

Intercultural and Multilingual Advocacy [CIMA], Kansas State University. His research emphasizes differentiated practices for cultural and linguistic diversity in the school and classroom.

**Debra Nakama** (debran@hawaii.edu) is a professor and articulation coordinator at Maui Community College. Her efforts have helped to significantly narrow the gap between Maui's K–12 and community college institutions. Her research initiatives include exploring collaborative leadership and the use of a county-wide student database to examine student preparedness for college.

**Maria Pacino** (mpacino@apu.edu) is a professor and chair of the Department of Advanced Studies in Education at Azusa Pacific University. She has several publications, including a book, in the area of diversity and equity in schooling. She collaborates on research with diverse school communities.

**Janet Penner-Williams** (jpenner@uark.edu) is an assistant professor of curriculum and instruction at the University of Arkansas. Her research interests include teacher professional development especially in the area of culturally and linguistically diverse student populations and assessment of higher education programs as it pertains to teacher success in the field.

**Della Perez** (dperez@ksu.edu) is an assistant professor of elementary education and the associate director of undergraduate programming at the Center for Intercultural and Multilingual Advocacy (CIMA), Kansas State University. Her research emphasizes teacher preparation for working with culturally and linguistically diverse student populations.

**Aline Maria de Medeiros Rodrigues Reali** (alinereali@ufscar.br) is a professor in the Department of Teaching Methods at the Federal University of São Carlo, São Paulo, Brazil, were she works with teacher education in preservice and inservice programs. Her research interests include the professional development of teacher and school–university collaboration.

**R. Martin Reardon** (rmreardon@vcu.edu) is an assistant professor in the Educational Leadership Department of the School of Education at VCU, Richmond, Virginia. He taught and held administrative positions in high schools for over 25 years before moving into the academy in 2001. His research interests include learning technology and school effectiveness.

**Cathy Risberg** (mindsthatsoar@comcast.net) is an educational consultant. As the owner of Minds That Soar, LLC (www.mindsthatsoar.com) she specializes in providing academic advocacy services for gifted and twice-exceptional children and their families. She is an adjunct faculty member for the Technology in Education program at National-Louis University in Wheeling, Illinois.

**Sheelagh Rusby** (rusbys@alc.dumgal.org.uk) is an experienced senior teacher at Castle Douglas High School, Kirkcudbrightshire. She is project coordinator for the School of Ambition initiative at the school, a role that includes curriculum development, coordination of practitioner research, and liaison with local authority officers and Scottish government advisors.

**Kathleen Shinners** (kds13@hotmail.com) is the external evaluator for the University of Rhode Island Office of Marine Programs, and community literacy and mathematics coordinator for Newport public schools.

**Elizabeth A. Sloat** (esloat@unb.ca) is an associate professor with the University of New Brunswick's Faculty of Education and a researcher with the Canadian Research Institute for Social Policy. Her research includes developing outcomes-based evaluation models to assess school program effects longitudinally, literacy development across the life-span, and teacher education.

**Adrienne Andi Sosin** (andisosin@andisosin.com) is a founding member of the Education & Labor Collaborative, and co-editor of *Organizing the Curriculum*. Her action research agenda includes labor and adult education, leadership, technology, and literacy.

**Joel I. Sosinsky** (jsosinsky@gmail.com) is a founding member of the Education & Labor Collaborative, and is assistant director of the Public Services Division, International Brotherhood of Teamsters. Joel contributed to *Organizing the Curriculum*.

**Regina Maria Simões Puccinelli Tancredi** (retancredi@gmail.com) is a professor at Mackenzie Presbyterian University in São Paulo-SP and Federal University of São Carlos, in São Carlos-SP, Brazil. Her research interests include professional development of teachers, school–families partnerships, and school–university collaboration.

**J. Douglas Willms** (willms@unb.ca) is director of the University of New Brunswick's Canadian Research Institute for Social Policy and the Canada research chair in human development. He is a fellow of the

International Academy of Education and the Royal Society of Canada, and president of KSI Research International Inc.

**Diana Gonzales Worthen** (dworthen@uark.edu) is director of Project Teach Them All, an ESL endorsement program for secondary inservice teachers at the University of Arkansas. She is a former ESOL assistant curriculum supervisor, science teacher, and Holmes scholar. Her research includes coaching teachers of English language learners and emerging diversity theory.

# Index

**A**

Academy for Urban School Leadership, 191

access, 15, 31, 35, 112, 143, 147, 162

action research, 36, 38, 39, 43, 57, 61–62, 73–78

Adequate Yearly Progress, 65

administrator role, 23, 61, 75, 79, 98, 100, 108, 148, 175

management style, 66, 158

American Federation of Teachers (AFT), 182, 210–211

assessment, 66–69, 162

academic, 131

alternative, 103

benchmark, 204

connect with student learning, 127

environment, 157

formative, 68

led instruction, 137, 140

needs, 196

reassessment, 100

skills based, 135–140

standardized, 61, 82, 99, 137, 165

standardized data, 135, 137

transformative, 65, 72

Australia, 126, 127, 132

authority, 22, 129, 130

central, 128

collective, 130

decision-making, 52

higher, 131

individual, 132

lack of, 138

shared, 92, 127

visible, 129

authorizer, 96, 98

**B**

benefits of collaborative research, 136 194

boundary (boundary crossing and boundary object), 45

encounters, 45

institutional, 194

maintenance, 148

spanners, 181

brokering, 37, 45

bureaucratic organizations, 121

structure, 12, 92, 131, 215

**C**

California Federation of Teachers (CFT), 210–211

career pathway, 143, 144, 156, 157

challenges of collaborative research, 58, 100, 107, 139, 159, 195, 212

operational, 43

public policies, 56, 71

resistance, 128

regulatory, 132

research, 137

sustainability, 131

change, 71, 93, 128, 131–132, 148, 182, 215–216

agents of, 78, 159, 170, 175, 182

anxiety, 16

efforts, 2

evaluation and, 67

funding, 37

holistic-organic, 19

institutional, 8, 169, 179, 204–205, 211–212

mandated, 61

mechanisms for, 5

planned, 10, 35

policy, 107, 152–153

resiliency of institutions, 108
resistance of, 6, 36, 38, 49, 59, 157, 172
school-led, 42
schools in, 1, 12, 132, 139, 151, 176
strategies, 16
sustainability, 2, 177
transformational, 36, 39, 40, 43
Chicago Public Schools, 191
collaboration, 1–12, 42, 118, 124, 216
    Collaborative Inquiry (CI), 127
    complexity of, 3, 100, 106, 116, 179, 215–216
        dissemination problems, 1, 8, 12, 35, 89, 162, 216
    informal, 47–49
    mentoring, as, 37, 40, 74, 75, 77, 97
    negotiating, 182
    participants, 43, 106–107, 186, 194, 195
    power relationships, 51–52
    research, 54, 57, 86, 136–139, 140
    school/university partnerships, 19, 45, 73, 110, 125
    social practice as, 45
collaborative types, 8–11
    consultation, 8, 35–38
    dissemination of, 35, 89, 145, 162, 216
    interagency, 8, 179–182
    multiple configurations, 8, 89–93
    one-to-one, 8, 61–63
    PDS, 8, 15–17
    postsecondary, 8, 143–145
    sustainability, of. See sustainability
    technology projects, 8, 169–170
collective, 3, 45, 126–127, 130, 145, 165
    activism and, 158
    process of, 158
college bound, 81
college placement exam, 203–204
collegial, 81, 102, 113, 165
    contrived collegiality, 43
    learning and, 43
    mutuality and, 91
community, 182, 183, 184, 186, 188
    communities of enquiry, 37, 42–45
    communities of practice, 45
    community involvement, 35, 36, 40, 84, 85, 86
community college, 8, 40, 90, 105, 143–145, 149–151, 179–180, 199, 212
    women in, 154–157

competition for resources, 149, 201, 203
computers (handheld computers)/technology, 171–172, 174
configuration, 147
constraints, situational, 43
    funding, 149
    time, 93, 201
constructivism, 103
    constructivist approach, 106, 162
contractual agreement, 8, 82, 104, 144, 148 149
cooperation, 6–7, 73, 84, 90, 92, 97, 207
co-teaching, 33
critical friend, 40, 43
critical reflection, 76
cultural evolution, 5
culturally and linguistically diverse populations, 161
culture, institutional, 33, 42, 92, 138, 172, 182
curriculum, 185, 187, 188, 189, 196

**D**

data analysis, 65, 67, 68, 71, 93, 162
    data-driven instruction, 135
decision-making, 16, 30, 52, 144, 156, 203
disadvantaged students, 126, 143
distance education, 161, 164
district leadership, 49
diversity, 20, 32, 82, 86, 161, 183

**E**

early field experiences, 26
early literacy, 134, 135, 138
ecological systems theory, 202
Education & Labor Collaborative, 179, 209
education change, 139
    educational policy, 66, 111
    educational practices, 208
    educational reform, 126, 191
elementary school and university partnership, 20, 22, 26, 32, 57, 59
ELL strategies, 161–163, 165
empowerment, 67, 73, 81, 208
English language learners, 145, 161
enriched curriculum, 83
equal partnership, 78

equity of collaboration, 137, 138, 140, 184
  goals of, 138
  partners of, 93
ESL teachers, 161–163, 165
ethnic and cultural diversity, 183
evaluation, 40–43, 84, 86–87, 127, 174
  assessment, 67–68, 81, 169, 173
  punitive, 35
  self, 40, 75, 188
  school district, 67
  teacher, 37

**F**
faith-based institution, 61, 82, 85, 87
federal programs, 66, 67
feminist standpoint theory, 154
Flow of Influence, 9, 12, 27
finding common ground, 158, 159
first-generation students, 151, 185–187, 189
flexibility, 173, 197
formal collaboration configuration, 147
formative assessment, 68
Freire, Paulo, 6, 67, 208
  praxis, 2, 6
functional interdependence, 22
funding, 9, 105–106, 111, 181, 211
  government support, 37, 137, 143, 163
  grant based, 2, 47–53, 90, 148, 196, 200
  lack of, 6, 37, 152, 188, 201–202, 205
  power wielding through, 216
  targeted, 40
  university, 30–31

**G**
gifted education, 61, 62, 80–83
goal conflicts, 92, 138, 144, 175, 202–203, 205
  among participants, 98, 100
  internal resistance, 48, 150
governance committee, 27, 28, 30, 33

**H**
hard-to-staff schools, 195–196
holistic partnership approach, 15, 19, 24
humanizing, 95, 100

**I**
impact of collaboration, 5, 104, 132, 165, 175, 184
  one-to-one, on, 63, 69, 70, 71

PDS, on, 16, 22, 25
impedance, 114, 115–116
incentives to participate, 9, 30, 105, 112, 116
informal configuration, 147
information flow, 45, 77, 93, 115, 136, 153, 170, 175, 216
initiation to teaching practice, 75
inquiry-oriented teacher education, 41, 119, 123–124, 129
inservice teacher professional development, 15, 36, 145
  consultation, 54–55, 59
  interagency, 195
  multiple configuration, 96, 113
  one-to-one, 73
  PDS, 19, 23
  postsecondary, 145, 161, 162
institutional context, public vs. private institutions/systems, 22
interagency collaboration, 4, 8, 179, 181, 182, 194, 205, 210–213
internal resistance, 48
intervention strategies, 54, 69, 70, 93, 136
  literacy for, 139, 140
  urban schools, 180, 192

**K**
K-20 education system, 20
knowledge base for teaching, 55–56
knowledge management, 68, 71

**L**
labor education, 182, 207–213
laboratories of innovation, 23
laboratory school, 27, 29
Latinos, 82, 147, 184
leadership, 21, 49, 51, 200, 216
  forward looking, 170
  relational, 159
  reconceptualizing, 155–159
  shared, 130, 154
  style, 144
learning community, 89, 97, 100, 149, 151, 172
  school as, 55, 60
  sustainable, 96
legitimacy of partnerships, 149
lessons learned from collaborative research, 24, 32, 53, 86, 122, 131, 137, 166, 176, 196, 213
levels of interdependence, 22, 73, 81, 97, 185

leverage, 111, 144, 152, 158
limitations, 2–3, 9, 24, 32, 35, 85, 99,
    115, 152, 157, 174, 187, 213
  between institutions, 62
  funding, 50, 165, 181
  inadequacy, 82
  logistical, 131
  time, 68, 123, 165
LINC (Learning Improves in Network-
    ing Communities), 126–127, 130
linkages, 107
longitudinal research, 134, 137
low-income students, 85, 147

**M**
macro-level resistance, 149
mandated collaboration, 144
mathematics education, 96, 102, 107,
    109
  mathematics anxiety, 99
memes, 2–7
  competition among, 3
  definition of, 3
  memeplex, 2, 4
  memes in use, 4
  memes of practice, 4
mentoring , 47, 50, 74–75, 185, 187
  peer, 188
  preservice teachers, 16, 30, 31, 32,
    33
  strategy, 40
micro-level resistance, 149–150
multiple roles of university partners, 77
multi-site professional development
    school, 26
multi-state university, 161
mutual professional development, 33
mutuality, 9, 83, 97, 113, 120. 127,
    148, 156, 195, 211
  consultation, 35
  interagency, 179, 180
  multiple, 90–92
  PDS, 15, 24, 26
  postsecondary, 143

**N**
navigating organizational contexts,
    145, 155, 157
New Teacher Center-Wisconsin, 49
No Child Left Behind, 65, 188

**O**
online learning community, 105
organic relationships, 24

organizational climate, 1, 172, 174,
    175
organizational involvement, 8, 20, 26,
    54, 80, 102, 110, 127, 147, 155,
    210
ownership, 32, 140, 150, 152, 180,
    186, 189, 201–202

**P**
parental involvement, 201
partnership, 41–42, 107, 118, 162–163
  essential considerations, 95–98, 100,
    122
  mutual interdependence, 185
  roles, 98, 100, 121
  trust, 166
PDS director, 31
pedagogical content knowledge, 97,
    176
  practices, 54, 59
  reasoning process, 54–56, 59, 60
performance monitoring, 134–136,
    139, 140
personal theories, 55
pilot study, 16, 26–33, 139, 140
planning, inadequate, 204
politics, 144, 157, 172, 176
postsecondary collaboration, 8, 143,
    155, 156, 158, 161
power, 6, 9, 37, 60–62, 121, 128
  relations, 51
  redefined/reconceptualized, 154–159
  flow of, 156
practitioner research, 41, 73, 74
professional development, 15, 65, 69,
    102, 105
  learning communities, 165
  learning, 127
  long term professional development
    model, 140, 144–145, 161–162,
    164
  mission and vision, 23, 25
  schools/teachers, 47–48, 50, 54–56,
    58, 59
  standards based, 104, 122, 163
  strategies, 55
project SCOPE, 19–22
public/private partnership, 80

**R**
research and development centers, 23
reading achievement, 134
reciprocity in collaboration, 81, 83, 85,
    144, 147, 153